Most of the early literature concerning women's religious experience is about exceptional women; those who diverged from the traditional female role to become nuns, mystics or charismatic leaders. While women were permitted to be prophets and visionaries they rarely played an important part in church organisation. This paradox is explored in this book and a number of themes emerge; in particular, the dominance of male symbolism within the great religions. The question of whether men and women apprehend religious systems and signs in the same way is also explored.

In considering the contemporary scene, the book is able to look at the ways in which religion affects the lives of women in different societies and in different historical periods; this gives us a larger view of the ways in which our own perceptions of 'femaleness' have been constructed out of the religious world views of both the past and the present.

Pat Holden is a Research Student in the Institute of Social Anthropology, University of Oxford.

WOMEN'S RELIGIOUS EXPERIENCE:
CROSS-CULTURAL PERSPECTIVES

Women's Religious Experience

EDITED BY PAT HOLDEN

CROOM HELM
London & Canberra

BARNES & NOBLE BOOKS
Totowa, New Jersey

© 1983 Pat Holden
Croom Helm Ltd, Provident House, Burrell Row,
Beckenham, Kent BR3 1AT

British Library Cataloguing in Publication Data

Women's religious experience.
   1. Women and religion
   I. Holden, Pat
   305.4'2   BL458
    ISBN 0-7099-1232-3
    ISBN 0-7099-1239-0 Pbk

First published in the USA 1983 by
Barnes & Noble Books,
81 Adams Drive,
Totowa,
New Jersey
07512
ISBN 0-389-20363-7

Printed and bound in Great Britain by
Biddles Ltd, Guildford and King's Lynn

CONTENTS

CONTRIBUTORS

DIANA BURFIELD was for many years a Social Science publisher. In 1975 she began research at Bath University on the Theosophical Movement. She now manages her own secondhand and antiquarian bookshop as well as continuing with her research.

JULIA LESLIE is at present doing research in the Faculty of Oriental Studies, University of Oxford. She has travelled extensively in South Asia. She recently won third prize in the BBC Bookshelf/Arrow First Novel Competition. Her novel, Perahera, a thriller set in Sri Lanka, is to be published shortly by Gollancz/Arrow.

JULIA NEUBERGER is Rabbi of the South London Liberal Synagogue, Lecturer in Bible at Leo Baeck College, London and member of the Executive of the London Society of Jews and Christians.

VIEDA SKULTANS is a Social Anthropologist with a special interest in the history of psychiatry. She is a lecturer in the Department of Mental Health, University of Bristol. Her publications include Intimacy and Ritual (1971), and Madness and Morals (1974).

LUCY RUSHTON is a Social Anthropologist at present doing research at Sussex University. She recently spent a year in Greece doing fieldwork.

NANCY TAPPER is a Social Anthropologist who teaches the anthropology of religion in the Department of the History and Philosophy of Religion, King's College, London. Her earlier fieldwork was with nomads in Iranian Azerbayjan and in Afghanistan. More recent fieldwork was carried out in Turkey.

ELIZABETH TONKIN is Senior Lecturer in Social Anthropology at the Centre of West African Studies, Birmingham University. She has taught in Kenya and Nigeria and done fieldwork in Liberia.

CATHERINE THOMPSON was until recently doing research in Social Anthropology at the School of Oriental and African Studies, University of London. She spent a year in India doing fieldwork. She is currently working as an MRC Research Fellow at the Institute of Medical Sociology, Aberdeen.

JONATHAN WEBBER is a Junior Fellow of the Oxford Centre for Post-graduate Hebrew Studies. He teaches the Oxford University course on the sociology of modern Jewish society, and is also chairman of the religious affairs committee of the Oxford Jewish Congregation. He is a Social Anthropologist who did his fieldwork in Jerusalem and is an editor of JASO, The Journal of the Anthropological Society of Oxford.

SUSAN REYNOLDS WHYTE is Senior Lecturer in Social Anthropology at the University of Copenhagen, Denmark. She has done fieldwork in Uganda and Kenya, and has recently been working in connection with a mental health programme for Tanzania.

PAT HOLDEN taught in Uganda, Malawi and Nigeria for a number of years. She is currently doing research in Social Anthropology at the Institute of Social Anthropology, University of Oxford and is an editor of JASO.

PREFACE

This book is the result of a programme of seminars organised by the Oxford University Women's Studies Committee in Michaelmas Term 1980.

Marina Warner gave a paper in the series but was unable to contribute it to this volume because it was committed elsewhere for publication. Catherine Thompson, Jonathan Webber and Susan Reynolds Whyte did not take part in the seminars but kindly contributed their papers to the book. Many people from different disciplines attended the seminars and provided stimulating discussion; thus making an important contribution to the volume.

A generous grant from the Ford Foundation made the series possible and the Warden and staff of Queen Elizabeth House kindly provided the venue. I would like to thank Shirley Ardener, the Oxford University Women's Studies Committee, and the members of the Oxford University Women's Social Anthropology Seminar who have provided continuing interest and support. Thanks are also due, especially, to Maureen Beck who typed the manuscript and advised on technicalities, and to Steven Seidenberg for preparing the Index and assisting with the proof-reading. Not least, the contributors have shown patience and understanding at all stages and for this I am grateful.

Pat Holden.

WOMEN'S RELIGIOUS EXPERIENCE:
CROSS-CULTURAL PERSPECTIVES

1 INTRODUCTION
Pat Holden

Religion and some Feminist Viewpoints

Most of the earlier literature concerning women's religious experience is about the 'exceptional' women, those who diverged from the traditional female roles to become nuns, mystics [1] or charismatic leaders. This type of literature forms part of the devotional body of works which provides the church with inspiration from the accounts of the lives of the saintly. There is thus a recognition in the Christian church, at least, that women have a part to play in the process of divine revelation. Mystical experience, in the Christian church is, nevertheless, always carefully controlled. It is a spontaneous union of the soul with God only achieved after the soul has been prepared according to a pattern of strict asceticism. The visions of women (and men) were thus carefully regulated and rigidly examined. It is arguable that the control exercised over female visionaries was particularly scrupulous; with the uncontrolled female visionary labelled as a witch or a mad woman. Fears of uncontrolled female enthusiasm are succintly expressed by Ronald Knox who says:

> from the Montanist movement onwards, the history of enthusiasm is largely a history of female emancipation, and it is not a reassuring one (quoted in I.M. Lewis, 1971, p.31).

What also emerges from this literature is that although women were permitted to be prophets and visionaries they rarely played an important part in church organisation. They have certainly always performed the tasks of deaconesses, and it is claimed that at certain periods in the Middle Ages abbesses exercised considerable power and ruled over combined male and female orders. Women, however, have generally been excluded from administering the Eucharist, and their power and influence in the church, it is said, has gradually declined. The endless processions of male clerics of all denominations who accompanied the Pope on his recent tour of Britain were a continuing witness to the 'invisibility' of women in this aspect of church life [2]. Paradoxically, women are said to attend church in much greater numbers than men (Lucy Rushton notes this also for the

1

Greek Orthodox church) and this largely concords with the commonly held view that women are intuitive, receptive to religious experience, and by 'nature' more devout than men.

More recent literature dealing with women and religion has attempted to widen the scope of discussion by considering material from different cultures and by placing the accounts of women's religious lives within historical and social contexts. It has often focused on areas of particular interest for female religious experience such as the worship of certain goddesses and women's cults. Perhaps more importantly it has turned its attention to the everyday religious experiences of ordinary women.

The argument put forward by feminist literature is that the picture presented by much of this material is not very favourable from a woman's point of view. Women are confined to the domestic sphere often in some form of 'seclusion'; and even if they are allowed to move in public spaces 'veiling' or the social conventions related, for example, to the dangers of their sexuality impose similar restraints on their freedom. They are excluded from formal religion, and from participating in important public rituals; they may be prominent in possession cults or healing rites but these can be seen as simply extensions of their traditional female roles. They are often either excluded or relegated to an area 'out of sight' in the church, the mosque the synagogue or the sacred area. This is sometimes justified by their state of 'pollution' or by the view that they are distracting to men.

Men, on the other hand, are prominent in religious organisation; they perform the important rituals, formulate dogma and hold the pens that write the 'divinely inspired' texts. They control the powers of female reproductivity and dictate the social and cultural roles of women. If women provide the important images of religious mythology and symbolism men manipulate these symbols.

These are some of the arguments which point to religions as male dominated systems in which women have little freedom to act [3]. The feminist viewpoint has of course correctly noted the repressive aspects of religion. If it has a major fault it is that the self perceptions of Western feminists, deriving mainly from the imagery of the Judaeo-Christian tradition, are at times, projected on to women in other cultures. The danger of such an approach is that women in these societies are not allowed to 'speak' (not only vocally but also through lack of examination of the religious action, mythology and symbolism which invariably 'speaks' more loudly).

Women and religion has not been a dominant issue in the women's movement in the West mainly because we live in a secular society, but also because religion seems to offer little scope for challenging dominant ideologies, as a number of contributors to this volume point out. However, it is generally accepted that the religious world-views of the past have been influential in shaping women's perceptions of themselves, and this is particularly important in relation to their sexuality.

The Christian church has been depicted as an instrument for the oppression of women and it is said that the Church has always linked anti-feminism with anti-sexuality. The Genesis myth, the writings of Paul, and the views such as those of Thomas Aquinas that woman was a 'misbegotten male' or of Jerome that she is 'the door of the devil' have all added flame to the fire which has brandished women with self-images of their own corruption and power to corrupt others.

Some of the Christian literature suggests that only by a symbolic denial of their femaleness could women achieve salvation. The church's oppression of women reached a gruesome climax in the witch-finding activities of the middle ages. Eva Figes points out that crimes of witchcraft were invariably linked to the male horror of sexuality;

But the gore of a woman's natural viciousness says Sprenger, lies in her insatiable lust, and it is her dreadful and perpetual appetite that allows her to copulate with the devil (1978, p.63).

In a recent book, Mary Daly (1979), a feminist theologian, argues that women can only be freed from these negative self-images by a complete re-creation of mythology and language. She makes a powerful and poetic plea for women to rewrite their own crone-ology [4]. Feminists have, however, rewritten their own charter myth by drawing largely upon religious mythology and ancient history. The myth presents an age of matriarchy in which women were powerful which preceded the present age of patriarchy. A rather tenuous framework has thus been constructed through which both the past and the present can be viewed. The construction of a mythology from the 'bricolage' of history is a necessary task of most ideologies; and for feminists, not least, the mythology provides legitimation for the search for equality and a share in power structures but it also provides an area for the exploration of 'mystical' feminism – the exploration of the nature of the feminine 'self'. (Diana Burfield's paper draws attention to one area in which 'mystical' feminism was developed).

The assessment of their own religious and historical tradition has exerted some influence on feminist concern with the lives of women in other cultures where religion still plays a dominant role. The frustration of Western feminists has become mirrored in readily available symbols like the veil. Outrage at sexual abuse (inherent perhaps in ideological systems which rigidly control female sexuality) is similarly reflected in the condemnation of such practices as polygamy, child-marriage and female circumcision, sometimes without consideration for the complex cultural and historical factors which underly these practices.

The familiar association of women with their bodies [5] which says, in effect, that 'woman is a womb' (de Beauvoir, 1972, p.13) has also provided some writers with what they consider to be a model for world-wide application. Thus Hoch-Smith and Spring (1975) claim that 'In no religious system do women's dominant metaphors derive from characteristics other than their sexual and reproductive status' (p.1) women can thus be viewed as vessels to be filled as much religious imagery suggests. They also say that most religions gener-

3

ate negative images of female evil, representing women as polluting, as witches and as prostitutes. It might be pointed out in connection with these claims that in some societies the metaphors associated with women's reproductive status can be very positively interpreted (see Catherine Thompson's paper). Words like 'witchcraft', 'pollution' and 'prostitution' may be negatively evaluated in our society but this does not necessarily mean that the same applies for other people. The words themselves may indeed be inadequate translations for comparable ideas and practices.

Hoch-Smith and Spring's work points also to one further area of interest in the study of women and religion; the prevalence of sexual imagery in religious description. There is wide cross-cultural evidence for the use of sexual metaphors in describing relations between people and the supernatural. To give just one example, in the Christian tradition the descriptions of the visions of female mystics often indicate an overt concern with sexuality. There are certainly those who would like to claim that the religious life of women represents a form of perverted sexuality. This is, of course, often said about nuns, 'the brides of Christ'. One simple answer to this was offered by the great authority on religious experience, William James, some seventy years ago; 'religious language clothes itself in such poor symbols as our life affords' (1907, p.11). The subject of the sexual psychology of women in religious systems is a matter of immense interest but some care has to be taken to ensure that the value of female religious experience is not seriously undervalued by it. After all, as in the case of Christian mystics, it may in the end tell us no more than that in describing states of religious ecstasy both women and men draw upon conventional literary forms. However, the fact that these forms may be the literature of chivalry and courtly love, written by men, is not without significance!

The Papers

The contributors to this volume take into account the view that religion is invariably male dominated, that it can repress and restrict women, and reinforce accepted female stereotypes. Some of the papers provide further evidence for this. The main focus of attention of the contributors, however, is to widen the discussion by considering how women perceive themselves and their roles within varying religious systems. They attempt to answer such questions as: can there be said to be a female experience of religion? Do men and women experience systems, symbols - even beliefs - differently? The answers, as might be expected from such a variety of approaches, both historical and anthropological, are varied and by no means exhaustive. The material is extremely varied and reflects the recent research interests of the contributors.

Since the book is about female religious experience it is neccessary to discuss briefly the implications of this term for both the readers and the contributors. When we speak of religious experience we are dealing with a topic which has long been problematic in social analysis [6] and one on which even theologians do not necessarily agree. For some it implies an extraordinary moment of revelation, for others it may be present in the monotony of everyday activities. It generally indicates something that is unique and individual, which as Tonkin says 'no-one can experience for anyone else' (p.166). The social analysts who write about religion have in the main concentrated on the 'collective' representations of religious systems rather on the workings of the individal psyche although the best accounts have shown clearly that 'collective' symbols can reveal much about the nature and working of the 'self' as a society perceives it [7]. It is also acknowledged that any examination of religion must consider the question of the individual experience. This lesson derives most firmly from some of the great world religions in which the individual inspiration or revelation of the founder has ensured the continuing importance of such experiences for the adherents. And even in those societies without comparable organisation or without written texts there are frequent examples in myth and ritual of dependence upon the 'revelations' of the intermediaries between people and the supernatural, the priests, prophets and diviners. In the end, however, these observations take us no further forward in deciding upon the methods for analysing religious experience. It may even be, as Tonkin says, that there is as yet no adequate methodology for dealing with the problem. We can certainly never be sure of any common consensus on its meaning. The important thing is that we acknowledge that it may mean different things to different people at many different levels. In this volume those who deal directly with the great world religions necessarily explore aspects of the individual experience. In others the individual is revealed through the biographical account. Those who adopt the approach of the social anthropologist follow the conventional methods of analysis; the exploration of religious action and symbolism 'understood in the light of a detailed examination of a people's entire categories of thought' (Evans-Pritchard, 1954, p.10). In these cases religious experience is that which is experienced in everyday life.

The papers in the book are linked together in pairs. Some deal with similar subject matter; others are linked by material from a common geographical area. There is no overall unity except that suggested above by the exploration of the complexity of female religious experience. However, within the diversity of material certain recurrent strands emerge; and there are distinct indications of new approaches to the study of women and religion which should provide important pointers to future studies.

Women and the Occult in the 19th Century

Vieda Skultans and Diana Burfield describe the participation of women in religious activities which were regarded as being outside 'institutionalised' religion. (A fact often reported of women in many different areas). In this case the papers deal with the resurgence of interest in the occult in 19th century Britain, with which women were particularly associated.

Spiritualism, the subject of Skultans paper, as an organised movement was first recorded in the home. It thus provided women with interests which allowed them to remain within their traditional environment. The practice of Spiritualism at this time, she says, reflected the polarization men/science/objectivity and women/religion/passivity [8]; a division which was particularly significant in an age which attempted to subject religion to scientific experimentation. The preponderance of male controls and female mediums further reflected the division and also asserted the superiority of science. The paper provides a fascinating picture of the sometimes strange relationships between the eminent men who were controls and the ordinary women who were mediums. These partnerships mirrored traditional male/female relationships but at the same time Spiritualism allowed women to step outside traditional roles whilst still remaining firmly within male control. Women were thus viewed as 'extraordinary' because of their psychic powers but they also remained 'ordinary' because, as Skultans points out, the ideal female medium conformed to the Victorian stereotype. There is in this observation a hint of the recurring theme in this volume of the recognition of the 'powers' of women, both positive and destructive, and the need to control them, apparent in many religious systems (see Tonkin, Tapper, Thompson in this book).

Theosophy sometimes included the practice of Spiritualism but this was only part of the picture. Diana Burfield draws upon material from the biographies of some of the women involved in the early part of the Theosophical movement and presents an 'inside' view of some of those who became involved in it. Theosophy, she says, represented an attempt to resolve the crisis brought about in the 19th century by the attack on both institutionalised religion and materialistic science. It did this by looking to a compilation of oriental religions. Its objects coincided with socialist and feminist ideals of the period and it further offered women the chance for leadership and self-expression which they had failed to find elsewhere. The material in this paper provides an interesting example of the appeal of certain doctrines to women. In Theosophical teaching the body was viewed as a temporary vehicle for the eternal spirit which passed through various stages and reincarnated in both male and female forms. Balance had to be restored between the masculine principle which was regarded as materialism and evil, and the feminine which was spiritual and superior. Interesting comparisons might here be made with those Christian doctrines which suggest the equation of women with the flesh and with matter, (see Lucy Rushton) while the masculine principle is associated with logos, the word. Theosophical teaching, however, also included the renascence of the feminine principle (Isis, Sophia, the great Mother), which in the form of the personified wisdom figure Sophia 'makes the universe of matter the body of God' (Herzel, 1978, p.113). The influence of this on Eastern orthodoxy is clearly apparent in Rushton's paper.

The mediums described by Skultans were lower middle-class, submissive and not very well educated. By way of contrast the women of Burfield's biographies were middle-class, intelligent, well-read, imaginative and assertive. The mediums operated in their homes but many of the Theosophists shunned domesticity; their maternal feelings were not strong and many of them travelled extensively. The movement contained a high proportion of divorced and separated women and there was an emphasis on companionate marriage. The women looked to a time when sex could be transcended. This is hardly surprising in view of the age in which they lived but it is tempting to suggest that this particular aim reveals one origin of the search for freedom outside the 'bondage' of heterosexual relationships which has been a preoccupation of more recent feminist thought.

Interest in the occult and in oriental religions thus provided women with the opportunity for reassessing and exploring their 'femaleness'. In the case of Spiritualism the conventional stereotypes of male/female relationships were reinforced; but in the case of Theosophy religion provided women with an alternative channel for the reassessment of their roles. It is possible to see in these movements the origin of 'mystical' feminism. Women began to explore their 'spiritual' or inner nature, often through attachments to alternative religions which provided them with doctrines relating to their femaleness; doctrines which often contrasted strongly with those of orthodox Christianity.

Women in Greece and Turkey

The papers on Greece and Turkey deal with widely contrasting subject matter but points of similarity are provided by the fact that both are concerned with the practice of world religions, Islam and Christianity (in this case the Greek Orthodox church) and in both cases religion continues to play an active part in people's lives in spite of the ever increasing importance of the state.

Lucy Rushton examines the religious lives of ordinary women in a village in northern Greece. She shows that although women are associated with nature and consequently given a place of nominal inferiority in religion they are actually far more involved in the religious life of the village than the men. The biological definition of their nature does not, as might be expected, exclude them from religion but rather emphasises the importance of their participation (a similar point is made by Catherine Thompson for Indian village women). Religion has, in this case, to be seen to extend beyond the formal sphere of the church and the priesthood into everyday lives, both inside and outside the home, which are shown to be rich in religious symbolism. The work of du Boulay (1974) Hirschon (1978) and others has amply demonstrated Greek views on the sexual nature of men and women. Rushton's material largely concurs with these views but her paper is more concerned with the ways in which women perceive themselves and their role compared with the view of themselves presented to them by the church and society. She does this by an exploration of the symbolism of the dove on the marriage crown and she shows how its central message is interpreted in the everyday religious activities of women.

The dove on the marriage crown, the symbol of submissiveness and gentleness, is referred to by the women of Velvendos as a magpie which like themselves 'caws' and gossips. It is this acceptance of 'reality' which symbolises their association with the world of matter and which makes them appropriate mediators between the physical and the spiritual. They are, Rushton says, continually involved in processes which transform the material world so that it is capable of manifesting God; the cleaning and display of the house, childbirth, rituals associated with death, and food preparation. Although women cannot become priests, or go behind the <u>iconostasis</u> – that is they cannot take formal religious roles, theologically their role is significant and they themselves acknowledge this by their own interpretation of religious symbols. Their challenge of the teaching of the church is symbolised by their wry comment on the marriage vows; 'How can we obey them (men) when they are such fools?' Elsewhere Elizabeth Tonkin also suggests that women may not always accept the surface message 'as men would like to think' (p. 171).

It is possible to see in Velvendos the working of a familiar system of 'complementarity' in which men seem to be prominent in formal religion while women 'spiritualise' the home, (a view which often masks underlying inequalities). Rushton, however, assigns to women a more fundamentally important theological role. She says Eastern orthodoxy emphasises the importance of the perfectability of the flesh in the doctrine of the Incarnation. In connection with this women play a central role, they 'make manifest the spiritual potential referred to in the sacraments, of themselves and their families' (p. 68).

Nancy Tapper's paper is concerned with Islam in Turkey, where the state system is secular and based on a European rather than an Islamic model. Nevertheless religion continues to exercise considerable influence on people's lives. She mentions some aspects of the role of women in Islam and in connection with this notes that there have been a comparatively large number of studies on the ideology of honour and shame and female seclusion but few studies of 'religious belief and practices and the conceptual systems of women' (p. 71). As a contribution to the latter she analyses a paired set of women's gatherings, one secular, the other religious. At the centre of her discussion is the contradiction between the domination by men of religious and social life and the fundamentally important honouring of motherhood (a contradiction noted in many religious systems). This contradiction, she says, is largely masked by the that men and women participate in separate sex-gatherings. The secular women's gatherings demonstrate male domination as in them women relate to each other as adjuncts of their husbands. In the religious gatherings, the mevlûds, the celebration of the birth of the prophet, women relate to each other as mothers both 'sacred and powerful'. A religious celebration thus provides women with an arena for the celebration of their own worth, away from male domination. However, Tapper says, the rituals do not act in any way as a <u>challenge</u> to the existing order. They are to be viewed rather as compensatory.

One interesting aspect of Turkish Islam mentioned by Tapper is what she calls the tension between the two conceptions of divinity, one abstract and revealed in the Koran and Sharia, and the other more highly personalised and experienced in Sufism as an almost cult-like relation with the prophet. In the mevlûds women would appear to be linked with the second. It is tempting to see parallels with female mystical experience reported in other areas which frequently entails close relationship with the divine, often expressed in intimate sexual or familial terms.

India: Ancient Texts and Village Life

Julia Leslie and Catherine Thompson provide complementary but very different pictures of Indian women and religion. Leslie looks at ancient Indian texts which cover a wide historical period while Thompson focuses on rural Indian village life.

The religious texts derive from Hinduism, Buddhism and Jainism. The written word forms an important part of the great world religions and the knowledge derived from it is often regarded as the means for attaining spiritual greatness. The fact that in many instances only men were literate, or were considered to be the rightful interpreters of the word has obvious implications for the consideration of women and religion. Leslie's paper provides important insights into these issues. The texts she discusses reveal 'male' views on the nature of women's religious life but they also provide the 'voices' of women themselves. The material is particularly interesting because of the rich variety of imagery it contains; imagery which vividly portrays perceptions of women.

The exclusion of women from esoteric knowledge is central to Leslie's discussion. Through the texts she explores the question of how far the invididual soul is affected by the existential fact of being a woman. This is the problem of 'essence versus existence' and women are associated with the latter. The problem is neatly reflected in the story of the rogue who ignores the lofty words of a woman because he sees only the beauty of her eyes; in response she plucks it out and offers it to him.

There are many fascinating aspects to Leslie's paper and some may be mentioned which have parallels elsewhere. One story she cites presents women as being required to cut off their breasts to achieve spiritual greatness (see above and Warner, 1978; 1981, for the suggestion that Christianity similarly implies that women in the truly religious life must become like men). Ironically Leslie also shows that in devotional worship the relationship between people and gods should ideally mirror the love of a woman for a man (not vice-versa) so that in some instances male devotees are said to imitate women.

Many religions claim to make no distinction between men and women in the religious life (see Webber). St. Paul said that in Christ 'there is neither male nor female' (Gal. 3.28) but also taught that the women of Corinth should not break the custom of wearing a veil in public thus conforming to the social norms of his day. Similarly the

9

Buddha taught the irrelevance of a person's sex for salvation but said that a woman joining the homeless life was like 'blight on a field of sugar cane' (p.94).

Nuns are a subject of continuing interest in the literature as well as in the popular imagination [9]. The nuns described by Leslie deliberately chose the life to avoid the woes of women; leaving parents to live with strangers, pregnancy, giving birth and having to wait on men. Women could only achieve salvation through the male-related roles of wife, mother or daughter. The dark side of a woman's nature was lustful, heartless, disloyal and malicious but she could overcome this by the performance of the idealised female roles.

Leslie's paper provides a rich background view of Indian women. Thompson provides the foreground; a case study of women's ritual participation in an Indian village. She challenges the often stated view that Hindu women have a low ritual status and are therefore excluded from religious worship. In the village she describes women participate in the worship of gods far more frequently than men. Menstruation and childbirth can be seen to make women impure and polluting in some ritual contexts but in others the same physiological processes enable women to become important mediators between men and gods.

Women in this Indian village system are regarded as important, powerful and necessary for the continuance of the structure but at the same time they threaten it. The function of women in some rituals, Thompson says, is to mediate between these contradictory forces socialising their sexuality. Her paper also raises the question of why women's religious roles aren't given more prestige and importance. One answer, she says, may lie in the tension between asceticism and eroticism in Indian religion. The important practice of asceticism is possible for men; they can be sexually active for procreative purposes but can then give up the world. A man can practice seminal retention whilst a woman cannot control her bodily secretions. The implication of this is that men are viewed in Hinduism as having greater religious potential.

Leslie explores the problem of the outer shell of womanhood and how far it defines the soul's potential. Thompson adds to the discussion by a case study which emphasises the importance of describing the nature of the social construction of female biology when considering the varying access of women to the sacred.

Judaism

Judaism often appears to be a male dominated system which exludes women from the synagogue and rigidly maintains its pollution laws. But set against this there is the figure, familiar in American fiction, of the powerful Jewish mother. Julia Neuberger and Jonathan Webber discuss the role of women in Judaism their papers necessarily touch upon aspects of these stereotypes.

Neuberger speaks from her own personal experience as a female rabbi of the Liberal Synagogue in a religion which is still reluctant to accept that a woman can legitimately perform such a role. Her paper argues that women should participate more in public religious life and she explains some of the reasons for their continuing reluctance to do so. She outlines some of the attitudes towards women in Judaism and gives examples of their disabilities and lower legal status. Beginning with the 'exceptional' women of the Bible she shows that the status of women in Judaism has gradually declined. The 'exemptions' which lift the burden of the Law from women, and generally keep them away from public worship, have gradually come to be interpreted as 'exclusion'. There is, she says, no need for this interpretation and women, if they wished, could be much more active in public spheres.

Webber takes the discussion a step further and looks to the deeper underlying reasons for this 'invisibility' of women. As he points out men and women in Judaism are considered spiritually equal before God but they clearly experience Judaism differently. Judaism, he says, is rooted in an unchanging legal system, the halacha which can provide commentary and explanation for a number of questions which arise in the environment (the social world which Jews inhabit). However halacha itself is a male model which cannot provide categories for the explanation of the female experience of Judaism. In terms of halachic Judaism questions such as 'What it is to be a woman?' belong to the realm of 'folk' explanation. As he explains, social behaviour cannot theoretically affect the law but in practice Judaism is viewed through a combination of both halacha and folk explanation. The folk view in fact generates its own life and possibilities for change. The internal logic of the system prevents women from gaining access to Talmudic Law but this 'freedom' from the law has in effect given them the opportunity to diversify their social and cultural life. Taking examples from Jewish communities in America he says that there is - movement away from religious activities towards an increased emphasis of the socialisation of children. This view, which presents halacha as Jewish culture rather than divine service is taken by Webber to indicate the strong possibility of a change of emphasis from a male to a female world-view and with it a new sense of legitimacy for a non-halachic outlook.

Africa: Masks and Little Spirits

The papers on Africa examine female participation in religious rituals in societies in which there is little written tradition and where religion is less clearly demarcated from other areas of social life. Women in these societies 'speak' through participation in ritual.

Elizabeth Tonkin explores the implications of the participation of women in masking societies in West Africa. The Gola myth which she describes is itself almost a charter myth for feminists. In the beginning women were the custodians of all the ritual and spiritual powers necessary for defending sacred tradition in the interests of the ancestors. But during great wars women prevented men from mobilising for defence. As a result men found a monster which subdued the women. After this it was agreed that Poro, the men's association, and Sande, the women's, should share control ruling for a number of years in turn. Although the sharing of the masking activities, she says, suggests symmetry, in fact the masks are intended to control and coerce women. The myth reflects the value placed on women's powers of fertility and their importance as mothers but it also justifies the subservience of women to men. Having said this Tonkin makes the interesting suggestion that if certain masks exclude women and justify their secondary position they may also leave women 'ideologically freer'. Although Gola women must share the religious assumptions of men they can also celebrate their own worth in an arena and a medium which is respected by men. Ideological freedom may mean that women do not always accept the 'male message of the masks. It is possible - who knows - that women do not always cower in their houses when the Masks go by outside, even though men would like to think so' (p. 171).

Susan Whyte's paper cites an interesting example of a system, in this case that of the Nyole of Uganda, in which certain spirits are clearly associated with women. As well as being a skilful analysis, the paper provides an appropriate conclusion to the volume because of the theoretical issues raised by the author [10]. She asks - if the little spirits (and we could add female religious experience in general) are said to be peripheral then from whose point of view is this true? The answer, in the case of the Nyole, is that they are peripheral from the point of view of a centre defined and dominated by men. Even if a specifically female view is expressed, she says, this is still 'determined and subordinated within a discourse having a male subject' (p. 190). As some of the papers have demonstrated, women do not challenge the dominant model but rather elaborate on an element of it. In answer to the question of whether women experience religion differently than men Whyte's material presents the conclusion that 'we cannot speak of separate realities, exclusive male and female models' (p. 190) nevertheless, she says, the dominant model sometimes relaxes its hold and a specifically female view comes through to be glimpsed by the analyst.

These observations about the Nyole may well have something to say about women and religion in a number of societies. It is hoped that this volume has provided some 'glimpses' of women's religious exper-ience. Religion may appear to repress women and to justify their subservience to men. The papers show that women do not generally challenge this; neither, however, do they necessarily share the view. To take up the point made by Tonkin, it may well be that exclusion or 'freedom' from dominant ideologies leaves women freer to explore and 'celebrate' their own worth sometimes within the same arena as men. It is clear from the papers that women in religious systems both 'speak' and effect subtle changes of emphasis. What is also cer-tain is that there is an immense and rich variety of female religious experience.

Notes

1. It is arguable that women who have mystical experiences are not necessarily 'exceptional'. In some parts of the Mediterranean it is quite common for adolescent girls to have visions of the Virgin Mary. Jean Buxton also reports for the Mandari of the Sudan that adolescent girls commonly manifest signs of possession; 'The Mandari seem to be aware of the mild neurosis or simply innate susceptibility which can be a symptom of growing girls' (1973, p.44).

2. The admission of women to the Christian Priesthood is a subject of continuing interest and concern. The work of Dr. Una Kroll should be particularly mentioned in connection with this. Two books which take up some of the arguments for and against are Montefiore, H. (1978) and Moore, P. (1978).

3. It is of course said that women do have room for some manouevrability by such strategies as the withholding of ritual services.

4. At the 'grass roots' level feminist theologians address prayers to 'Dear Auntie God' and propose attempts to re-write the Bible in a neutered form (Time Magazine Dec. 8th 1980). Although it is easy to ridicule such efforts they represent a serious attempt to discover the meaning of 'What it is to be a woman' today in the context of a historically male dominated and repressive religion.

5. See McCormack and Strathern (1980) for a discussion of the nature/culture question as it relates to women. They argue that the association of women with nature is itself the result of certain traditions in Western historical and intellectual thought.

6. See e.g. Needham, R. (1973).

7. See e.g. Lienhardt, G. (1961).

8. This division still persists today and particularly links women with intuitiveness and receptivity to mystical experiences. It is connected with the view that women are associated with their bodies and therefore more likely to 'hear'. The attentive listening female is common in literature, art and everyday life!

9. See for example Campbell-Jones, S. (1979) and Williams, D. (1975).

10. Whyte draws particularly on Ardener, S. (1975) and Feuchtwang, S. (1975) in her analysis.

References

Ardener, S. 'Introduction' in S. Ardener (ed.) Perceiving Women. London, Dent/Malaby, 1975

Buxton, J. Religion and Healing in Mandari. Oxford, Clarendon, 1973

Campbell-Jones, S. In Habit. London, Faber and Faber, 1979

Daly, M. Gyn/Ecology. Boston, Beacon Press, 1978

de Beauvoir, S. The Second Sex. Middlesex, Penguin, 1972

du Boulay, J. Portrait of a Greek Mountain Village. Oxford, Clarendon, 1974

Evans-Pritchard, E.E. 'Religion' in The Institutions of Primitive Society. Oxford, Blackwell, 1954

Feuchtwang, S. 'Investigating Religion' in M. Bloch (ed.) Marxist Analysis and Social Anthropology. London, Malaby, 1975

Figes, E. Patriarchal Attitudes. London, Virago, 1978

Herzel, S. 'The Body is a Book' in P. Moore (ed.) Man, Woman, Priesthood. London, SPCK, 1978

Hirschon, R. 'Open Body/Closed Space' in S. Ardener (ed.) Defining Females. London, Croom Helm, 1978

Hoch-Smith, J. and A. Spring (eds.) Women in Ritual and Symbolic Roles. New York and London, Plenum, 1978

James, W. Varieties of Religious Experience. London etc. Longmans, Green Co. 1907

Lewis, I.M. Ecstatic Religion. Middlesex, Penguin, 1971

Lienhardt, G. Divinity and Experience. Oxford, Clarendon, 1961

McCormack, C. and M. Strathern (eds.) Nature, Culture and Gender. Cambridge, CUP, 1980

Montefiore, H. Yes to Women Priests. Essex and London, Mowbray and Mayhew-McCrimmon, 1978

Moore, P. (ed.) Man, Woman, Priesthood. London, SPCK, 1978

Needham, R. Belief, Language and Experience. Oxford, Blackwell, 1972

Warner, M. Alone of All Her Sex. London etc. Quartet, 1978
___ Joan of Arc: The Image of Female Heroism. London, Weidenfeld, 1981

Williams, D. 'The Brides of Christ' in S. Ardener (ed.) Perceiving Women. 1975

2 MEDIUMS, CONTROLS AND EMINENT MEN
Vieda Skultans

The early history of Spiritualism is full of peculiar events: apart from trance mediumship, there were rappings, levitations, ectoplasmic apparitions, the spontaneous playing of musical instruments and automatic writings, telekinesis and apports. This startling array of activities makes it difficult to decide whether nineteenth century Spiritualism was a new religion, a form of science or a society game. When a famous nineteenth century sceptic remarked that even if Spiritualism were proved to be true he would find it uninteresting, I think he was referring to this preoccupation with odd manifestations and trivial messages. One early Spiritualist has described it thus:

> What have these latter-day dead to tell us? To begin with it is a remarkable thing that they appear to be much more interested in events here below than in those of the world wherein they move. They seem above all jealous to establish their identity, to prove that they know everything, and to convince us of this, they enter into the most minute and forgotten details with extraordinary precision, perspicacity and prolixity. They are also extremely clever at unravelling the intricate family connexions of the person actually questioning them, of any of the sitters, or even of a stranger entering the room. They recall this one's little infirmities, that one's maladies, the eccentricities or tendencies of a third (Maeterlinck, 1913, p. 89).

Perhaps these family and domestic preoccupations stem from the beginnings of Spiritualism which are exceptionally unexalted. Elements of Spiritualist belief have existed as part of other religions for a very long time. However, Spiritualism, as an organized movement, originates at a quite specific time and place: namely, in March 1848 loud rappings were heard by two young sisters, Kate and Margaret Fox, in a farmhouse near Hydesville in New York State. These rappings were attributed to the spirit of a murdered travelling salesman. The noise made by this spirit was such as to prevent the family from sleeping and it soon attracted crowds of inquisitive neighbours. Conan Doyle in writing the history of Spiritualism was apologetic for these unlikely and, indeed, prosaic beginnings. He therefore reminds

15

his readers that the first message transmitted by cable across the Atlantic was a commonplace enquiry from a testing engineer. 'So it is that the humble spirit of the murdered pedlar of Hydesville may have opened a gap into which the angels have thronged' (1926, p.56). Whether subsequent Spiritualist activities involved throngs of angels might be disputed, but it is certain that within two years the Fox sisters and their mother had established themselves as mediums in New York city and gave public sittings which attracted large crowds. Thus the first conclusion to draw is that Spiritualism grew from domesticity and this domesticity is reflected in both the style and the content of its activities.

Secondly, from its beginnings Spiritualism has accorded a special place to women. Generally, women's role in the development of religious movements has been restricted. For example, Joan Morris in her book The Lady was a Bishop (1973) acknowledges the part played by women in the administration of the church but argues that they were barred from participation in the more specifically religious activities such as the celebration of the Eucharist because of their supposed ritual impurity. Mary Daly (1968) points out that whilst there have been women saints and mystics, the example of whose lives has enhanced Christian experience, women have not held hierarchical positions of authority within the Church. It is clear that Christian moral practice is shot through with the idea of the natural defectiveness or inferiority of women in relation to men. No doubt with such thoughts in mind, Teresa of Avila wrote: 'The very thought that I am a woman makes my wings droop' (quoted by Daly, 1968, p.56).

By contrast, Spiritualist mediumship has been and is primarily a female vocation. Doyle wrote:

> The early Spritualists have been compared with the early Christians and there are indeed many points of resemblance. In one respect, however, the Spiritualists had an advantage. The women of the older dispensation did their part nobly, living as saints and dying as martyrs, but they did not figure as preachers and missionaries. Psychic power and psychic knowledge are, however, as great in one sex as in another, and therefore many of the great pioneers of the spiritual revelation were women (ibid., p.50).

The requirements of successful mediumship are more typical of what is or was taken to be a woman's character than of a man's - passivity and submissiveness being among the most important. Another requirement which women were attributed with was absence of high intelligence or at least lack of education. Again Doyle wrote: 'It has been the habit to say that great intellect stands in the way of personal psychic experiences. The clean slate is certainly most apt for the writing of a message' (1926, p.2). Whatever may have been thought about women's brain size and intelligence in the nineteenth century, their lack of education would make them seem peculiarly fitted to mediumship. This congruity between stereotypes of femininity and the requirements of mediumship opened up career opportunities within Spiritualism for women. Feminine stereotypes have always attributed great intuitive and mystical powers to women. The biologist, Geddes, wrote that women have 'greater patience, more open-mindedness, greater appreciation of subtle details, and consequently what we call more rapid intuition' (1889, p. 250). Certainly, it is worth bearing in mind that stereotypes of femininity were highly developed at this time and played an important part in medicine (particularly psychiatry), education and law. Spiritualism consolidated and developed this tradition.

A Census of Hallucinations carried out by the Society for Psychical Research between 1889 and 1892 reaffirmed the connection between women and Spiritualism [1]. The census concluded that women were almost twice as likely to experience hallucinations (by which the report meant psychic experiences) and that these experiences seem to be most frequent between the ages of twenty and thirty.

An earlier study by Gurney, Myers and Podmore (1886, pp. 707-23) had looked at 882 cases of Spiritualist experiences and also found a preponderance of women. An analysis of the cases showed 58% of the percipients to be women and 42% men. A further finding was that 63% of the spirit agents were male, 37% were female. In other words, the typical spiritualist experience involves a female medium and a male spirit or control. The authors account for the preponderance of male spirit controls by the fact that men are more likely to die violent deaths away from home and therefore to return in spirit form. Sudden and violent death is thought by Spiritualists to create an uneasy and difficult transition to the spirit world and such spirits are more likely to need to communicate with this world. A reason of a different order may be that the typical Spiritualist experience grew out of and was enhanced by traditional male/female relationships. Whilst permitting women to step outside the traditional feminine role, the conditions under which this is done are controlled by norms of traditional femininity. The role of the Spiritualist medium has a similarity with that of the nun as described by Marina Warner: 'The nun's state is a typical Christian conundrum, oppressive and liberating at once, founded in contempt of yet inspiring respect for, the female sex' (1976, p. 77). The elements of oppression and liberation are both there for women Spiritualists but in a different combination. The nun's state involves a repudiation of women's traditional and reproductive roles, providing an exalted status for certain categories of women at the expense of others. Mediumship, however, capitalizes on existing relationships and transfers them to a spiritual plane. So far I have remarked upon the domestic and familial preoccupations of Spiritualism and the peculiar suitability of women's supposed character to mediumistic activities. A closer look at the career of nineteenth century mediums now follows.

There is huge Mrs. Guppy, 'famous in the annals of levitation'; (Clodd, 1917, p. 57), Mrs. Emma Hardinge Britten, the young Englishwoman who arrived in New York with a theatrical company, and Madame d'Esperance from East London, otherwise known as Mrs. Hope. Autobiographies and biographies reveal a pattern of shared and recurring features. Most mediums come from lower middle class homes. A large number appear to have lost their fathers at an early age and had to fend for themselves. Annie Besant, who was involved in Spiritualism and later became a theosophist, also lost her father at the age of five. Emma Hardinge Britten 'being deprived of her good father's care at a very tender age, the young girl, like the rest of her family, was compelled to depend upon her own talents for subsistence' (1900, p.5). Many other examples can be found.

Whatever the psychological impact of such early bereavement, it clearly had consequences for the need to gain a livelihood. Emma Hardinge Britten likened by Doyle to a St. Paul of the movement, came to New York in the 1850s with a touring theatrical company. She had originally trained for the opera but found her mediumistic activities irritated her vocal chords and her operatic career was therefore curtailed. When her six month contract in New York expired, she turned to Spiritualism. Obviously, there was nothing inevitable about this, but the pattern is fairly typical. Anna Kingsford is another medium whose career developed along similar lines. Her early interests were also in opera but she was dissuaded from pursuing such a career. Instead she took up poetry and writing. She wrote for the Lady's Own Paper where she could publicize her views on the women's movement. Although she initially started out as a wholehearted supporter of women's rights, her views changed as her commitment to Spiritualism deepened. Her biographer, Maitland, writes,

> though sympathizing to the last in the movement for the enfranchisement of women, she did not long continue to take an active part in it. The reasons for her withdrawl were manifold ... one was her strong disapproval of the spirit in which the movement was coming to be worked. This was the spirit which manifested itself not only in hostility to men as men, but to women as the wives and mothers of men. But that which most of all she reprobated in this connection was the disposition which led women to despise womanhood itself as an inferior condition, and accordingly to cultivate the masculine at the expense of the feminine side of their nature (1896, pp.19-20).

In many ways her views were typical of the Spiritualist position which enthrones women in their traditional roles and relationships. By this time Spiritualism was flourishing on the East Coast of America. A correspondent of the Spiritual World in 1849 estimated that there were 100 mediums and 50 or 60 'private circles'.

The area where this enthronement of traditional femininity is most clearly manifested is in the relationship between mediumship and psychical research. The Society for Psychical Research came into being on 20th February 1882 in order to make 'an organized and systematic attempt to investigate that large group of debatable phenomena designated by such terms as mesmeric, psychical, and Spiritualistic' (1882, p.3). It would aim to investigate psychical phenomena 'without prejudice or prepossession' (ibid., p.4). Eligibility for membership was not to depend upon belief in psychical forces and, most importantly, 'Ladies are eligible either as members or associates' (ibid., p.6). The first president of the Society was the philosopher, Henry Sidgwick, and he saw the purpose of the Society as being to provide sufficient evidence for Spiritualism to convince the scientific world. Members of the Society for Psychical Research present an impressive array of well-known names. They include Lord Balfour, William James, Sir William Crookes, Andrew Lang, Henri Bergson, Gilbert Murray and William McDougal. In Italy the criminologist Lombroso became convinced of Spiritualism after his meetings with the young Neapolitan medium Eusapia Palladino.

The alliance between the Society and Spiritualism is probably quite unique in the history of religion. The Society for Psychical Research purported to be scientific and it certainly attracted scientists as members. Harry Price, a long term president of the Society described the differences between psychical research and Spiritualism thus:

Psychical research is a science and Spiritualism is a religion. The genuine researchers have their laboratories and scientific equipment, their special apparatus for eliminating human testimonies, as far as possible, their scientific methodology, their critical analyses of the results obtained. Their reports are published in Bulletins and Proceedings (1939, p.1).

In contrast to this: 'Spiritualism is, at its best, a religion, at its worst, a "racket". Spiritualists, though badly organized, have their churches and lyceums' (ibid., p.2). A further difference related to money. 'If there is no money in psychical research, there is plenty in Spiritualism' (ibid., p.3). Whether or not the medium chose to accept payment for their psychic gifts was hotly disputed but what is certain is that they had the opportunity for making money if they so wished. Many mediums became household words, travelling the world and being entertained by Royalty. Spiritualism could offer a career of star quality.

A good example of this alliance between research and Spiritualism is seen in the career of Sir William Crookes, the physicist and chemist, who was involved with psychical research for a number of years. Between 1870 and 1874 he gave up research in electronics to devote himself exclusively to the investigation of psychical phenomena. The Biographical Dictionary of Parapsychology attributes to Crookes the somewhat dubious achievement of having attended more seances than any other scientifically qualified investigator before or since his time. During the year 1874 he directed his attentions almost exclusively to Florence Cook. Their extraordinary and unlikely partnership is the subject of a quite fascinating book by Trevor Hall called The Spiritualists (1962). Florence was the eldest daughter of a compositor in Hackney. Her age is uncertain except for the fact that she was certainly a few years older than she claimed to be. Contemporary accounts lay much emphasis on her youth and innocence. At the time of her meeting with Crookes she had already acquired a considerable reputation as a medium which had been thrown into jeopardy by the discovery of trickery. Florrie Cook's spirit guide was an ectoplasmic apparition or materialisation called Katie King who could 'move, talk and act in all ways as an independent entity'. A spiritualist called Volckman had been invited to the Cook's domestic seance. During this seance Katie took Volckman by the hand. Volckman was struck by Katie's resemblance to Florence and retained his grasp on the proffered hand. Eventually Katie was rescued from his struggling grasp and retired behind curtains. Volckman was convinced that he had detected imposture and the incident was reported in all the national papers. At this point in her career Florence offered herself as a subject of investigation for Crookes. She herself wrote, 'I went to Mr. Crookes myself without the knowledge of my friends, and offered myself a willing sacrifice on the alter of his unbelief. It was immediately after the unpleasant incident of Mr. Volckman and those who did not understand said many cruel things of me' (quoted by Hall, ibid., p.32). Crookes appears to have been completely won over by Florence's charms and immediately took up cudgels on her behalf.

The precondition of his investigating her gifts was that he should remove her from her parents' house to his own in Mornington Road in the north of London. From the very outset he felt it his duty to defend Florence particularly if

a few lines (would) assist in removing an unjust suspicion which is cast upon another. And when this other person is a woman – young, sensitive and innocent – it becomes especially a duty for me to give the weight of my testimony in favour of her whom I believe to be unjustly accused (quoted by Hall, ibid., p.35).

At his house in Mornington Road, Crookes had constructed a small laboratory leading off from his study. The two were separated by a doorway draped with a curtain. Histories of Spiritualism recount how night after night Miss Cook would lie entranced upon a couch in the inner room whilst Sir William Crookes observed in a subdued light from his study. During these seances Katie King would materialize and walk around. She was said to have been very beautiful and was always dressed flimsily in white. Several witnesses attest to the fact that she wore no stays. She possessed every feminine virtue and charm and was the daughter of a pirate. She was so real that on one occasion Sir William 'embraced her and kissed her as he himself tells us' (Price, 1939, p.26). The wholly convincing interpretation which Hall advances is that Crookes became infatuated with Florence and that the two became lovers. At the time of their first meeting Crookes was a married man of forty-two whose wife was expecting their tenth child. Hall's detailed and plausible account suggests that he was totally and helplessly captivated by the young and pretty Florence who was then about eighteen. He agreed to protect her professional reputation and conceal her imposture in return for sexual favours. In an extraordinary letter to The Spiritualist describing the appearance of Katie King, the spirit guide, his susceptibility to her physical charms is all too apparent:

But photography is as inadequate to depict the perfect beauty of Katie's face as words are powerless to describe her charms of manner. Photography may, indeed, give a map of her countenance; but how can it reproduce the brilliant purity of her complexion, or the ever-varying expression of her most mobile features, now overshadowed with sadness when relating some of the bitter experiences of her past life, now smiling with all the innocence of happy girlhood when she had collected my children round her and was amusing them by recounting anecdotes of her adventures in India (quoted by Hall, ibid., p. 86).

Psychical research provided a good pretext for introducing her into his home where she stayed for weeks at a time. It also provided an opportunity for a trip to Paris. Whether Sir William and Florence were lovers, as they appear to have been from a reading of Hall's historical detective work, is not the concern of this paper. What is beyond dispute is Sir William's attitude of prayerful adoration towards the spirit guide Katie and his protectiveness towards the medium Florence - on account of her youth and innocence.

This case is an important one because Florence Cook is one of the most famous of nineteenth-century mediums and because Katie King is recognised by Spiritualists as the most perfect materialization. One writer in <u>Psychic News</u> (8th May, 1948) went so far as to claim, 'I feel that the materialization of complete figures which behave as ordinary persons in every way stands or falls by this one case.' Spiritualists have also claimed that the materialization of Katie King has implications for the Resurrection. Whether or not the comparison is an appropriate one, it has been made. Certainly some of the contemporary observers of Katie King's seances would not have endorsed the comparison. One observer is recorded as having described Crookes as 'half-showman and half playactor, on more than respectful terms with the ghost' (quoted by Hall, ibid., p. 62).

Yet another medium to achieve fame through her spirit guide was Madame d'Esperance. The guide was a beautiful young Arab girl called Yolande who vied in beauty with Katie King. Madame d'Esperance gave the following coy description of her spirit guide.

Her features were small, straight and piquant, her eyes were dark, large and lively; her every movement was as full of grace as those of a young child, or as it struck me then as I saw her standing half-shyly, half-boldly, between the curtains like a young roe-deer (E. D'Esperance, 1897, p. 251).

The description comes from her autobiography <u>Shadowland, or Light from the Other Side</u> (1847). Like many Spiritualist autobiographies, it fails to give precisely the details which a social anthropologist wants to know. However, this is a drawback which appears to be shared by much theological writing which can be infuriatingly abstract. St. Theresa of Avila, for example, wrote at great length about her sins without telling us what they were.

In America the medium, Mrs. Piper, entered into a long-term re-

search alliance with William James, yet another 'eminent man'. Mrs.
Piper's control was the former president of the American branch of
the Society for Psychical Research - Richard Hodgson. During his
lifetime Hodgson had known Mrs. Piper well and, in fact, had said

> that if ever he passed over and Mrs. Piper was still officiating
> here below he would control her better than she had ever yet been
> controlled in her trances, because he was thoroughly familiar with
> the difficulties and conditions on this side (James, 1909, p.2).

Hodgson, as control, was supposed to have had a 'marvellous dis-
cernment' of the inner states and anxieties of his sitters and to be
able to speak straight to their heart. And James adds: 'with all due
respect to Mrs. Piper I feel that her own working capacity for being
a spiritual adviser, if it were compared with the Rectors would fall
greatly behind' (ibid., p.3). This theme of the relative naivety and
lack of worldly knowledge of the mediums, particularly in relation to
the psychical researchers, is a constant one. In many ways the attitude of William James is typical of the psychical researchers. His
biographer describes him as longing for a religion, for faith in a
spiritual world existing back of or parallel to the visible material
world (Allen, 1967, p.378).

In summary, mediums and scientists entered into a longstanding alliance of a strictly controlled nature. The spirit guides or controls
captured and emphasised the desired qualities of the mediums themselves. In most cases the scientific outcome of the researches proved
to be contradictory or at best inconclusive. Many mediums who were
credited with great psychical powers were acknowledged, even by
ardent spiritualists, to have been fraudulent at certain periods of
their lives. The temptation to fake spiritual messages has been recognised by spiritualists and non-spiritualists alike and does not in
itself discredit Spiritualism. It simply testifies to the power and attractiveness of a Spiritualist career. As has been the case in science
genuine commitment to a theory may account for what appears to be
falsification of the evidence or cheating.

An example of the attractiveness of a mediumistic career is provided by Kate Cook, younger sister of Florence. From the first appearance of Florence's mediumistic gifts, the Cook family had acquired as patron a rich Manchester businessman and committed Spiritualist, Charles Blackburn. The net result of this patronage was that the
entire Cook family could live on the allowance which he regularly
supplied. When the 'struggling ghost' scandal erupted, Blackburn
withdrew his support from Florence but continued to support Kate
and the family. In fact, his financial beneficence continued throughout
his lifetime and after it, for he left almost his entire possessions to
Kate and her family. Trevor Hall has documented the financial
fortunes of the Cook family in order to discredit their mediumistic
activities. Whilst this documentation does not cast a flattering light on
mediumship, the story of the financial dependence of Kate on
Blackburn emphasizes the fact that mediumship could provide women
with a livelihood which was often much better than any they might

otherwise have had. Certainly, the financial support saved her from having to give public sittings and meant that she could decide for herself whom she invited to her domestic seances. Precisely for this reason the practice was condemned by Emma Hardinge Britten and used by her as an argument in favour of the professionalization of mediumship. Where the seance takes place in the home of the medium and the investigators are simply guests any suspicion would be a form of impoliteness. Just as one would not quibble about the quality of food served at a dinner party so one could not question the authenticity of the hostess's mediumship. However, although the domestic setting was safer and more protected it was limited and ultimately less rewarding than the more dangerous career of the fully professional medium. Although professionalization increased the risk of exposure, it also increased the possibility of financial rewards, fame and travel – in short it offered glamour. These two types of mediumship have coexisted from the beginnings of Spiritualism to the present day, each offering its own peculiar rewards and constraints.

In conclusion I would like to make the following five points:

1. From the start Spiritualism has been preoccupied with domestic and family matters. This preoccupation emerges in the messages received from Spirit which are concerned with intimate details of domestic life and with psychological problems and relationships. Thus, there is a remarkable coincidence between the preoccupations and interests of women and those of Spiritualism. Futhermore the domestic nature of Spiritualism is frequently emphasized by its setting within the home of the medium.

2. Victorian stereotypes of femininity (which to a greater or lesser extent persist today) bear a remarkable resemblance to the conception of the ideal medium. The following adjectives can equally well describe the ideal woman as the ideal medium: unsophisticated, innocent, passive, young, tender, feeling, intuitive and so on. The stereotype has such a strong hold on our attitudes and behaviour that any one could extend the list indefinitely. The title of my paper has set limits to its subject matter. It is by definition concerned with women's role within Spiritualism and yet it may be objected that there <u>were</u> male mediums. Daniel Dunglass Home was one such medium who achieved international fame and a high reputation. However, the men who did pursue a mediumistic career were few and exceptional and almost invariably doubts were cast on their masculinity. (In this respect they appear to be rather similar to the Somali men who participate in spirit possession cults and have been described by Ioan Lewis (1966, pp. 307-29)).

3. The first two points lead on to the next. Namely, that – because of the characteristics of Spiritualism just described it provided ideal career opportunities for women. It did not involve stepping outside women's traditional sphere of interests either literally or metaphorically. It provided one of those rare and still sought after opportunities of working from home. Moreover, it allowed women to draw upon talents and resources which they already possessed without any threat to their feminine nature or transgression of social

norms. It allowed for individual advancement without threat to an essentially conservative system of relationships between the sexes.

4. Despite the existence of a few male mediums and an occasional woman member within the Society for Psychical Research, it is true to say that spiritual mediumship was essentially a feminine enterprise whilst psychical research was predominantly masculine. Moreover the relationship between the two mirrored several aspects of traditional male/female relationships. For example, there appears to be a considerable age difference between mediums and psychical researchers. Whilst mediums at the outset of their career and particularly during the time when they excited most interest were young women, the scientific investigators were decidedly middle-aged. Another differentiating factor is that of class. Whilst the investigators appear to come from secure and solid middle-class homes, the mediums came from rather precariously balanced lower-middle-class homes. Perhaps for that very reason their social origins are frequently glossed over or left imprecise. The mediumistic career thus certainly provided them with opportunities, though often short-lived, of social advancement. Thus money constitutes another area of difference. Whilst Price is right in one sense to say that there was money in Spiritualism but none in psychical research, in another sense he is wrong. For the non-involvement of psychical research with money was really an indication of the investigators' privileged financial standing. They could afford to do it for nothing. For the mediums financial reward was frequently necessary for obtaining a livelihood. Finally, there is a great difference in values and attitudes. The Society for Psychical Research saw itself as being impartial, unemotional, critical and observant, in short, scientific. It embodied many stereotypically male attributes. The mediums laid no claim to qualities of impartial criticism but emphasized the sincerity of their convictions and the genuiness of their spiritual experiences. As a footnote to the description of this alliance it should be added that although the relationship between mediums and investigators was in many cases longstanding and devoted, it was nevertheless temporary. Many mediums spent the latter half of their lives in isolation and destitution. Alcoholism has been recognized as a common problem among ageing mediums by several historians of Spiritualism. Certainly, this trouble afflicted the Fox sisters. Florence Cook died in poverty and alone. This pattern appears to be fairly common.

5. Finally, I would like to note the development of Spiritualist activities. The earliest noted spiritual manifestations were rappings, loud noises heard in different parts of a house coming from no obvious source. By means of these raps (one for Yes, two for No) answers could be sought from the spirit. When mediums established seances for a wider audience another activity was introduced. This was a type of partial materialization behind a screen with holes in it when parts of a materializing body would appear; usually floating limbs. In fact, early Spiritualists were presented with a kind of Punch and Judy show. Later, as materializing mediums gained confidence the entire body of the spirit appeared sometimes behind a screen, always in subdued light. With the advent of Florence Cook,

the materializing spirit began to walk and talk among the seance audience. Katie King was conducted on the arm of Sir William among the Spiritualist visitors. Finally, around the turn of the century, with a very few exceptions, materializations disappeared. Instead, mediums concentrated on diagnostic messages dealing with individual problems and relationships and healing activities. The progression of activities is towards greater abstraction and completeness: from noises, to the appearance of parts of a body, to a total body, and finally, to concern with inner feelings and relationships. I would like to make the tentative suggestions that perhaps the development of Spiritualist activities mirrors in a small way the development of relationships between the sexes.

Notes

1. The census prided itself on its impartiality. It was carried out by 410 inquirers, 223 women and 187 men. One third of the collectors were members of the S.P.R. A further sixth were friends of members. Yet others were identified through advertisements in learned journals such as Mind. Most of the collectors were professional, highly educated people. The informants were mostly friends and colleagues of the collectors, and therefore also educated and professional people. The informants replies were collected over three years and numbered 17,000. In general, the census adopted a cautious approach and a number of affirmative answers were excluded on the grounds that the experiences occurred during illness or dreams for example. Also where information about the experience was withheld it was excluded from the census figures. The census takers felt confident that no significant deceptions were taking place. Roughly 21% of the collectors had themselves experienced hallucinations. Each collector was instructed to obtain information from 25 respondents. Hallucinations were found to be most common in the age group 20-29.

References

Allen, Gary Wilson, William James: A Biography. London, Rupert Hart-Davis, 1967

The Biographical Dictionary of Parapsychology. London, Helax Press, 1964

Britten, Emma Hardinge, Nineteenth Century Miracles. Manchester, William Britten, 1883
___ Autobiography. Manchester, John Heywood, 1900

Clodd, Edward, The Question: If a Man Die Shall He Live Again? A Brief History and Examination of Modern Spiritualism. London, Grant Richards, 1917

Daly, Mary, The Church and the Second Sex. Boston, 1968

D'Esperance, E. Shadowland or Light from the Other Side. London, George Redway, 1897

Doyle, Conan, The History of Spiritualism. London, Cassell, 1926

Geddes, Patrick, The Evolution of Sex. London, 1889

Gurney, Edmund; Myers, Frederick, with Podmore, Frank. Phant-
asms of the Living. 2 volumes. London, Trubner and Co., 1886

Hall, Trevor, The Spiritualists. The story of Florence Cook and William Crookes. Place Duckworth, 1962

James, William, 'Report on Mrs. Piper's Hodgson Control', in Proceedings of the Society for Psychical Research. Vol.23, Part
LVIII, (1909) pp.1-126.

Lewis, I. M. Ecstatic Religion. Middlesex, Penguin, 1971

Maeterlinck, Maurice, One Eternity. London, Methuen and Co., 1913

Maitland, Edward, (1896) Anna Kingsford. Her Life, Letters, Diary
and Work. London, George Redway, 1896:

Morris, Joan, The Lady was a Bishop. New York, Macmillan, 1973

Price, Harry, Fifty Years of Psychical Research: A Critical Survey.
London, New York Toronto, Longmans Green and Co., 1939

Proceedings of Society for Psychical Research 1882-3

Proceedings of Society for Psychical Research 'Report on the Census
of Hallucinations', Vol.X, (1894) pp.25-426

Warner, Marina, Alone of All Her Sex: The Myth and the Cult of the
Virgin Mary. London, Weidenfeld and Nicholson, 1976

3 THEOSOPHY AND FEMINISM: SOME EXPLORATIONS IN NINETEENTH-CENTURY BIOGRAPHY

Diana Burfield

'Human beings are too important to be treated as mere symptoms of the past' Lytton Strachey, preface to Eminent Victorians (1918, p.viii)

Lytton Strachey's dictum may serve as an epigraph to this paper and as an indication of the pitfalls encountered in getting to grips with the past through the lives of individuals. There is a temptation on the one hand to treat them rather distantly as expressions of historical forces, which can lead to some variant of determinism, and on the other hand to draw so close through empathetic understanding that the fascinating person seems unique and autonomous. In the first instance persons are reduced to being carriers of ideas, and in the second degenerate into case histories. Steering between these hazards entails working simultaneously, or perhaps alternately, on two levels. One takes in the wider social, economic, and political context that provides the opportunities and constraints influencing individual lives, and constructs the framework of experience for whole classes and categories of people. The other concerns the individual subject with a unique biography, responding more or less creatively to the given circumstances. This approach is guided by Marx's observation that:

Men [and women] make their own history, but not of their own free will; not under circumstances they themselves have chosen, but under the given and inherited circumstances with which they are directly confronted (Marx [1852] 1973, p.146).

In seeking this balance, I have been collecting biographical material about a large number of individuals who were associated with the progressive movements of the late nineteenth century - with 'advanced thought', as it was then called - among which I would include the Theosophical Society. There is a vast amount of information about the more prominent men and women - Radicals, Freethinkers, Fabians, social reformers, and so on - but I am equally interested in the lesser figures and the rank and file, about whom also much has been recorded. For in trying to understand a social movement it is as important to discover something about the membership, the people it reaches out to and who in turn carry it along, as it is to know about the founders and the leaders. Furthermore, when data have been amassed about considerable numbers of people connections emerge that suggest new lines of inquiry. It becomes possible to discern patterns both in personal experience and in the hard demographic data - age, sex, class, family background, education, marital status, occupation, and so forth - that are characteristic of particular groups. To take just two factors, age and class, the first Fabians were born around 1856, formed the Society when around the age of thirty (thirty was then considered middle-aged) and recruited predominantly thirtyish people from the professional middle class (Mackenzie and Mackenzie, 1977). The first Theosophists were in their forties or older (Ransom, 1938), and the Theosophical Society has continued to attract people in the second half of life, a bias that Theosophists interpret favourably as demonstrating that Theosophy appeals to maturity. The notion of spiritual search as the proper occupation of the latter part of life is, of course, found in Brahminism, and in the analytical psychology of C.G. Jung. That the Theosophical Society (TS) was an overwhelmingly upper and middle-class preserve needs no further demonstration than to note that its London meetings in the 1880s closed at the end of the Season. Reproaches of social exclusivity were made and taken to heart, but various initiatives to 'evangelize the masses' not surprisingly petered out. However, in order to make more specific and meaningful connections between class and ideology than such gross correspondences, it is necessary to define more closely the fractions of these classes from which Theosophists were drawn and the features of the Theosophical system of thought that appealed to them. It is here that biographical material provides evidence about an individual's location in a network of family and friends that discloses the channels through which certain ideas reached them, the contacts that led them to join certain organizations, and so on. This point will be deferred until later, together with general considerations of method, in order, first, to sketch in the historical background; second, to give an account of the TS and its place among contemporary social movements; and, third, to discuss some of the Theosophical feminists individually.

The Historical Context

The Theosophical Society was founded in New York in 1875, but it really took off in the 1880s, when its activities turned on an axis between London and Madras. It was a cosmopolitan organization from the outset, but as I am here mainly concerned with English Theosophists I will refer to the historical background from the standpoint of England, which was, in the heyday of British imperialism, pretty determinate for the rest of the world.

The era in which the TS became established, which coincided with that in which the Women's Movement gathered momentum, was one of massive turbulence in British society. The eighteen-seventies inaugurated a new stage in industrial capitalism when Britain's supremacy as the workshop of the world was challenged by the USA and Germany, and the mid-century economic boom was followed by the Great Depression of 1873-96. Recovery from this was associated with the transition from industrial to finance capital and with the scramble for overseas markets of the Age of Imperialism. The crisis of the 1880s, accompanied by widespread unemployment, low wages, and appalling misery among the working class, led to the rebirth of militancy in an eruption of strikes and demonstrations and to a revival of trade unionism, specifically the New Unionism of the unskilled and the women workers. Now also came the 'second spring' of socialist ideas in England, informing sections of the working-class movements as well as the predominantly middle-class organizations such as the (Social) Democratic Federation (formed in 1881), and its offshoot the Socialist League, and the Fabian Society (1884), elements from all of which came together to form the Independent Labour Party in 1892-3 (see Mackenzie and Mackenzie, 1977; Williams, F., nd).

The extremity and enormity of the social and economic plight of the mass of the population, contrasted with the luxury of the few, forced a widespread recognition of the urgent need for change, if not by reform then by revolution. The existing structures - moral and religious as well as political and economic - seemed strained to breaking-point, and their critics were drawn from all strata of society and motivated by a variety of concerns. Members of charitable and religious organizations, of radical and secularist societies, of socialist and anarchist cells, and of discussion circles like the Zetetical Society attended by George Bernard Shaw, came together to form new groupings and alliances that to some extent crossed class boundaries.

This interaction was aided by the increasingly complex structuration of the class system corresponding to changes in the mode and relations of production. New fractions arose within the working class, and with increased bureaucratization there emerged new 'intermediate classes' (in Marx's phrase). These included that nouveau couche sociale, as the Fabians termed themselves, represented by the salariat of civil servants, jounalists, and clerks - 'workers by brain' as distinct from 'workers by hand'. A fair proportion of these were women. According to census returns, during the period 1861-1911 around 30% of the working population were women, and in 1881 12.6% of these were employed in middle-class occupations (nursing, teaching, and clerical work predominantly, for at this time there were only 25 women doctors, 100 law clerks, and no architects). One factor influencing the admission of women to the professions and semiprofessions was that since the mid-century there had been much public concern about the problem of 'surplus women'. There were over half a million more women than men in 1851, and of over six million women over the age of twenty, two million were independent and self-supporting (see Marsh, 1958, pp. 128-9; also Holcombe, 1973). The need for respectable paid employment among so sizable a proportion of the population immensely strengthened the feminist demands for educational and occupational opportunities and for the

29

parliamentary franchise that had gathered force in the eighteen-sixties (see Strachey, R., 1928)

However, women were also well represented in the rentier class. According to Hobsbawm (1969, p.119), in 1871, 'Britian contained 170,000 "persons of rank and property" without visible occupation – almost all of them women, or rather "ladies"; a surprising number of them unmarried ladies'. A number of Theosophical ladies owed their freedom of action to such private incomes. By the 1880s, then, there were significant numbers of women who were economically independent, and it was from their ranks, and from the ranks of those with sympathetic parents or husbands, that the first candidates for School Boards and Boards of Guardians as well as for County Councils were drawn, as well as the activists in the numerous organizations for social and political reform. Collectively they created the image of the New Woman, who was to be a model for countless others less privileged than they were.

The theme of the New, which ran like a leit-motiv through the eighteen-eighties, expressed not simply a fascination with novelty and modernity, but also a recognition of changing social reality, as in the phrase 'the New Journalism' (attributed to Matthew Arnold) in reference to the rise of the mass-circulation press (Havighurst, 1974, p.1) [1]. More deeply, it reflected a desire for renewal and regeneration, which might take inspiration from the future or the past – from the technological fix exemplified in Bellamy's Looking Backward: 2000-1887 (1888) or from the imagined harmony of Blatchford's Merrie England (1894). Or it might attempt a genuine synthesis of marxist economics and utopian dreams as in the work of William Morris (Thompson, 1977). At this time when the nature of capitalism was undergoing a shift and new classes were in process of formation, it was not possible to discern one dominant class and one dominant culture, in the sense of a hegemonic ideology. The oft-quoted statement of Marx and Engels (1846) that 'The ideas of the ruling class are in every epoch the ruling ideas, i.e. the class which is the ruling material force of society, is at the same time its ruling intellectual force', needs to be understood in the context of a society in which there was a struggle for dominance among the ruling interests – landed, manufacturing, financial – as well as a challenge from an increasingly well-organized working class, with the new intermediate classes poised between them. Consequently there were competing ideologies, i.e. competing versions of political and economic philosophy within and between the traditional parties, and competing religious interests, with Nonconformists and Roman Catholics attenuating the privileged position of the Church of England, and Christianity itself severely shaken by the cumulative assaults of biblical criticism, scientific materialism, and the general heritage of ideas from the Enlightenment. These conflicts were to a large extent contained because, as Macintyre (1967) has argued, in the religious and moral sphere there was a tacit agreement to differ about ends – a recognition of pluralism, in effect – based on a general acceptance of certain means, the 'secondary virtues' of tolerance, fair play, and so on, which constituted the ground rules of behaviour.

From the viewpoint of the 1980s we may look back on Victorian certainties with nostalgia only by overlooking the fact that 1888 was as exciting and tumultuous a year as 1968, and considerably closer to being a genuinely revolutionary situation. Indeed, it was regarded as such by many of the groups active at the time, among them the Theosophical Society.

The Theosophical Society [2]

As mentioned above, the Theosophical Society was formed in New York in 1875. Its founders, Helena Petrovna Blavatsky and Colonel Henry Steel Olcott, were at the centre of a dilettante circle of spiritualists, freemasons, occultists, and bohemians, most of whom dropped out quite early. HPB (as she was generally referred to) was a colourful, temperamental, and much-travelled Russian aristocrat with inter alia a considerable reputation as a medium, the precise details of whose life, as the first of her many biographers had reason to complain (Sinnett, 1886), were exceedingly difficult to verify. It seems likely that she drew no hard line between factual and imaginative truth in life as in literature, but she well understood how to manipulate others through a persona that seasoned mystery and unconventionality with charm and robust humour. In most respects she conformed to the copybook image of a charismatic leader, to whom Olcott provided the necessary practical and administrative complement. Indeed, they called themselves the Theosophical Twins, a pair of 'chums' who scrapped but always made up. Olcott was an agronomist turned soldier, who fought an adventurous campaign in the Northern army during the American Civil War. He subsequently combined a legal practice with journalism, and it was while on an assignment for his paper investigating the strange phenomena produced by a family of mediums in Vermont, that he encountered HPB. This bluff, likeable, if rather naif, man-of-affairs quickly became HPB's chela, or disciple, in esoteric matters and thereafter threw himself into the Theosophical cause as the principal organizer and publicist of the young society.

The initial period in New York had a somewhat surrealistic flavour. The founders' bizarrely decorated apartment - jokingly called the lamasery - where HPB conducted her salon and demonstrated her mediumistic arts, became the focus of lively curiosity. Further publicity resulted when they staged a rather rowdy Orphic funeral for one Baron de Palm, 'principally famous as a corpse', for his was the first to be cremated in the USA. Already Theosophy was showing an affinity with avant-garde ideas - vegetarianism, homoeopathy and other forms of natural medicine, anti-vivisectionism, anti-vaccinationism, dress reform, etc. - which are the hallmark of alternative or underground movements then as now. At this time spiritualism was falling into disrepute in the USA owing to exposures of fraudulent mediums, and HPB became involved in public controversies, putting the case for a 'spiritual spiritualism' as against the 'materialistic' kind then in vogue. The publication in 1877 of Isis Unveiled brought her

31

international attention, respectful and otherwise. Subtitled 'A Master-Key to the Mysteries of Ancient and Modern Science and Theology', the work launched a spirited attack on the 'twin tyrannies' of contemporary institutionalized religion and materialistic science, lambasting the Pope and T.H. Huxley with equal fervour. The resolutions of the strife between the two 'conflicting Titans' was to be sought in the restoration of the Hermetic Philosophy, that Ancient wisdom which she held to be the true and timeless basis of knowledge and the esoteric heart of all religious systems. In a synthesis of reconstructed religion and a science purged of materialism, the Divine Plan of cosmic evolution would be made clear. HPB had been called by the Masters of Wisdom, the cadre, so to speak, of the Occult Hierarchy responsible for governing human affairs, to the somewhat ungrateful task of forming the Theosophical Society as the vanguard of a world-wide movement to awaken humankind to its spiritual destiny of fulfilling that plan.

The response to the call in New York was not overwhelming, and the founders accordingly set sail for India, on the invitation of an organization called the Arya Samaj concerned with the revitalization of Hinduism. Olcott was under the mistaken impression that this was a sort of Indian TS, and the Arya were similarly misinformed about them, but for a time the two societies worked together. En route for the Orient in 1879, the founders stopped off in London, to meet a group of friends who had already started a branch of the Society. It is with this group that I am principally concerned here.

Its members were mostly ex-officers of the British National Association of Spiritualists, which was then in some disarray (see Nelson, 1969). The TS offered a more serious and theoretical approach to spiritualism, as well as an introduction to the religious philosophies of the East, which were seen as the source of the Western esoteric tradition of which some members were already students. The three Objects of the Society, which with slight changes of wording soon assumed the form they retain today, were acceptable to a wide range of seekers who were coming to terms with the Victorian crisis of faith. They read:

1. To form a nucleus of the universal brotherhood of humanity, without distinction of race, creed, sex, caste, or colour.
2. To encourage the study of comparative religion, philosophy, and science.
3. To investigate unexplained laws of nature and the powers latent in man.

There was, of course, an inherent contradiction between the tolerant open-mindedness of the Objects of the Theosophical Society and the truth-claims made for the Theosophical cosmology, and this was to be a ground of recurrent disputes and schisms. Although, at the level of cosmic ideation, all religions are one, at the level of human institutions they are distinct and various, and orthodox believers are not generally prepared to concede more than a courtesy validity to other confessions. However, in the last quarter of the nineteenth century, the syncretistic vision of the Theosophists had considerable appeal to those who needed to reconstruct their shaken faith, to come to terms with advances in physics and biology, particularly Darwinism, and to justify personal experiences of a mystical or occult nature. The TS provided a setting for the exploration of ideas and phenomena usually dismissed or prohibited by the established churches and sects, and it offered women an equal part in the enterprise.

Some Other Contemporary Societies

As already indicated, the Theosophical Society was one of a plethora of organizations centred on late-nineteenth-century London - Heterodox London, as it was termed by a contemporary observer (see Smith, 1967) - which attracted a shifting and overlapping membership of intellectuals and socialites, some of whom were also involved in working-class politics. I have referred to the British National Association of Spiritualists, some of whose members joined the Cambridge group around the Sidgwicks in founding the Society for Psychical Research in 1882 (see Gauld, 1968). After a brief honeymoon with the TS based on mutual misperception, the SPR published a damning Report (1885) on HPB and her Madras entourage, which rocked the Society and lost it many members. However, the TS recovered, HPB settled in London, while Olcott successfully expanded activities in India, and the TS became a feature of the London social round.

In 1884 the Fabian Society had been formed, following a split in the Fellowship of the New Life, a group dedicated to the 'cultivation of a perfect character in each and all'. According to Bernard Shaw, the two factions went their separate ways, 'the one to sit among the dandelions, the other to organize the docks'. Fissions along these lines also occurred in the TS from time to time. At this juncture Annie Besant was one of the most militant of the Fabians, but she, like Shaw, and Frank Podmore, a founder of the Fabian Society who later became secretary of the Society for Psychical Research, was also interested in spiritualism. The reason given at the time was that the seance-room would prove to be the laboratory in which the existence of the superphysical world would be put to definitive test, where evidential proof would be forthcoming to settle once and for all the question of survival after death, the existence of a spirit world, and the validity of various religious claims. Such was the deference accorded to science, even by those who opposed the scientific world-view, that the endorsement of what was taken to be scientific method (and sometimes was) was sought for beliefs relating to non-physical realms of experience. However, biographical material suggests that for many, including some of the most professedly rationalist, seances offered comfort and hope in coping with the death of relatives and friends, so often untimely in the Victorian era.

Some of the Fabians were drawn deeper into occultism and followed Annie Besant and Herbert Burrows into the Theosophical Society. A few, including E. Nesbit (now best known for her children's stories) were attracted to magical orders such as the Stella Matutina, an offshoot of the Golden Dawn, with which W.B. Yeats and Maud Gonne were for a time associated after leaving the Theosophical Society. Fabians who were Christian Socialists, such as the Rev. Stewart Headlam, founder of the Guild of St Matthew (in 1877), had little time for the occult, and neither perhaps had those who gravitated towards the Ethical Society, founded in 1886, or the anarchist Freedom Group, whose mainstay, Mrs Charlotte Wilson, had been prominent in the Fabian Society. There were groups enough for all shades of opinion, and those who differed politically might come together at meetings of the Vegetarian Society or the Humanitarian League, or unite for the defence of civil rights under the umbrella of the Law and Liberty League.

For many Fabians and other socialists at this time, women's suffrage was not the paramount issue it was to become after the turn of the century. Many felt that it was subordinate to the wider question of adult suffrage, a view taken by Beatrice Webb and E. Nesbit. Others felt that 'Votes for Women' meant votes for ladies, who would inevitably support the Tories. The Suffrage Societies, which had started in the eighteen-sixties, and were not amalgamated into a National Union of Women's Suffrage Societies until 1897, were sedate law-abiding bodies which did not appeal to the energetic Fabians. Impatient with their lack of militancy, Dr and Mrs Pankhurst, who were at that time Fabians, formed the Women's Franchise League in 1889, but according to Mitchell (1977, pp. 21-3), it had collapsed by 1893 because it attempted to embrace too many issues and set its sights too high.

At the end of the 1880s it was becoming clear that the hoped-for revolution was not around the corner, although considerable gains had been won by organized labour, and by the women's movement as regards increased educational and employment opportunities and some social legislation. The creation of the Independent Labour Party from a coalition of trade-union and socialist interests represented a new political force with parliamentary objectives, but while it won the support of left-wing feminists it offered little backing for their cause. It is not surprising, therefore, that when the Pankhursts and their followers decided to launch a mass campaign with the single-minded aim of obtaining the vote, the resultant organization, the Women's Social and Political Union, formed in 1903, was a very different proposition from the earlier societies. This phase of the women's movement falls outside the scope of this paper, but it may be noted that many Theosophists, including Annie Besant, were involved in the campaign, and many suffragists, notably Charlotte Despard (see Linklater, 1980) became Theosophists. As will be suggested below, Theosophical doctrines were highly consonant with the outlook of many militants.

34

Biographies: the Theosophical Feminists

From the preceding account it will be evident that the Theosophical Society in the 1880s was very much in tune with the utopian mood of the times. Its Three Objects expressed notions of brotherhood, equality between the sexes, progress, perfectibility, toleration, and so on that were in harmony with socialist and feminist ideals, although, as with Fabian doctrines, they could also be, and sometimes were, interpreted in an elitist and authoritarian manner. The fact that the co-founder and charismatic leader of the TS was a woman, H.P. Blavatsky, was no guarantee that other women would be encouraged to play a prominent role, but they did so from the first. The first secretary of the London branch was Miss Emily Kislingbury, former secretary of the British National Association of Spiritualists, and its treasurer a Miss Arundale. Mabel Collins, a prolific novelist and mystical writer, co-edited the journal Lucifer with HPB before Annie Besant appeared on the scene, and Annie became de facto leader of the movement worldwide on HPB's demise in 1891. Nor were women just carrying the burden of administration behind the scenes - in fact, if anyone could reasonably have complained of office drudgery it was Olcott - they took an equal share in lecturing, travelling, and writing, and a number of them put their private fortunes at the disposal of the Society. As far as one can judge, women were equally well represented among the rank-and-file. Insofar as the TS can be regarded as a religious sect, it offered women opportunities for self-expression and leadership denied them by the established churches and by most of the other sects - Quakers, the Salvation Army, and to some extent the Unitarians apart, though respect for women in these groups still relegated most of them to a secondary role. Regarded more broadly as a social movement, the TS offered greater scope than did the Secular Societies, which often regretted the lack of interest shown in them by women at the grass-roots level (see Budd, 1971), and by the political organizations, apart from the Fabian Society. Women supporters of the two main parties were sidetracked into their own organizations, such as the Women's Liberal Association, or fan clubs, such as the Primrose League. Only in the field of social reform, in the temperance societies and the Charity Organizations Society, for instance, were women allowed real openings, since these were regarded as suitable interests for females.

The appeal of the Theosophical Society to women was twofold. In the first place, there was the explicit statement in its first Object concerning absence of sexual discrimination; in the second there was the content of Theosophical teaching. This depends on the idea that the body is the temporary vehicle for an eternal spirit, which in its evolutionary progress passes through all material forms from the mineral to the angelic, and reincarnates innumerable times in male and female guises. Furthermore, the dynamic of the cosmic process requires the interaction of two principles differentiating out from the Absolute, and these may be seen as matter and spirit, yin and yang, male and female. Thus Theosophy provides a theoretical legitimation

at the highest cosmological level for mundane notions of equality between the sexes. Since, in the everday world, this balance has mani-
festly not been achieved, some Theosophical feminists were inclined to
identify the male with materialism and evil, and to assert the
superiority not just of the feminine principle but of the female sex.
This was stridently asserted by some of the militant suffragettes, inspired by the Theosophical writings of Rosa Swiney [3] (e.g. 1906),
and expressly condemned by Charlotte Despard in Theosophy and the
Woman's Movement (1913).

By no means all the women in the Theosophical Society would have
described themselves as feminists, any more than all members would
have regarded themselves as socialists, but there were elective affinities between these groups, which were quite pronounced up to the
First World War. Many Theosophists who had little interest in women's suffrage and the political aims of the women's movement were
nevertheless sympathetic to its social and educational objectives, if
only because they themselves exhibited the self-determination necessary to obtain higher education, pursue a professional or artistic career, or engage in writing and public speaking. Indeed, it would
have been difficult for a Theosophist, male or female, of however
quietistic bent, not to subscribe to many of the views on the status
of women and relations between the sexes put forward by the feminists. But this did not necessarily entail any compulsion to support
reforms in the real world, which for some occultists has inferior reality to the ideal world and is therefore something of a distraction.

It will be seen from the biographies that follow that individuals
differed widely in their commitment to feminism as a movement, and
in some cases changed their stance as they grew more involved with
Theosophy.

Dr Anna Kingsford (1846-1888)

Dr Kingsford is still remembered as one of the first Englishwomen to
qualify as a physician, as a pioneer in the campaign against vivisec-
tion and for the rights of animals, and as a mystic and the author of
several inspirational works. She was born Annie Bonus in 1846, the
youngest of twelve children of a prosperous merchant and shipowner,
to whom she was devoted. A solitary and imaginative child, with un-
restricted access to her father's library, she enacted the myths and
legends that absorbed her in dramatic performances with a vast
collection of dolls and in conversation with flowers and fairies. Her
creative capacities were expressed in stories and poems, some of
which had been published before she was thirteen, but similar en-
couragement was not given to her musical talents, and lessons were
discontinued when teachers hinted at a professional career. Her
precocious exhibitions of clairvoyance were regarded as symptomatic
of disease and referred to a physician. Later, at the finishing school
where she was sent to undergo 'the lopping and trimming considered
necessary to fit girls for conventional society' (Maitland 1896, I,
p.6), while her literary abilities were appreciated her critical

interest in religion most emphatically was not. On leaving school she devoted herself to writing; her Dreams and Dream Stories [4] was a posthumous republication of some of this material. Her family frustrated her desire for more mundane work, and prevented her taking up a position as a clerk to a solicitor whom she had prevailed upon to try her out. In 1865 her father died, settling on her an income of £700 a year, and she determined to marry her amenable cousin Algernon Kingsford, then a civil servant, on whom she had impressed conditions guaranteeing her independence. Owing to family opposition her plan had to be deferred until she attained her majority. In the meantime, between bouts of illness, she led 'a fairly hedonistic life', and was passionately addicted to hunting, until suddenly revolted by its brutality. The reflections thus prompted on the relations between humans and animals led to her espousal of vegetarianism and antivivisectionism. She was already wholeheartedly committed to female emancipation, on which she later published an essay (Kingsford, 1868). It was while canvassing for signatures to a petition for the protection of married women's property that she met a lady medium, who first aroused her interest in spiritualism. Shortly after this, in December 1867, Anna and Algernon were married. The following day, incapacitated by an attack of asthma, Anna returned to her mother's home, remaining there until the birth of her only child, Eadith. As Maitland puts it, her marriage was a marriage in little more than the name. Perhaps for this reason Algernon decided to take holy orders, and together they studied Anglican theology.

At this time Anna had no settled religious convictions. She was repelled by the 'hardness, coldness, and meagreness' of the Evangelical religion in which she had been reared (Maitland I, p.15), which seemed unresponsive to her awakening spiritual needs, but found sympathy in her medium friend, who transmitted messages purportedly from her father encouraging her to search and pray, and also from her putative ancestress Anne Boleyn, who suggested an affinity between them. The visions and trances she began to experience were viewed by her family as fits, and she was submitted to painful medical treatment for these, and for nervous panics, neuraligia, and sudden losses of consciousness. She then underwent surgery for an internal complaint from which she never completely recovered. The visions persisted, and it was at the prompting of a nocturnal apparition of St Mary Magdalen, who told her that a great task lay ahead, that she turned to Roman Catholicism. The artistic and devotional aspects of a faith practised by several of her friends had long appealed to her, and since her new religious mentors accepted her visions as marks of special grace, her conversion was hardly surprising. She was received under the names of Mary Magdalen in 1870 and confirmed two years later by Archbishop Manning with the additional names of Maria Johanna [5].

Although she had opted for Catholicism as against Protestantism, Anna had not yet arrived at what Maitland calls the 'alternative presentation' of Christianity – the mystical and subjective, as against the ecclesiastical and objective – but she by no means surrendered herself to her new church, declining spiritual direction and availing herself of its offices as the impulse took her. She asserted her independence also in the secular sphere when her husband was appointed to a country curacy and she, on the grounds of boredom and ill health, arranged to spend half her time in London editing The Lady's Own Paper: a Journal of Progress, Taste and Art. Her object in buying the weekly was to promote social reform, particularly with regard to the position of women, but even at this stage her ultimate concern was with restoring the due balance between the masculine and feminine principles of humanity rather than with female emancipation as such. Among the contributors to her paper were such notable feminists as Emily Shirreff, Julia Wedgwood, Sophia Jex Blake, Elizabeth Wolstenholme, Barbara Bodichon, and Frances Power Cobbe. After two years Anna was forced to close the magazine for the familiar reason of lack of advertising revenue due in this case to her refusal to promote products of which she disapproved on humanitarian grounds.

While remaining committed to the enfranchisement of women, Anna henceforth ceased to take an active part in the movement, after about 1873, giving the following reasons. She felt that women should demonstrate their capacity for serious work rather than clamouring for freedom and power; she disapproved of the growing tendency in the movement to exacerbate divisions between the sexes and to express hostility towards men; she deprecated the exaltation of spinsterhood over wifehood, which she saw, interestingly, as an assertion of inexperience over experience; and she reprobated the disposition among women to regard womanhood as an inferior condition evidenced by their cultivating the masculine over the feminine side in their nature. These views represent a prise de position on some controversies about female emancipation within the women's movement that have by no means been resolved over a century later.

In line with her first point, Anna had already formed the intention of studying medicine, not because she wished to practise but in order to acquire the scientific knowledge and status to equip her to wage an effective campaign against animal experimentation and for dietary reform. After passing the examinations of the Apothecaries Hall in November 1873, Anna had to continue her studies in Paris, since the English medical schools were then closed to women. She had recently met Edward Maitland, a widowed relative some twenty years her senior, who became her spiritual partner. He shared with Algernon the duties of chaperoning Anna during her frequent trips to the Continent and supporting her through the arduous course of study. In 1880 her doctoral thesis, L'Alimentation végétale de l'homme was accepted, not without considerable opposition. It appeared in English a year later as The Perfect Way in Diet, a manifesto for 'purity in diet, compassion for the animals, the exaltation of womanhood, and mental and moral unfoldment through the purification of the organism'. On her return to England she occupied herself with a successful London medical practice, mainly with women patients, and continued her association with Maitland, with whom she shared the mystical experiences described in their joint work The Perfect

Way (1881), based on a lecture series that won them considerable acclaim and led to an invitation to join the Theosophical Society. Anna was almost immediately elected president of the London Lodge in 1883, but owing to differences about the Masters and the emphasis to be placed on Christian as distinct from Oriental sources, formed a separate Lodge, which then split off to become the Hermetic Society. Its meetings were attended by many of the Theosophists, and papers (on Kabbalism and alchemy) were also contributed by Dr Wynn Westcott and MacGregor Mathers, who were shortly to inaugurate the Order of the Golden Dawn. Anna and Maitland maintained friendly relations with the TS, including HPB, who characteristically dubbed them the 'Perfect Wayfarers'. However, in spite of her success as a physician, writer, and lecturer, and the near adulation of her coterie, who were as charmed by her beauty and elegance as a woman as they were impressed by her vision and profundity as a teacher and seer, Anna was frequently prostrated by illnesses, for which she resorted to chloroform and laudanum, and increasingly tormented by depression and suicidal thoughts as her fortieth birthday approached. Her diary entries poignantly express her despair:

9 months since I wrote a line in my Diary. Time enough in which to have conceived and borne a child ...[yet she felt she was only marking time.] 'I know what I want ... to be away in strange places - prairies, fjords, etc. I want a friend with whom to visit solitudes. Is it Love that I want? No, not the common, vulgar cry, the cry of all sickly women-folk, the sing-song of drawing-room misses. I want a friend. There are too many men and women; there is too little Humanity ... There is a dearth of understanding, of nakedness of spirit. All of us are over-dressed ... Truth is dead, is dead - or has she never yet come to birth? (June 22, 1886, cited by Maitland II).

Here is more than a hint of her ambivalence towards Maitland, her protector and nurse as well as spiritual collaborator, who also exercised a restraining, or restrictive, influence. He discouraged her interest in 'practical occultism' and 'experimental methods' in alchemy (also deprecated by HPB), which took the form of hurling 'spiritual thunderbolts' against the vivisectors Claude Bernard and Pasteur with murderous intent. He also diverted her from responding to an intimation received while asleep that 'she could not expect to have given to her a revelation of the mysteries of the Kingdom of Love while leading an ascetic life' (Maitland II, p.1). The explanation of these destructive and erotic impulses was gradually revealed through a dream horoscope and other signs. Anna's previous incarnations - as Faustine, Anne Boleyn, et al. - indicated for her the 'Path of the Harlot', and her refusal to follow it in her present incarnation was bringing on her the evil Karma (here is introduced an Oriental concept) created in her previous lives, hence her misfortunes and suffering. The early deaths of her previous selves protected her from the experience of ageing, preserving her youth but also luring her to re-enactment through suicide. According to Maitland, she had 'no substantial permanent personality' (II, p. 351), and accordingly he had to act as the guardian of her mental continuity.

Diagnostically, the occult interpretation of Anna's experience and behaviour was satisfying and constructive, in that it formed an integral part of their evolving mystical system. It is not difficult to translate this occult psychopathology into the terminology of some conventional psychiatric paradigms, substituting multiple personalities, split-off parts of the self, archetypes of the collective unconscious, etc. for the past selves, and dissociation, repression, sublimation, etc. for the mechanisms responsible for karma and reincarnation. From a relativist standpoint these are simply different metaphors for systematizing phenomena, and both Freud and Jung explored mythological and symbolic meanings in the content of the psyche. Therapeutically, however, interpretation and understanding are not usually sufficient to resolve conflicts and complexes, and in Anna's case the elaboration of a mystical cosmology on the spiritual plane (or fantasy level) performed no abreactive function and left untouched her mundane situation. Maitland's protective collusion prevented her integrating the split-off destructive and sexual elements into a whole personality, and she was denied the opportunity of 'working through' her dependence on the father (actual and surrogate) to an adult sexual relationship with her husband or a fully maternal relationship with her child. It could be that her obsession with pet guinea-pigs was an acting-out of her inability to come to terms with the child in herself and a fortiori with her daughter.

Unfortunately Anna never received the disinterested psychological support that might have enabled her to struggle through to maturity, and the medical treatment she underwent proved disastrous. It is little wonder that on reaching the menopause with the emotional tasks of the first half of life unfulfilled she was unable to survive the 'mid-life crisis' and found a way out through virtual suicide. Her death in 1888 was attended by unseemly bickering about her status as a member of the Roman church.

Maitland survived to write her biography and republish her writings, and to found the Esoteric Christian Union devoted to the 'New Gospel of Interpretation'. This was 'neither an invention nor a compilation, but first, a discovery, and next, a recovery' – discovery because it ascertains the nature and method of existence, and recovery because it proves to be the 'basic and secret doctrine of all the great religions of antiquity, including Christianity, – the doctrine commonly called the Gnosis, and variously entitled Hermetic and Kabbalistic' (Kingsford and Maitland 1887, p. li). Essentially, the Divine Mind, bent on self-manifestation or creation, conceives the Ideal Humanity as a vehicle in which to descend from Being into Existence. Human Nature in its perfection (Christ) is twofold in operation, expressing the opposites of Will/Love, Justice/Mercy, Energy/Space, Life/Substance, Positive/Negative, i.e. Male/Female. Male/Female qualities are in their union and cooperation the life and salvation of the world; in division and antagonism its death and destruction.

According to Kingsford and Maitland, as to other contemporary occultists, 1881 was a pivotal year between two dispensations, the one evil and adulterous (the product of conflict between opposites), and the other the prelude to 'heaven on earth' (their reconciliation). The time was therefore ripe to promulgate the Doctrine: the product of the Woman (Intuition), whose office is Interpretation, was to be submitted to the manipulation of the Man (Intellect), whose office is Manifestation. This Doctrine was adapted for promulgation into a world in which intuition was nearly extinct and intellect alone active, but bound to sense-nature (materialism). The renascence of the feminine principle (Isis, Sophia, the Great Mother) with its mission of renewal was a dominant theme in the esoteric teaching of the time, and one that recommended itself to mystical feminists. Nor is it too far-fetched to see its secular analogue in the image of the New Woman referred to above.

The next subject of biographical exploration was a devoted friend of Anna Kingsford, but a far more robust character.

Isabelle de Steiger (1836-1927)

Unlike Anna Kingsford, who achieved fame in her own time and is still remembered today, Isabelle de Steiger (née Isabel Lace) [6] was known to a relatively small circle in her lifetime and is now forgotten. Nevertheless, she was a painter and the author of several articles and books on mystical subjects, as well as a highly entertaining autobiography (de Steiger, 1927), which, though unreliable as to dates and extremely prejudiced in its judgements, provides much insight into the upper-middle-class society in which she grew up and the genteel fringes of Bohemia she inhabited in her widowhood. She was one of seven children born to a Liverpool solicitor of artistic inclinations whom she describes as one of the younger sons of County families with money and university education who formed the 'Upper Ten' of Liverpool society. Her mother died when she was five, her father when she was fifteen, and she completed her education in the care of an aunt. At twenty-five she married a Swiss cotton merchant, who died ten years later. These 'regular decimal cycles' punctuating her life assumed great importance in her eyes. Instead of returning to her family on the death of her husband in Egypt, she decided to study art, first in Cairo and Florence and then, after settling in London in 1874, at Heatherley's School and the Slade. She managed to support herself on the proceeds of her work, supplemented by a small private income, and was sufficiently talented to exhibit in most of the leading galleries, including the Royal Academy and the Society of Women Artists (see Wood, 1978). She painted portraits of several Theosophists, including Anna Kingsford and Patience Sinnett, but unfortunately much of her work was destroyed in a fire.

At first, while seeking to establish herself, she went through 'a somewhat rough time' occasioned partly by depression over her husband's death and partly by the usual obstacles to independence placed in the way of a well-bred lady by family and friends, and in her case by the art establishment. Women artists found difficulty in renting studios, and were not admitted to life classes at art schools, so Isabelle and her women colleagues organized their own, and thereby became aware of the plight of the models, then regarded as little more than tarts. Recognition of their common condition as working women produced a feeling of solidarity and efforts to improve their status and treatment. While Isabelle did not associate herself with any organized branch of the women's movement, she identified with the feminist outlook with regard to issues that came within her own experience, such as education and employment. Her attitude to the women's movement, and later to the Theosophical Society, exemplifies a strain of individualism and radical conservatism very characteristic of English thought (cf. George Eliot). She was dismissive of the constraints of Victorian bourgeois society, and birth, character, and some talent enabled her to override them to a considerable extent. This independence manifested itself in her religious development. Even as a girl, she was 'not devoted to the church and clergy'. Her mother's family were Evangelicals, 'like all Irish Protestants', but there were Unitarians on her father's side, and later she had to endure the dour Calvinism of her Swiss in-laws. None of these variants of Christianity afforded spiritual satisfaction, and in her early widowhood she experienced a 'black period': 'I do not think I was completely born until I was about thirty-six' (de Steiger, 1929, p.1). Her spiritual rebirth, during which she 'evolved a deeper philosophy' came about through an interest in spiritualism – to her family's disgust she contributed to the periodical Light – and through her study of hermetic philosophy. She was a friend of Mrs Penny, a student of Jacob Boehme, and of Mrs Atwood, author of A Suggestive Inquiry into Hermetic Philosophy and Alchemy (1850). Above all she admired Anna Kingsford, whom she held in higher esteem than she did the rebarbative HPB. Through her association with the medium Mrs Hollis Billing, and with Miss Kislingbury (see above, p.35), she became a member of the first Theosophical group in London. Many of these people shared Isabelle's reservations about HPB's eccentricities, and gravitated towards Anna Kingsford and her Hermetic Society as well as aligning themselves with A. P. Sinnett, the pupil of HPB who was often at loggerheads with her and came to dominate the London Lodge of the TS. The advent on the Theosophical scene of Annie Besant at the end of the eighties dismayed the Sinnett faction (who were almost defiantly Conservative), and they were further alienated when HPB's new-found favourite took over as her virtual successor when the Old Lady passed over (or pegged out, as she herself would have put it) in 1891. Like many others, Isabelle withdrew from the TS, her disillusionment deepened by the refusal of the Theosophical Publishing Company to accept her first book, On a Gold Basis, allegedly on account of its Christian character. The book eventually appeared under another imprint in 1907, and was followed by Superhumanity, and by a translation of Karl von Eckertshausen's Cloud upon the Sanctuary. The latter work originated in papers presented to the Alchemical Society of London, which flourished just before the First World War. After the war Isabelle became acquainted with the work of Rudolph

Steiner (who had left the TS in 1913 to form his own Anthroposoph-
ical Society), and it seems that in his presentation of mystical
philosophy she at last found a summation that resonated with her own
experience. In many ways she was a typical 'seeker', whose lifelong
quest took her through a succession of phases – spiritualism,
Theosophy, Rosicrucianism, alchemy, Anthroposophy – but, as her
own writings show, this was no dilettante sampling of current fads,
but a consistent attempt to find a social milieu responsive to her
developing spiritual needs. But where her mentor Anna Kingsford was
a leader, Isabelle de Steiger was essentially a loner, in her art and
her mysticism as in her feminism.

Isabel Cooper-Oakley (1854-1914)

The younger Isabel offers a striking contrast to her namesake, who
regarded with some amusement this personification of the New Woman
of the eighties, who so rapidly became the intimate of HPB and Annie
Besant. She was born in Amritsar, the daughter of Henry Cooper,
C.B., Commissioner of Lahore, a supporter of the cause of Indian
education, including the education of women. No doubt he encouraged
his daughter's desire for higher education, but her entry to Girton
was delayed until 1882 owing to illness following an accident in her
early twenties. In the intervening years she became interested in
spiritualism, studied Isis Unveiled, and became involved in the women's suffrage movement and the Social Purity Alliance. At Cambridge
she met a group of young men who were soon to become prominent
in the Theosophical Society, including Bertram Keightley, who acted
as amanuensis to HPB, G. R. S. Mead, who became HPB's secretary, and married Isabel's sister Laura, and her own future husband,
A. J. Oakley. Isabel and Laura joined the TS in 1884 during a visit
to London of HPB, who was gratified by this accession of younger,
university-educated supporters, some of whom accompanied her on
her return to India, including the recently married Cooper-Oakleys
(in true feminist style they had hyphenated their names); apparently
they sunk all their resources in the venture. In December of that
year, the Theosophical convention assembled in Madras, and Isabel's
speech was especially well received. However, these deliberations
took place against the gathering storm of the press campaign
orchestrated by Christian missionaries against the Theosophical
Society, and specifically accusing HPB of fraudulent mediumistic
practices. Characteristically, HPB wanted to fight a libel action, but
a committee that included the Cooper-Oakleys vetoed litigation, and
the dejected HPB departed for Europe never to return. The scandal
that exploded following the investigation carried out by the Society
for Psychical Research (SPR, 1885) split the TS and nearly finished
HPB. After a period wandering round the Continent (during which
she was visited by Anna Kingsford), HPB was persuaded by Bertram
Keightley and others to settle in London to complete the writing of
her magnum opus, The Secret Doctrine. Isabel and Laura joined her
household, and became pillars of the Blavatsky Lodge, founded in

what can only be described as opposition to the London Lodge dominated by the Sinnetts. It seems that Cooper-Oakley remained in India as editor of The Theosophist, but left the Society in 1887 on account of doctrinal differences with HPB, who cabled that the entire Blavatsky Lodge would resign were he readmitted. It seems that this may have been the parting of the ways for Isabel and her husband, for no further mention of him appears in the official history of the TS.

Undoubtedly Isabel had plenty to occupy her in London, and not simply Theosophy. About 1890, under the name of Madame Isabel, she opened a hat shop in New Bond Street. According to Isabelle de Steiger, this was so unheard-of an event that it 'excited Mr Labouchere, the Editor of Truth, into many words ... Extravagant prices were asked and willingly paid by society Theosophists and their wealthy friends ... who expected that Mr Labouchere's Girton-Lady-Milliner would produce rare, weird, and wonderful bonnets. She did not. She only produced inordinately expensive ones' (de Steiger, 1929, pp.159-60). After the failure of this enterprise, Isabel, undeterred, started no less than two Dorothy Restaurants, one for West-End working girls and one for ladies. No doubt it was to the latter, with 'its neat little tables and special china' and Kate Greenaway décor, that Isabelle de Steiger repaired on opening day, together with a bevy of advanced Society ladies - and the press. Leading lady artists ('society had not by then entirely dropped the word "lady" - we had not all become "women"') exhibited their pictures, and Isabelle's 'Spirit of the Crystal' - a work inspired by Anna Kingsford and fresh from the Grosvenor Gallery - was voted the prize ('a nice five-pound note').

Working girls of a different sort were catered for in another establishment that Isabelle was unlikely to have patronized, for it had been set up by Annie Besant with money anonymously donated to HPB 'for the service of humanity'. This was the HPB Club for Working Girls situated in the Bow Road, an area of the East End by then stiff with 'settlements' set up in imitation of, or rivalry with, Toynbee Hall. However, this one was exceptional, since it was inspired by Theosophy rather than Christianity, and its clientele was composed of factory girls, and in particular the Bryant and Mays matchgirls whom Annie Besant and Herbert Burrows had so spectacularly helped to unionize during their aptly named strike. Relays of Theosophical ladies, led by Laura Cooper and her sister, helped to run the hostel and club. The premises were also used for meetings by trade unions and by the Social Democratic Federation, as George Lansbury (who himself later joined the TS) gratefully records in his autobiography (Lansbury, 1928, pp.6-7).

For the rest of her life, Isabel was engaged in official duties of one kind and another on behalf of the Society, and spent much time on lecture tours in Australia and various European countries as well as the UK, but after the turn of the century her base was in Italy. In 1900 she published Tradition in Masonry and Medieval Mysticism (a work that was reissued in 1977), and in 1907 presided over an international committee set up by Annie Besant for research into mystical traditions. Her study of the Comte de Saint Germain was re-published posthumously in 1927. According to Theosophical teaching, the Comte was one of the incarnations of the Master Rakoczi, a member of the Occult Hierarchy with a special concern for ceremonial magic. Isabel was believed to have been in direct contact with the 'Hungarian Adept', so it is perhaps of some significance that her death in 1914 occurred in Budapest. At the annual White Lotus Day meeting commemorating the founder, Annie Besant paid tribute to Isabel Cooper-Oakley as a 'devoted pupil of HPB'. She was also un-usually loyal to the TS, having remained in active membership for thirty years, and having accepted the leadership of Annie Besant whose innovations had proved too much for other members of HPB's entourage. G. R. S. Mead, Laura Cooper's husband, for instance, became increasingly estranged from Annie Besant, and in 1909 resigned from the Society to form the Guild of the Quest. In the words of Clara Codd, a militant suffragette who became the first paid national lecturer for the TS, commenting on such defections: 'It is quite a common practice in the TS; so many attracted by the thought, drift in and out. A small proportion can never leave it again; for them it is life and eternity' (Codd, 1951, p.96). Isabel was undoubtedly one of these.

Some Problems of a Biographical Approach

The variations in the quantity and nature of the information given about the three subjects of the preceding accounts point to a few of the problems encountered in gathering biographical material about substantial numbers of people involved in a movement, which ideally should result in a kind of Namierization of the Theosophical Society. Because of the diversity of the sources, it is difficult to obtain com-parable data for everyone, even as regards the main events of their lives. In the case of Anna Kingsford, there is Maitland's two-volume biography (sans index), which is undoubtedly selective, but never-theless contains diary extracts, letters, poems, sketches, and other material by the subject herself. There are also many contemporary references by Theosophists and others, and she features in biographical dictionaries of the day and in some modern works on occultism and vegetarianism. There are also her own writings, which read in relation to the biography, provide what it is legitimate to regard as an accurate reflection of her states of mind. Not only the events of her life, but her personal experience, are accessible, since she was concerned to make them so. Her mystical ideas were in fact an exegesis of her experience or, more accurately, of the experience shared with Maitland. On this solid base of information, it would be perfectly feasible - and very worth while - to write a full biography of Anna Kingsford.

In the case of Isabelle de Steiger, there is her own autobiography, largely written when she was over eighty and after her diaries had been lost. The official Theosophical view is that it is unreliable, and it certainly contains errors of fact and date; but these are easily adjusted, and when one is primarily interested in the experience of an individual it is the openness of self-revelation that counts. Furthermore, Isabel's mordant comments on controversial personalities provide a salutary corrective to the bland portrayals by their partisans. Her astute and witty observations convey something of the flavour of occasions and their participants, including, as we have seen, Anna Kingsford and Isabel Cooper-Oakley. Isabelle herself features in the correspondence and memoirs of contemporary Theosophists, in various histories of the movement, and also in reference works on Victorian painters, so her self-portrait is rounded out. In general they reflect the image of the vivacious, forthright, humorous lady wearing a becoming Greenaway dress and casually holding palette and brushes, who appears in a photograph in her autobiography.

Isabel Cooper-Oakley presents much greater difficulties, since there appears to be no biography or autobiography, and information about her has to be pieced together from the other types of source. Undoubtedly this could be greatly amplified by following up the indications provided, and by laborious recourse to TS records and periodicals. Such an exercise in depth is hardly feasible in dealing with scores of individuals, but the fact that there <u>are</u> scores of them, about all of whom something can be discovered, means that a composite picture emerges of a number of types about whom inferences may be drawn. Networks and groupings of people may be discerned in terms of affinities and antagonisms, and against this densely textured background reflections are projected of their individual experience. On this basis it is possible cautiously to adumbrate a number of orientations to Theosophy and feminism, and to speculate about the subjective reasons and even the objective determinations operative in each of them. Taking the three women as exemplars, three 'ideal types' may be proposed: Leaders, Loners, and Disciples.

Types of Orientation

Leaders

Anna Kingsford undoubtedly falls within this category, along with Madame Blavatsky and Mrs Besant. All were innovators possessed of the personal charisma that attracts a devoted following. But they operated in very different ways. Although the titles of seer, magus [7], prophetess, initiate, or occultist can properly be applied to HPB and Anna Kingsford (and were acceptable to them, though 'medium' emphatically was not), they do not fit Annie Besant, who showed no spontaneous psychic gifts and had to work hard to develop such powers after becoming a Theosophist. Annie, in fact, played the militant organizing and publicizing role in the movement (as she had earlier done among secularists, Malthusians, and Fabians) originally taken by Olcott, whom she followed as president of the TS on his death in 1907. She built various institutional frameworks within which others, notably C. W. Leadbeater and her protege Krishnamurti, could exercise their occult powers. Whereas there was a rather neat

division of labour between HPB and Olcott, the even closer partnership of Anna Kingsford and Edward Maitland involved joint activity.
Immersed in their shared experience (amounting at times to folie a
deux), they were neither of them disposed to undertake the organiz-
ational labours required to build a large scale movement, preferring
the select coterie attracted by their writing and lecturing. In terms of
Weber's typology (1965, p.46 et seq.), Anna Kingsford approxim-
ated to the exemplary and HPB to the ethical prophet. Both Olcott
and Annie Besant were concerned with the routinization of HPB's
charisma in consolidating the TS as a world-wide organization, but
the groups founded by Anna Kingsford and Edward Maitland – the
Hermetic Society and the Esoteric Christian Union – did not survive
their inspirers.

Loners

This term will serve to characterize Isabelle de Steiger, for whom
independence was the keynote of existence. Although she participated
in various groups, there is no evidence of her having held office,
and she moved on when they ceased to satisfy her needs. She was
clearly suspicious of large-scale organizations, and was drawn to the
small intimate circle of Anna Kingsford and to the reclusive Mrs
Atwood. She was equally unwilling to become involved in the art
world, and had little time for the Chelsea 'art set' [8]. Nor, after her
husband's death, did she seek another partner or lapse into dependence on one spiritual teacher. She was undoubtedly unusual in dis-
playing so high a degree of autonomy and ego-strength while remaining an isolate. Such individuals are hard to locate because they lack
salience. Mrs Atwood, who was revered as a Theosophical teacher,
is a case in point. She never joined the TS, though she donated her
extensive library to the London Lodge. Confirmation of the existence
of a sizable number of temperamental non-joiners is however,
provided by the creation of a special category of 'non-attached
members' for individuals who subscribe to the TS but do not belong
to a Lodge or commit themselves to participate in activities.

Isabelle's individualistic stance is characteristic of the aristocratic
rebel, whose disdain for bourgeois convention provides a vicarious
thrill for the bourgeoisie itself. It is plausible to interpret Isabelle's
rebellion in this sense, for her family's 'county' antecedents inclined
her to identify with the professions and the arts and to regard the
commerical world of her husband and his friends as distinctly odd.
Distaste for industrial society and the parvenu middle class was
motivated as much by the apprehensions of the landowning interest
(witness the struggles over the 1832 Reform Bill) as by the suffering of the masses and the conscience of reformers. Among Theosophists, as among other contemporary critics of industrialism, two
bases of dissent may be discerned. On the one hand there were those
such as Annie Besant and her fellow-Socialists Herbert Burrows and
Mrs Despard who argued from a socialist standpoint for forward-
looking political and economic change, and saw Theosophy as integral

to this movement. HPB herself, despite her attachment to her aristocratic Russian family, was democratic in outlook and expressed sympathy for these aspirations in her endorsement of Edward Bellamy
(Blavatsky, 1889). On the other hand were many members of the
upper-class London Lodge of the TS centred on the Sinnetts, who regarded Theosophy as the vehicle for spiritual progress among a
(self)-chosen elite and abhorred the efforts of the 'left wing' to offer
Theosophy to the masses. According to Isabelle de Steiger: 'The
words "Mr Gladstone" made Mr Sinnett smile gently at anyone men-
tioning his name! I felt very much akin to him. I never was a Demo-
crat' (de Steiger, 1927, p.158). It is not surprising, then, that
she took an instant dislike to Annie Besant:

> As an Irish woman, she was, of course, 'agin' all governments and
> 'agin' everything that did not meet with her approbation. This is a
> vulgar but true statement. I remember especially the speech to in-
> cite the match girls to their first strike. What a cruel and second-
> rate policy that was (ibid., p.150).

These trivial but revealing comments serve as indicators of a deep
division in the TS between those who understood the first of its Objects in an egalitarian sense, regarding the 'nucleus of the universal
brotherhood of humanity' as a kind of revolutionary cadre dedicated
to struggle on behalf of humankind on the political as well as the
spiritual plane, and those who saw in it a charter for a small company of the elect to accelerate their evolutionary progress towards
membership of the Occult Hierarchy presiding over the affairs of the
universe. The not infrequent rifts in the Society tended to follow this
'basic fault', with the militants on one side and the mystics on the
other (to borrow the useful distinction made by Adam Curle, 1972).
These two factions may be located within the scheme proposed by
Raymond Williams (1973) for the analysis of cultural forms. In this,
the 'effective dominant culture', understood as a process rather than
a static entity, refers to 'a central system of practices, meanings and
values' that perpetuates its hegemony by incorporating and modifying
new trends, and constantly reinterpreting itself. The new, or
'emergent' forms are notably associated with new classes, and may
appear as 'alternative' or 'oppositional' to the dominant culture, either
as 'incorporated' elements (the 'loyal opposition') or as 'resigned
areas' (excluded or neglected, and with some degree of autonomy).
Similarly, 'residual' forms associated with earlier social formations
(such as the feudal landed gentry) may persist as alternative or
oppositional, and may likewise be incorporated or resigned.
  As suggested above, the mid-to-late-Victorian era was one in
which the hegemony of the values of industrialism had by no means
been completely established, being challenged on the one hand by
'residual' aristocratic and land-owning interests, many of which were
incorporated, and on the other by 'emergent' socialistic trends represented by the industrialized working class and by new fractions of
the middle class, which at that stage were largely oppositional (later,
of course, they became largely incorporated). The Theosophical

Society may be seen as a microcosm of this design ('as above, so below'), embodying these contradictory tendencies within its own membership and, at the same time, relating to the wider culture both as an innovative oppositional force and as a conservative influence harking back to traditional religious themes – the revival of the 'ancient wisdom' or, in the idiom of the nineteen-eighties, 'rejected knowledge'. The traditional, mystical, and holistic aspects of Theosophical doctrine correspond to Mannheim's delineation of conservative thought (1953).

Disciples

The enthusiastic group that assembled around HPB, and later Annie Besant, were certainly disciples in the Weberian sense, for their presence was essential to that routinization of the movement whereby the permanence of the preaching and the continuity of the religious community is assured (Weber, 1968, p. 70). Indeed, these people regarded themselves explicitly as disciples, pupils, chelas, and in many instances threw up other commitments to put themselves and their incomes at the disposal of the TS. This path was followed by the Cooper-Oakleys, but whereas the husband departed after a decade or so, Isabel remained until her death, having transferred her loyalty from HPB to Annie Besant. Others who had been closely associated with HPB, such as Countess Wachtmeister and Miss Arundale, continued to serve in official capacities under her successor, while others such as Miss Kislingbury could not accept her innovations and drifted away. Generally speaking, it was the male disciples who, having clashed with Annie Besant, set up their own organizations. The most notable was W. Q. Judge, one of the original 'Founders' and head of the American Section, who after a long-drawn-out constitutional battle with Annie and Olcott, split the Society and formed the independent Theosophical Society in America in 1895. Henceforth there were to be two Theosophical Societies claiming the apostolic succession from HPB and competing for the affiliation of lodges internationally.

Annie Besant had the capacity to inspire strong personal attachments, as in the case of Esther Bright, daughter of her old friends the Radical MP Jacob Bright and his wife Ursula, campaigners for the suffrage (Bright, 1936), and Lady Emily Lutyens, who took maternal charge of the young Krishnamurti. But many disciples experienced considerable strain, torn between loyalty to the Society, personal attachment to one of its leaders, and fidelity to Theosophical doctrines. The contradictions built into the Society's constitution: on the one hand, tolerance and freedom of conscience for all members; on the other the proclamation of certain specific doctrines, set up an instability that was bound to lead to disagreements and schisms. The situation parallels that of the Rationalist and Humanist organizations described by Budd (1977). Faced with these paradoxical injunctions to be both loyal and independent, committed TS members had to negotiate their own modus vivendi or, as so many of them did, move on. The three biographies sketched above illustrate some typical dilemmas.

Some Recurrent Features

These biographical explorations of a few individuals seek to show some of the ways in which women with feminist aspirations used the Theosophical movement as a means to express and realize their needs and beliefs. Although these women related to the movement in very different ways, they had some features in common.

As regards religious background, they tended to have had Evangelical upbringings, but to have been exposed to other sectarian influences, such as Unitarianism, in youth. Often one or other parent had held unorthodox views. Dissatisfaction with the Church of England, combined with awareness of alternatives, initiated a spiritual quest that sometimes included a period of agnosticism or even atheism, as in the case of Annie Besant. Several turned to Catholicism (Mrs Despard, Anna Kingsford, Miss Kislingbury) before or after becoming Theosophists, but almost universally they became involved in spiritualism before moving on to Theosophy. This transition occurs in individual after individual (male and female), and there seem to be no cases in which the movement was in the reverse direction, presumably because Theosophy represents a more sophisticated and elaborated philosophical system and those who abandon it join (or rejoin) one of the established denominations or proceed to another esoteric sect (as W. B. Yeats and Maud Gonne turned to the Golden Dawn, and Isabelle de Steiger to Anthroposophy) or, occasionally, to a more authoritarian sect such as Christian Science.

Not uncommonly one or both parents had died while the subject was a child, with some disruption of family life and her education. Many regretted the lack of formal education, but often they had much broader opportunities for self-education through access to private libraries and the company of stimulating adults. In some ways they were fortunate in being spared the brutalizing and academically restricted schooling endured by their envied brothers. Since these women were intellectually gifted, awareness of the discrepant treatment accorded to boys and girls was an early stimulus to feminism. Private incomes were in many cases the key to the later pursuit of higher education and a career.

Some of the women remained single, and of those who married a high proportion were widowed relatively early or separated from their husbands. Even the happy marriages seemed to have involved some measure of sexual trauma, and it seems that subsequent close relationships were platonic. The partnerships of HPB and Olcott, and Anna Kingsford and Edward Maitland, were indispensable to their mission. Annie Besant had a series of close collaborators, from Charles Bradlaugh in her secular phase, through Edward Aveling, Bernard Shaw, and Herbert Burrows in her socialist phase, to Professor Chakravati and C. W. Leadbeater when she became a Theosophist. Mrs Despard, who formed emotional ties with other women after her husband's death, was convinced of continuing communication with him through the planchette and seances.

During the period under review there was a heavy emphasis on 'purity' in advanced circles. The model for man-woman relationships was that of 'comrades' (or 'chums' in the case of Olcott and HPB), as though equality between the sexes could be achieved only by the renunciation of sexuality, which was associated with male domination and the degradation of woman. Companionate marriage, as between Havelock Ellis and Edith Lees (members of the Fellowship of the New Life) and Beatrice Potter and Sidney Webb (the paradigmatic Fabians) were much admired; while not entirely trouble-free platonic relationships, including that with Annie Besant, were widely indulged in by Bernard Shaw before he escaped into what was probably a mariage blanc with Charlotte Payne-Townsend. For most emancipated women, freedom implied freedom from sex, rather than sexual freedom. Eleanor Marx who 'set up' with Edward Aveling after his fervent but 'pure' interlude with Annie, was exceptional among women in her milieu in wanting her free union to be a union in all respects (Kapp, 1976). Although there was some talk of 'free love' at the time, and even some practice of it, notably among spiritualist communities in the USA, it was in general frowned upon by English socialists and severely castigated by Theosophists. Theosophists looked forward to a coming stage in human evolution when sex would be transcended, though they were not averse to recalling amorous exploits in their past lives. Such fantasies were virtually institutionalized means of dealing with untamed libido.

It would seem that maternal feeling was not very strong, or was displaced onto other objects, among the female Theosophists. Isabelle de Steiger, Isabel Cooper-Oakley, and Caroline Despard were childless as, it goes without saying, were those who were unmarried. Anna Kingsford's daughter is rarely mentioned by Maitland, and then only in ominous terms as having 'much improved' under the tutelage of a new governess. Anna's apparent preference for her guinea-pigs may, of course, be a reflection of her biographer's bias. Ironically, Annie Besant, who was devoted to her children, lost custody of them for long periods to her vindictive husband on account of her then atheism. Whatever their private feelings may have been, it seems that the Theosophical women tended to limit domestic commitments, including children, as did many Fabians and feminists.

It is sometimes alleged that there was an unconscious lesbian element in the close attachments formed by Annie Besant with other women, including HPB and Esther Bright, and their admittedly florid correspondence is referred to with patronising amusement even by Nethercot, Annie's scholarly biographer. What he and other male commentators contrive to miss is the degree to which these women supported and learnt from each other, instead of depending on masculine direction and authority in spiritual and intellectual as in all other matters in the way society required them to do. The recognition by women of the contribution made by their own sex in fields hitherto claimed by men is a powerful reinforcer of their self-esteem. Since signs of female competence are still viewed with incredulity and resentment, allowances must always be made for the tendency among male writers to present these pioneering feminists as mildly deranged and faintly laughable. Hell hath no fury like a man upstaged.

In Conclusion

I have tried to situate the early Theosophical Society in the context of the emergent social groups of the eighteen-eighties which express-ed the protest of sections of the middle and upper classes against what they perceived as a monstrous and life-denying orthodoxy. I have also tried to show that the dominant ideology was by no means monolithic, because this was a period of transition when capitalism was entering a new phase with new interests struggling for express-ion. In terms of Raymond Williams's analysis of culture, both residual and emergent forms provided an opposition to a divided dominant culture, and some of them became incorporated in it. The Theosoph-ical movement contained both residual elements, in its appeal to the ancient wisdom and occult tradition, and emergent elements in its future-orientated psogsamme for humanity, which allied it wmth soc-ialist and feminist aims. Individual biographies can show how these strands are interwoven and suggest their social origins in the class structure, specifically among the intelligentsia – the wilder fringes of that 'intellectual aristocracy' anatomized by Noel Annan (1955) [9] – which included members both of the traditional aristocracy and of the professional middle classes.

Notes

1. Socialists and Theosophists made good copy for the New Journal-ism, with its brighter, more gossipy, even sensational choice of topics and presentation. Massingham of the Star, a friend of Herbert Burrows and for a time a Fabian, covered the Match Girls' strike and also various doings of the Theosophists, including the opening of the Dorothy Restaurants (see below). Annie Besant, whose Fleet Street colleagues included the crusading editor (and spiritualist) W. T. Stead, could always be certain of widespread press coverage from the popular papers to the heavies.

2. It would be tedious to detail all the works consulted on the his-tory of the TS, many of which repeat each other and perpetuate well-loved myths. Among primary sources may be noted: Besant (1893); Bright (1936); Ransom (1938); Sinnett (1886, 1922); de Steiger (1927); Wachtmeister (1839), together with Olcott's diary (1895) and the collected writings of HPB (de Zirkoff, ed. 1960 onwards). Among secondary sources is Nethercot's exhaustive biography of Annie Besant (vol. II 1963). Mention should here be made of a recent work (Campbell, 1980) giving a straightforward scholarly ac-count, based on the standard sources, of the movement primarily seen from the American point of view.

3. Rosa Swiney (born in 1847), suffragist, food-reformer, foun-der of the League of Isis, and leading light of the Higher Thought

Centre in London, regarded woman as the 'first and most beneficent Inventor and Discoverer, while man was the Ravisher and Destroyer of Nature' (Mitchell, 1977, p.8).

4. This volume appears in the bibliography of Freud's Interpretation of Dreams (1900), but unfortunately he does not discuss the work.

5. These and other names were of great significance to Anna Kingsford, and represented different aspects of her personality. Annie Bonus became Mrs Algernon Kingsford, and later Dr Kingsford; her husband called her Nina, her brother Ninon, a name she used for some of her literary work and which expressed a more masculine side. Maitland addressed her, and wrote of her, by her mystical name, Mary.

6. To avoid confusion, the form Isabelle will be used in referring to Madame de Steiger, and Isabel for Mrs Cooper-Oakley (see below), although each lady used both forms.

7. In her interesting study The Myth of the Magus (1948), E. M. Butler lists ten 'stock features' some or all of which recur in the magus-legend: supernatural or mysterious origin; portents at birth; perils in infancy; an initiation; wanderings; a magical contest; a trial or persecution; a last scene; violent or mysterious death; a resurrection or ascension. She concludes that HPB can be properly placed in this tradition. To a lesser degree Anna Kingsford too satisfies her criteria.

8. As is shown in the following anecdote:

> The last time I saw Oscar Wilde was at a private view in the Grosvenor Gallery. He addressed me on my entrance: 'Where have you been, Madame de Steiger, and where are you going?' I said briefly: 'I am going to leave London and live in Liverpool.' He drew himself up (he was a tall, fat, large man) and addressing the crowd around about us, said in a clear, loud, vibrating platform voice: 'Liverpool? Where is Liverpool?', whereupon there was a buzz of delight. What idiots we were! (1927, p.85).

9. Annan traces the linkages between a series of families distinguished for intellectual achievement in the nineteenth century and after, who constitute 'a new class emerging in society' - Wedgwoods, Darwins, Stracheys, et al. Members of some of these families were involved in the groups referred to above (pp.7-9), for instance, Henry Sidgwick, Nora Balfour, and Edmund Gurney in the SPR; Beatrice Potter (Mrs Webb) and E. H. R. Pease in the Fabian Society; and James Ingall Wedgwood and St George Lane-Fox in the TS. What is important here is not so much the individuals as the milieu, the common social and intellectual background from which sprang both conformist and critical elements, thus ensuring that radical or heterodox ideas would to some extent become incorporated in mainstream thought.

References

(TPH = Theosphical Publishing House; TPS = Theosophical Publishing Society).

Annan, N. 'The Intellectual Aristocracy' in J. H. Plumb (ed.). Studies in Social History. London, Longmans, 1955

Bellamy, E. (1888). Looking Backward, 2000-1887. London, William Reeves, nd

Besant, A. An Autobiography. With an additional survey of her life by G. S. Arundale, reprinted 1939. Adyar, Madras, TPH, 1893

Blavatsky, H. P. Isis Unveiled: a Master-Key to the Mysteries of Ancient and Modern Science and Theology. New York, Bouton, 1887
___ The Key to Theosophy. London, TPS, 1889

Bright, E. Old Memories and Letters of Annie Besant. London, TPH, 1936

Budd, S. Variations of Unbelief: A Sociological Account of the Humanist Movement in Britain. London, Heinemann, 1977

Butler, E. M. The Myth of the Magus. Cambridge, Cambridge University Press, 1948

Campbell, B. F. Ancient Wisdom Revived: a History of the Theosophical Movement. Berkeley, Los Angeles, London, Univerity of California Press, 1980

Codd, C. M. So Rich a Life. Pretoria, Institute of Theosophical Publicity, 1951

Cooper-Oakley, I. (1900). Tradition in Masonry and Medieval Mysticism. Reissued London, TPH, 1977
___ The Comte de St Germain: the Secret of Kings. 2nd edn. London, TPH, 1927

Curle, A. Mystics and Militants: a Study of Awareness, Identity and Social Action. London, Tavistock, 1972

Despard, C. Theosophy and the Woman's Movement. London, TPS, 1913

Gauld, A. The Founders of Psychical Research. London, Routledge, 1968

Havighurst, A. H. Radical Journalist: H. W. Massingham. London, Cambridge University Press, 1974

Hobsbawm, E. Industry and Empire. London, Weidenfeld, 1968, Harmondsworth, Penguin, 1969

Holcombe, L. Victorian Ladies at Work. Newton Abbot, David and Charles, 1973

Kapp, Y. Eleanor Marx. 2 vols. London, Lawrence and Wishart, 1972, New York, Pantheon, 1976

Kingsford, N. (Anna) An Essay on the Admission of Women to the Parliamentary Franchise. London, Trubner's, 1868

Kingsford, A. B. and Maitland, E. The Perfect Way, or the Finding of Christ. Rev. edn, 1881, London, Field and Tuer, 1887

Lansbury, G. My Life. London, Constable, 1928

Linklater, A. An Unhusbanded Life: Charlotte Despard, Suffragette, Socialist and Sinn Feiner. London, Hutchinson, 1980

Macintyre, A. Secularization and Moral Change. London, Oxford University Press, 1967

Mackenzie, J. and Mackenzie, N. The First Fabians. London, Weidenfeld, 1977

Maitland, E. Anna Kingsford: her Life, Letters, Diary, and Work, by her collaborator. 2 vols. London, Redway, 1896

Mannheim, K. 'Conservative Thought' in Essays on Sociology and Social Psychology. London, Routledge, 1953

Marsh, D. C. The Changing Social Structure of England and Wales, 1871-1961. London, Routledge, 1958

Marx, K. (1852). The Eighteenth Brumaire of Louis Bonaparte. in D. Fernbach (ed.), Karl Marx: Surveys from Exile. Harmondsworth, Penguin, 1973

―――― and Engles, F. (1846). The German Ideology, ed. C. J. Arthur. London, Lawrence and Wishart, 1974

Mitchell, D. Queen Christabel: a Biography of Christabel Pankhurst. London, Macdonald and Jane's, 1977

Nelson, G. Spiritualism and Society. London, Routledge, 1969

Nethercot, A. H. The Last Four Lives of Annie Besant. London, Hart-Davis, 1963

Olcott, H. S. Old Diary Leaves. Vol I. New York, Putnam, 1895

Ransome, J. A Short History of the Theosophical Society. Adyar, Madras, TPH, 1938

Sinnett, A. P. Incidents in the Life of Madame Blavatsky. London, Redway, 1886

―――― The Early Days of Theosophy in Europe. London, TPH, 1922

Smith, W. S. The London Heretics, 1870-1914. London, Constable, 1967

Society for Psychical Research. Report of the Committee appointed to Investigate Phenomena connected with the Theosophical Society. Proceedings, Vol II, part ix, Dec. 1885

Steiger, I. de. Memorabilia: Reminiscences of a Woman Artist and Writer. London, Rider, 1927

Strachey, L. Eminent Victorians. London, Chatto, 1918

Strachey, R. (1928). The Cause: a Short History of the Women's Movement in Great Britain. London, Virago, 1978

Swiney, R. The Cosmic Procession, or the Female Principle in Evolution. London, 1906

Thompson, E. P. William Morris: Romantic to Revolutionary. 2nd edn. London, Merlin, 1977

Wachtmeister, C. and others. Reminiscences of H. P. Blavatsky and 'The Secret Doctrine'. London, TPS, 1893

Weber, M. (1922). The Sociology of Religion. London, Methuen, 1965

Williams, F. Fifty Years' March: the Rise of the Labour Party. London, Odhams, nd (c. 1950)

Williams, R. Base and Superstructure in Marxist Cultural Theory. New Left Review, No 82, Nov-Dec, 1973

Wood, C. Dictionary of Victorian Painters. 2nd edn. Woodbridge, Suffolk: Antique Collectors' Club, 1978

Zirkoff, B. de (ed.). H. P. Blavatsky: Collected Writings. 11

vols. London, Adyar, Wheaton, TPH, 1960 onwards

4 DOVES AND MAGPIES: VILLAGE WOMEN IN THE GREEK ORTHODOX CHURCH

Lucy Rushton

Introduction

The material presented in this paper provides another instance of the familiar equation of woman with nature and of women's consequent formal inferiority to men in religious ritual.Its main theme, however, is to show how in the village of Velvendos in Macedonia, northern Greece, women are placed, both through their social role and through biological and cultural definitions of their nature, in a position of greater involvement and responsibility in religious affairs than is the experience of most men. This responsibility is not something apparent only once in a while on occasions devoted to sacred performances, but constantly, in all the trivia of daily life.

An explanation of why this occurs can be found in the Greek Orthodox theology of the potential redemption of the entire natural world, of the physical part of creation as well as human souls (Ware, 1963, p.239). This redemption is, however, dependent on humanity. As will emerge from what follows, this theological concept does not have to be completely grasped by individuals for their conception of the world about them to accord in some degree with its principles. Even matter, it is known, especially in relation to icons and to miracles, can reveal God to humanity and be a manifestation of the spiritual world, and this notion of the potential of all material things is associated with the tendency to distinguish exterior appearances from 'more real' interiors. To illustrate the theological point about the redemption of matter, Timothy Ware selects a passage from Romans:

> The created universe waits with eager expectation for God's sons to be revealed... for the universe itself will be set free from its bondage to corruption and will enter into the liberty and splendour of the children of God. We know that until now the whole created universe has been groaning in the pangs of childbirth (Romans viii 19-22, quoted Ware, 1963, p.239) [1].

The two suggestions of gender in this passage ('God's sons' and 'childbirth') are relevant to my theme - it is the men who are held to be more morally responsible, but women who are more involved in the struggle implied by Orthodox aspirations. Through an account of certain symbolism relating to marriage we can see how these differing roles are allotted to men and women. Women are given a place of formal inferiority both in the family and in the church. This is sometimes justified in terms of women's failure in the role they accept (or rather are supposed to accept) at marriage. This failure is expressed by the women of the village themselves in terms of a metaphor.

Women are supposed, according to the traditional symbolism of the wedding ceremony, to be as doves - pure, gentle and innocent [2]. These 'feminine' qualities of submission are, as we shall see, qualities also required of the aspiring Christian. Women of the village of Velvendos have, almost jocularly, altered the metaphor and interpret the little figure of a bird which surmounts their marriage crown as a magpie because, it is said, it is the bird which caws, like women who talk too much. This symbolism must be seen in the context of the women's whole lives and preoccupations. Whether pure, obedient dove, or impure, disobedient magpie, a Velvendos woman belongs to, and, more important, acts upon, the physical, non-human world (whether she is thought of as the bird of the village rooftops or the bird of the fields and beyond), and is continually involved in processes which transform the material world so that it is capable of manifesting God. These processes include childbirth, and also the preparation of food, the cleaning and display of the house, and particular rituals performed when somebody has died.

Women's Activities

The material used here was gathered during 1979-1980 in the large village of Velvendos in Macedonia, northern Greece [3]. It has a population of well over four thousand. Most families are at least partially dependent on the peach orchards which surround the village, though many men combine farming with some other occupation or small business. The community is self-sufficient containing most kinds of shops, schools, and essential offices, and has, in addition to the large central parish church, about fifty smaller chapels located round the periphery of the village. There are four resident priests who serve the community's ritual needs. There is no real poverty, and virtually all migrants return after a period away.

As Friedl observed, elsewhere in Greece, male activities have predominance in public life, but the extent to which women are restricted and kept from 'public' areas is, in Velvendos, not nearly so marked as Friedl found in Vasilika or Hirschon in Piraeus (Friedl, 1962, Hirschon, 1978). In fact the associated sense of familiarity and confidence which women feel within the community was noticed by its absence when there were many outsiders present in the village during a period of major engineering works nearby. Women's lives do indeed centre round their homes and families, and to be lax about household duties is felt to be both immoral and a matter for intense shame. Commitment to household obligations is made visible in a very high standard of cleanliness and order, often at the expense of convenience. Also very important is the provision of food, and this is not done simply on a day to day basis, but implies the processing all the year round of whatever is abundant at the time. Most farmers' wives have to combine these tasks, in the summer, with work in the fields. On the whole women are required in the fields only for the harvest (but with strawberries and grapes as well as peaches, this can cover all the summer months). Women leave pruning, irrigating, thinning and spraying to their husbands. Traditionally hoeing was a springtime task for women (one they remember with hatred), but they have been almost entirely relieved of this since the introduction of tractors. A third way for women to contribute to the material continuity of their families is by the provision of dowries for their daughters to ensure that they make successful marriages. Dowries include an element of property or cash if the girl's parents can afford it, but, in Velvendos, more stress is laid on the collection of household software, mostly handmade, which is prepared and displayed at the time of the wedding. It includes rugs, blankets, linen and all kinds of ornamental cloths. What Velvendos women see as the primary importance of dowry is that the new couple should have the wherewithal to 'dress' the house (Na stolizoun to spiti).

Women's obligations are not restricted solely to the house and family fields. In such a large community the celebration of namedays is frequent, and, except when one of the parea (the group of closest friends of a married couple) or most immediate neighbours is celebrating, it is left to the woman of the house to visit and convey good wishes to the family concerned. On the days of popular saints such as St George or St Nikolaos there are so many houses to visit, even though the compliment is owed only to those one knows best, that most women spend the day going from house to house. Women are also much more frequent church attenders than most men. This applies particularly to the services in the many little chapels at which liturgies are performed on their saints' days and maybe on other occasions. For those who attend regularly this means that they go through an annual cycle of outings into the countryside immediately surrounding the village, with coffee and maybe a picnic after the service. On Sundays large numbers of men do turn out for the liturgy in the parish church but they are still outnumbered by women. Usually women with children take them with them to church and often take them to communicate (since children can do so without fasting). As well as attending church services, women take responsibility for visiting the cemetery on the three occasions when those with recent dead are expected to do so.

Many household tasks easily assume the form of religious acts. If, for example, the housewife crosses the loaves of bread when setting them to rise they become imbued with all the many meanings that bread has in Orthodox ritual. To exhibit this tendency in its more general form I will concentrate on two main areas of women's activities; the preparation of food and cleaning of the house.

59

Symbolic Connotations of Women's Activities

Everyday eating is done with very little ceremony in most families but the idea of eating to maintain the body is given considerable import- ance. After I had been in the village for some months the woman of the house I first lived in admitted to me that her greatest worry on my joining the household was that I would fail to eat the strange food and become thin. The village women are unadventurous cooks and are suspicious of any food beyond their knowledge. Food is a serious matter, not to be treated frivolously. Food for hospitality follows certain very strict customary rules. At a nameday celebration women guests are given a sweet liqueur, a chocolate, coffee if they have not had some elsewhere, and a piece of cake. Men are offered wine, beer or raki with savoury snacks, especially stuffed cabbage leaves and pieces of roast meat. They take a piece of cake away with them. The choice of recipe for the cakes offered on these occasions exer- cises housewives considerably. As with other kinds of display, they are torn between conformity and virtuosity.

These positive ideas about food have their opposite in the notion of fast. Fasting is essential for all adults in preparation for receiving Holy Communion. Also part of this preparation is attendance at con- fession, and sexual abstention for two weeks (these requirements represent the ideal, and in fact are not always fulfilled). The impur- ities of food, sex and sin may often keep people from taking Holy Communion, for although it is available at every Sunday and weekday liturgy, few take it more than once or twice a year. Children do not have to fast 'because they have no sins'. Insofar as it relates to food, the degree to which a household fasts is very much in the control of the women. Strictly, it means abstention from all animal products, oil and wine. Usually, in the last week before a major festival, people will graduate their abstention, avoiding only meat for the first two days, all animal products for the next two, and even oil for the last days. The fulfilment of this programme depends on the cook since although men usually do the shopping, the exclusion of oil, in particular, requires a special kind of cooking. Despite its expression in terms of food, fasting is not meant to be solely phys- ical. The most important abstention of all, according to one of the village priests, is from hatred and all that makes a gulf between one person and another. One young woman, on being asked to what ex- tent the family were fasting for Easter replied that there was no point, they were in such a bad state anyway (there had been a dis- pute with her mother-in-law).

The almost obsessive cleaning of the house and display of its con- tents is not without its symbolic connotations. This becomes apparent when one sees the extent of preparation before a name day or other festival when visitors may be expected. The housewife's standard of what is acceptable goes far beyond the visible. She may sponge the floor twice, launder already spotlessly white curtains and change crocheted cloths and cushions for almost identical 'better' ones. In the preparation of cakes which in most households is now done with the assistance of an electric beater, the mixture will be beaten for twenty minutes or half an hour when ten minutes would have had the same effect, so that the cake will be (undetectably) 'better'. The stated purpose of all this activity is to show that it is a 'good' house and a 'good' family. The exterior, physical aspect is required to say something about the interior, spiritual aspect of the family, and it is the woman who creates this supposed concurrence of physical and spiritual. One of the fathers of the Church (of the second century) explained in these words how in the end a saint's true qualities become apparent:

> At the day of resurrection the glory of the Holy Spirit comes out from within, decking and covering the bodies of the saints - the glory they had before but hidden within their souls. What a man has now, the same comes forth externally in the body (Ware, 1963, p.238).

On certain occasions, all that pertains to a family is required to be 'decked and covered' in such a way as to symbolically display (or even to actually reveal) the glory of a Christian family.

Concern with display and appearance is also manifested in relation to women's clothes. Young women, particularly, are expected to be meticulous about their presentation (both before and after marriage) especially when they are going to church. Nowadays most can afford to be competitive about keeping up with fashions, although usually competitiveness takes the form of seeking conformity to very limited seasonal norms. But a woman's style of dressing changes dramatically as she gets older. Usually the change originates with the death of a parent or parent-in-law, when she will go into black for mourning. Most women do not change back into normal clothes. Even if she has not been in mourning an older woman may assume black and will certainly never wear bright colours. Men do not wear mourning except for a black band on the sleeve for the first few days. Women who wear black are probably those who can no longer contribute to the replenishment of the family and each may be recording the fact that the particular nexus of generations represented by her marriage is beginning to disintegrate from the top.

One effect of the adoption of black by women is that it likens them to priests (who also have long hair tied back in a bun in the way traditional for women). Although women can never become priests there is one circumstance in which a priest and a woman are interchangeable [4]. This is for exorcism of the 'evil eye' or mati. Certain women know spells (or prayers) which they have learned under special circumstances and they will be summoned for all minor cases of 'overlooking' (the symptoms are headaches, nausea, fractiousness in children). This again accords with the notion of women as those who deal with the physical in such a way as to manifest the 'spiritual' element behind it; physical symptoms respond to spiritual treatment.

There are several ritual acts more associated with women than with men. As we have seen the preparation of food contributes both to the purity and to the healthy integrity of the family; but there is one special kind of food which is associated with disintegration. This is kollyva which must be prepared in large quanities after someone has died and is given with bread to the congregation at memorial services (which must be held a minimum of three times, forty days, one year and three years after the death). It consists of wheat which has been pounded in one of the large hollow stones set at certain street corners throughout the village. Relatives of the deceased take it in turns to wield the enormous asymmetric wooden hammers (their curious shape makes them resemble hoes). Although men may join in the pounding of kollyva, the parties which gather round the stones are mostly women. The wheat is afterwards boiled to a stiff porridge and nuts are added. It is also required that kollyva should be made on a small scale every week, in households which have recently lost a member, to be taken to the graveyard on Saturday. Kollyva is explicitly likened to wheat seeds in the earth in the spring; they are softened and ready to burst into new life. Candles, which are also used at rituals for death and memorial, provide similar imagery. Although individuals may make their own interpretations the 'correct' interpretation given by priests, teachers and others who consider themselves authorities is that as the candle softens and melts, so the individual is to soften and melt into God through the light of the Orthodox faith [5]. Everyone lights candles as the first act on entering a church. But women do so more often than men and it is usually they who go to the cemetery to light candles for the dead. During the three years between burial and the third major memorial the flesh of a dead person is supposed to decay so that when exhumation takes place at the end of that period the bones are clean. 'The sins', they say, 'have melted away', and the deceased is ready for new spiritual life. Weeping for the dead is a third way in which this softening, melting process is suggested.

Marriage as a First Step Towards Death

It is easy to demonstrate that marriage in a Greek community is a social necessity. There is no satisfactory role for a girl once she has completed her education until she gets married, unless she leaves the village to work in a town, and that requires considerable determination and, probably, assistance from relatives. For young men the imperative is not so urgent, but in many contexts a man is not taken seriously until he is married and has 'taken on life'. It is also quite clear that much of the need to be married is the need to have children [6]. Reproduction sanctions sexual relations, continues the family name, and, filling the house, provides the promise of well-being and wealth that that replenishment implies [7]. But further to this there is the fact that it is a bad thing in itself to remain un-married; with almost astonishing vehemence sometimes, middle-aged women exhort younger ones to do all they can to avoid being left un-married. While painting a far from rosy picture of the married state, they stress its intrinsic goodness. Marriage is a spiritual state as well as a social one, and its ritual necessity for all people of appropriate age is demonstrated by a special kind of funeral ceremony.

It is always the case that the funeral ceremony echoes a wedding in some particulars. Both feature a procession through the village led by children; in both cases bread is prominent in the customs surrounding the actual ceremony and wine is used in the ritual; lighted candles are used, and kisses of farewell are given in the church. But when a young person of marriageable age but not yet married dies, the parallel is made much more marked. Visitors to the house before the funeral (and there will be many, who go 'to cry', or 'to see the mother cry') , are given roasted chickpeas and sugared almonds, as is done in the interval between an engagement and the marriage. Then when the body is prepared for the coffin it is dressed, if male, in a best suit, and if female, in a wedding dress, before being wrapped in a white cloth and surrounded with flowers. At this stage a silver marriage crown is placed by the godparent (who, in the case of a man, would have been the marriage sponsor and would have crowned him at his wedding) on the dead person's head. The crown is a simple ring of metal from which four uprights curve to meet over the top of the head. Surmounting this meeting point is either a cross (for the man) or a bird (for a woman). Metal crowns are no longer used at weddings although they were in the past [8]. Instead the koumbaros (marriage sponsor) provides, as in the rest of Greece, two wreaths of artificial twigs which are later kept with the family icons. In the view of the Church the crowns symbolise the gift of grace from the Holy Spirit which the couple receives in the sacrament of matrimony. The cross on the man's crown represents the Christian faith and the strength from Christ of the head of the family (Tzinikou Kakouli, 1979, p.294). The bird on the women's crown is properly a dove and, according to Tzinikou Kakouli, the village's historian and folklorist, represents purity, gentleness and innocence. However, one woman informant when describing the crown said, 'It has a bird on it, the one that goes "Caw!", the magpie. Women talk a lot, they gossip, that's why.' ('echi ana pouli, afto pou kani 'kaa', i karakaxa. I yinaikes milane poli, koutsomboulevoun, y'afto.') I will deal with this particular aspect of the magpie image below. The more general implication of the crowning is that in some way it makes a person fitter for death.

This can be related to those symbols discussed earlier which refer to a softening of the individual in readiness for new life. Such symbols are central to Orthodox practice, and their theological significance is summed up in a sentence of the Russian theologian Vladimir Lossky:

> Man created in the image (of God) is the person capable of manifesting God in the extent to which his nature allows itself to be penetrated by deifying grace (1974, p.139).

Marriage, in that it is a lowering of personal boundaries to become part of a greater unit, is an instance of this softening, and the marriage ceremony is the medium through which divine grace is channelled.

As Ware points out, the crowns are also crowns of martyrdom (and the modern circlets of twigs bear a striking resemblance to a crown of thorns). But the nature of the sacrifice required is rather different for men and for women. The cross marks the man out as the leader of the new unit, head of this mini-Church which is being established. As Christ is head of the Church which is his 'Body', so the married man is to be spiritual (and of course practical) head of the family. As Christ took ultimate responsibility for the sins of men, so the head of the family is to be responsible. The self-sacrifice represented by the women's dove is that they should be submissive and indeed, obedient. Since the metal crowns are no longer used for living brides many women may not be aware that they are likened to doves (though women are referred to as magpies without concrete symbolic stimulus) but they are fully aware of the nature of the role they are expected to fill as it is clearly stated in the words of the marriage service:

> and give to this Thine hand-maid in everything to submit to the man, and to this Thy servant to be the head of the woman, that they may live according to Thy will (the Sacrament of Holy Matrimony, p. 16).

These words may not always be noticed and understood as they come in the middle of a long passage and the language of church service is very different from everyday Greek, but even if they are not, the following words are always listened for and understood:

> ...let every one of you in particular so love his wife even as himself; and the wife see that she reverence her husband (p. 21).

The word translated here as 'reverence' is in fact the everyday word for 'to fear', and as this sentence is chanted it is customary in Velvendos for the man to attempt to step on the woman's foot, to assert his authority from the outset. She is expected to try to evade the foot.

In normal life a woman's relation to God and submission to God's will is meant to be mediated. Obedience to God means obedience to her husband, however inadequate he may be. When telling me about the requirement that they should 'fear' and obey their husbands certain women made comments to the effect of 'How can we obey them when they're such fools?' but, as with the priests and bishops, the office of husband is not meant to be regarded as degraded by the deficiencies of him who holds it. Frequently women fail in their submissive role, and possibly it is consciousness of this that is expressed in their interpretation of the bird on the marriage crown as a magpie.

Women as Inadequate Doves

There are certain concrete ways in which almost all Velvendos women fail to live up to the qualities of the dove. First there is the question of disobedience. It is not common for a man to give his wife orders unless some disagreement has arisen. When that occurs, perhaps over disciplining children, or the question of how often the wife should go out, even the mildest may adopt a tyrannical tone. Wife beating is not uncommon, particularly, according to a male informant, during the early part of a marriage so that the wife 'learns to listen' (Na akouei). Women are not often particularly respectful of their spouses (though there are exceptions) and this exacerbates such disputes.

Then there is the problem of impurity. William Christian's remarks about Spanish women have a relevance here:

> It seems likely ... that behind the ... religious activities of the women lies a sense of impurity that has been laid on by the Church and its ministers. Ever since Eve, women have been seen as ... the cause of man's downfall. With an overwhelming emphasis on female models who were pure and virgin ... adult sexually active women ... feel they are unworthy, that they have something to expiate (1972, p.153).

These factors affect Greek women too, and even if there is no evidence to suggest that they are trying, in their religious activity, to expiate impurity, there is plenty to show that they are felt to be responsible for purity. We have already considered fasting as purification, and women's responsibility for it. In the light of Hirschon's material showing that Greek women in Piraeus are held to be capable of resisting sexual impulses whereas men are not, the main responsibility for sexual abstention may here also rest with women (hence the point of certain jokes about the sexual voracity of priests' wives). To whatever degree they succeed or fail in this, the model of the Virgin is inimitable. For one thing, most Velvendos women are not virgins at the time of their marriage, though the customs relating to the bridal night as a test of virginity are still remembered. It is not infrequent for a couple to start sexual relations from the time of their engagement, and it is apparent from the records of the births of first children that this has been customary, at any rate in some families, for up to fifty years. It is associated with very binding engagement, and illegitimacy is virtually unknown. Not everybody approves of this way of conducting matters, however, and even families whose elders condone the cohabitation of engaged couples may show a trace of embarrassment. One potential daughter-in-law was required by her fiance's mother to induce a miscarriage (this occurred during my fieldwork). Many women, then, will start married life with a failure to live up to the highest ideals of their society with relation to sexual purity.

Added to this there is the tendency to believe that women are weaker and therefore more inclined to sin and folly. Women themselves sometimes express this belief. Both sexes attend confession very rarely, but women attend more often than men. It happens that of the major sins which must be confessed (infringements of the Ten Commandments) the only one to occur with any frequency is committed by women. Abortion has to be confessed as murder, and, considering that it is prohibited by both Church and state, it occurs surprisingly frequently, sometimes being resorted to by married women who do not particularly want another child.

The idea that women are more prone to wrong-doing gains an added dimension if we consider the extension of the notion that women are magpies that is made by the village women themselves. Women are magpies 'because they gossip'. Gossip is, of all vices, the one most frequently noticed and discussed [9]. An examination of the experience of women in and beyond the household can do much to explain why it is thought of as a particularly female weakness. There is no doubt that men may talk about other people in exactly the same sort of way without incurring the same criticism. The Greek word koutsombolia covers exactly the same range of instances as the English term. It can mean simply talking about the affairs of others, but it can imply that this is done with critical or malicious intent. It is often associated in peoples' minds with envy. Women frequently said that it was regrettable that people should gossip, but inevitable in such a closed community, and especially among the women who are 'closed' in the house all day and have no other interests [10]. They fully admit to adjusting their behaviour to avoid becoming an object of gossip, never carrying an item, however inoffensive, through the village without a wrapping, and if doing anything which might seem peculiar, explaining themselves to all who pass by. Gossip has two aspects – it can unite a group within which news is exchanged and opinions expressed, yet it can also be highly divisive. In its less innocent form this may be its intention. Any outsider is particularly vulnerable both to gossip and to the sense that she is being gossiped about. But wherever the subject of gossip is a villager there will almost inevitably be an element of betrayal behind it. Someone who has inside knowledge allows it to cross boundaries it should not cross. The information involved may not be accurate but it is effective if it may be supposed to be so. A great deal of gossip takes the form: 'She appears to be virtuous, but it is to conceal her true nature of which I have special knowledge'. It is an accepted, oft-remarked fact that one can never know what is going on inside other people: 'We don't know what tobacco he smokes, what he hides inside him' (Then xeroume ti kapno foumarei, ti kryvei mesa tou). When the cover-up is thought to have failed, gossip is the consequence.

The boundaries most frequently abused by gossip are those around the household. Thus it creates a gulf where there should be unity, and in particular it creates gulfs between mothers-in-law and daughters-in-law who frequently live under the same roof. As in the other parts of Greece in which dowries do not customarily include a house, the bridegroom's parents traditionally provide houseroom for a newly married couple. If resources are not available for the building or purchase of a new house it is common practice to extend or alter the

existing one. Although there will be two kitchens in such an arrange-
ment it would be thought very strange if the two housewives did not
in fact cook and perform almost all household tasks together. This is
important since few girls will have learned to cook or keep house
before their marriage. So the relations between pethera
(mother-in-law) and nifi (daughter-in-law/bride) are crucial to the
well-being of the joint family. It is the women who will make the two
units as one or the one unit as two. There are various traditions
relating to the state of harmony between nifi and pethera, as it is a
relationship which is almost certain to become strained at some
point. The nifi has the disadvantage of being both the outsider and
the junior [11]. The temptation must be greatest for her to betray the
secrets of her new family by complaining to her mother or sisters.
Obviously not all gossip originates in bad relations between pethera
and nifi, but when it does it shows that cracks are appearing even
in the external facade of what is supposed to be the most secure and
integrated unit. Just as it was Eve's failing to talk to the outsider,
so it is felt to be the failing of women today.

The Redemption of Bride and Body

The extent to which women feel that they have something to expiate
stems from ideas of their moral nature and the incompleteness of
their submission and commitment to their new family of marriage. It
does not seem inappropriate to them that they are kept at a distance
from the holiest things of their religion. They remain at the back of
the church except when taking Communion. They are not supposed to
go behind the iconostasis (screen) and cannot become priests or
deacons. But there are two very important ways in which women's
lives have a positive religious value. The first is that in so far as
she acquires the characteristics of a good wife, a woman acquires
the characteristics of a good Christian. Although women may not be
'by their nature' more 'penetrable' in Lossky's sense than men (and
we cannot exclude the possibility that they are seen to be so), in
the social and religious role of wife, they certainly are to the extent
that they achieve the ideal. This is not the case for a man, upon
whose efforts to manipulate others and assert himself in the community the economic welfare and social standing of the family largely
depends (the economic role of women must not be underestimated,
however, and it is not impossible for a woman to run a business or
a farm on her own). The feminine, penetrable, submissive role does
not only refer to the individual Christian, but also to the entire
Church, which is 'the Bride of Christ', and which, before Easter, is
prepared in a manner comparable to the week of preparations
traditional for a bride. Christ's 'Bride' is also referred to as Christ's
'Body'. The equation of bride and body, while it places women in the
'inferior' physical realm, refers to redeemed flesh (which became
possible because of the submission of a woman) and thus indirectly
to the place of women in the redemption process. Eastern Orthodoxy
does not overstress the tendency present in some of the writings of

the Church's fathers to totally separate the spiritual from the physical. For example, St Jerome wrote:

> you must act against nature or rather above nature if you are to foreswear your natural functions ... and, while in the body, to live as though out of it (Ruether, 1974, p.176)

Such goals fit better with a mainly 'redemption' theology (Lossky, 1974, p.99) in which personal salvation is given priority over deif-ication and the redemption of the whole world. If Christ could be truly incarnated in human flesh, then human flesh must be seen as perfectable, and capable of becoming united with God. The reminder of this comes to every Orthodox believer almost daily in the venera-tion of icons. Icons are intended to show a kind of ideal perfection, a beauty never directly encountered on earth, and this perfection applies not just to the saints depicted but also to animals and plants. They are to be glimpses of the transfigured, redeemed world. There are rules applied to their painting so that they conform to the convention whereby it is the 'inside' of the saint which is depicted. A saint has transfigured his 'inside', his spiritual part, and in the case of miraculously preserved relics, his physical part as well (Ware, p.239).

Whatever their formal failure, Velvendos women are in most of their everyday activities concerned with the perfectability of human flesh and with the aspirations both to make manifest the spiritual po-tential referred to in the sacraments, of themselves and their families, and to make their bodies fit vehicles for that spiritual po-tential.

Notes

1. The Authorized Version renders it slightly differently: 'For the earnest expectation of the creature waiteth for the manifestation of the sons of God ... for the creature itself also shall be delivered from the bondage of corruption unto the glorious liberty of the children of God. For we know that the whole creation groaneth and travaileth in pain together until now.'

2. Tzinikou Kakouli p.294: 'The bride's had a dove, symbol of purity, gentleness and innocence. But the playful people of Velvendos called it a magpie, and they call all women magpies'.

'To nyfiatiko eiche peristera, symvolo agnotitos, praotitos kai athootitos. Oi filopaigmones omos Velvendinoi tin onomazan karakaxa kai karakaxes onomazan oles tis yinaikes'.

3. The research upon which this paper is based was made possible by a studentship from the Social Science Research Council to whom I am extremely grateful.

4. Hirschon comments that the woman's role in the house parallels the priest's role in the church (Hirschon, 1981, p.183); this is true in a certain sense in that the priest prepares and offers 'food', but there are many aspects of the priest's role, for example as a

sacrificer, which does not have its equivalent. The similarity of cost-ume of priests and women is noted below.

5. Indicative of the fact that it is not the <u>light</u> which carries most meaning when a candle is lit is the distinction between the use of candles and lamps. Simple olive oil lamps are kept alight near icons to represent God's presence in the icon. Candles are never used for this purpose.

6. Virtually all ethnographies of Greece point out the importance of having children (e.g. du Boulay, 1974, p.135 and 164, Hirschon, 1978, p.68).

7. Almost without exception, Velvendos housewives use plastic dolls as ornaments, particularly large collections being displayed on name days. When asked why they like dolls some reply, 'I love them, they are like children', or, 'They fill the house'.

8. Tzinikou Kakouli p.334. It seems that in the past the godparent of a dead girl or youth provided a tin crown which was left in the tomb. The silver marriage crowns were hired from the church.

9. Much of Juliet du Boulay's analysis of 'Lies, Mockery and Family Integrity' (1976) would apply more or less unchanged to Vel-vendos. Here I concentrate on women's gossip as a particular part of that complex.

10. The opposition of 'open' and 'closed' is not quite the same as for urban Greeks (Hirschon, 1978) but being 'closed' has the same inauspiciousness. The same 'need' to control women's speech is also apparent.

11. One young married woman said ironically to her sisters one day: 'All mothers-in-law are "good"; all daughters-in-law are "bad".'

References

Apostolikis Daikonias tis Ekklisias tis Ellados <u>Mikron Evhologion.</u>
1974

Christian, W. <u>Person and God in a Spanish Valley</u>. Seminar Press, 1972

du Boulay, J. <u>Portrait of a Greek Mountain Village</u>. Oxford, Oxford University Press, 1974

____ 'Lies, Mockery and Family Integrity' in J.G. Peristiany (ed.), <u>Mediterranean Family Structures</u>. Cambridge, Cambridge University Press, 1976

Friedl, E. <u>Vasilika - a Village in Modern Greece</u>. New York, Rine-hart and Winston, 1962

____ 'The Position of Women: appearance and reality' Anthropological Quarterly, Vol. 40, (1967), pp.97-108

Hirschon, R. 'Open Body/Closed Space: the Transformation of Female Sexuality' in S. Ardener, (ed.), <u>Defining Females</u>. London, Croom Helm, 1978

____ 'Essential Objects and the Sacred: Interior and Exterior Space in an Urban Greek locality' in S. Ardener (ed.), <u>Women and Space: Ground Rules and Social Maps</u>. London, Croom Helm,

1981

Johnson, P. A History of Christianity. Middlesex, Penguin, 1976

Lossky, V. In the Image and Likeness of God. Oxford, Mowbray, 1974

Ruether, R. Religion and Sexism. New York, Simon and Schuster, 1974

Tzinikou Kakouli, A. Laografikoi Antilaloi tou Velvendou. Thessaloniki, 1979

Ware, T. The Orthodox Church. Middlesex, Penguin, 1963

Wiles, M. and Santer, M. Documents in Early Christian Thought. Cambridge, Cambridge University Press, 1975

Williams and Norgate. The Sacrament of Holy Matrimony. London, Williams and Norgate, 1929

5 GENDER AND RELIGION IN A TURKISH TOWN: A COMPARISON OF TWO TYPES OF FORMAL WOMEN'S GATHERINGS

Nancy Tapper

In recent years anthropologists and others have become increasingly interested in the relation between gender and religious ideology and practice. The feminist perspective often adopted is a general one: as Hoch-Smith and Spring write in the preface to their volume, <u>Women in Ritual and Symbolic Roles,</u>

> religious ideas are paramount forces in social life, and relationships between the sexes, the nature of female sexuality, and the social and cultural roles of women are in large part defined by religious ideas (1978, p.v).

As such, this perspective is applicable to the study of religious systems of any scale, from the parochial or tribal to world religions. Of the world religions of Semitic origin, a number of studies have now appeared which adopt this perspective vis-à-vis Judaism and Christianity (e.g. Ruether, 1974; Warner 1976). In the case of practical Islam, however, the main themes to have received comparative and theoretical discussion have been the ideology of honour and shame and female seclusion (e.g. Peristiany, 1965; Antoun, 1968; Papanek, 1973; Nelson, 1974; Meeker, 1976) and the involvement of women in spirit possession (e.g. Lewis, 1971; Constantinides, 1977; Morsy, 1978). As yet there are few studies of religious belief and practices and the conceptual systems of women (cf. R. and E. Fernea, 1972); those by Mernissi (1975) and Dwyer (1978) are among the first to remedy this neglect. The present paper is intended as a further contribution in this latter direction [1].

My immediate aim is a limited one: I seek to compare two types of formal women's gathering - one determinedly secular, the other intensely religious - which occur with considerable frequency in small provincial towns and elsewhere throughout Turkey; but my conclusions suggest several areas in which formal Islamic images and prescriptions relating to women are at once qualified by and qualify the social life of Turkish Muslim women.

So far I have spent only a very brief period - a total of five weeks - in one Turkish provincial town, that of Egridir. However, even in this short time, during which I participated in both types of women's gathering, I became convinced that these two types of gathering pose a number of general questions for the study of gender roles and religion. In this paper I set out some of the issues. To do this I shall use both my own limited material on Turkey and that which has been published by other anthropologists. I approach these data from two different angles: first, I consider the institutional structure and meaning of these gatherings, and second, I attempt to discover their place in relation to the whole spectrum of women's social life, as part of the general system of relations between women and men and that system which includes the whole range of religious and ceremonial practices in the provincial town.

I argue that though the dominant gender ideology in the town contains a major contradiction, it is one which is not consciously confronted by either men or women. The contradiction lies between the clearly articulated and effectively enforced model of male domination and the highly valued status of motherhood. Though both male dominance and the importance of motherhood are given secular and religious recognition, the contradiction is masked, in part at least, because both men and women regularly participate in two types of single sex gatherings. The exclusively male gatherings take place in the clubs and cafes of the town, on the one hand, and in the mosques, on the other. In this paper, these men's gatherings can only be mentioned in passing, but it is important to note that, with the exception of a certain ideological continuity between them, they seem in many ways parallel in structure and function to the two types of women's gatherings which I examine in detail. I consider that the women's gatherings, when treated as a paired set, so condition the women's perception of relations among themselves, particularly by focusing on the areas of equality and inequalities between them, that they discourage women from examining the underlying issue – the position of women vis-à-vis men – which determines relationships among women.

The Women's Gatherings

Reception Days

The first type of gathering I discuss is known in the literature as 'reception day' or sometimes as 'acceptance day', a more literal translation of its Turkish name, <u>kabul günü</u>. I shall use the former phrase, 'reception day', which in English indicates something of its formal qualities. In spite of the general paucity of material on women in Turkish towns, women's reception day activities have been relatively well described (Dobkin, 1967; Mansur, 1972; Benedict, 1974a; Aswad, 1974 and 1978; L. and M. Fallers, 1976; Good, 1978; Kandiyoti, 1977).

Reception days are explicitly secular occasions when, for an afternoon once a month, a woman holds an open house for up to sixty or so invited women guests – kin, affines and friends, who come to gossip and enjoy an elaborate meal provided by the hostess. Women spend much time on their personal appearance on reception days and, if they are hostess, on the cleanliness and decor of their house. Moreover, since continuing participation in reception days depends on strict reciprocity, individual townswomen may spend a great deal of time on such visits and may even attend several separate receptions during a single day. Benedict notes that in the small town of Ula in southwestern Anatolia, reception days were originally introduced in 1954 by the non-local wives of civil servants who came to live in the town when it was elevated to the status of a sub-provincial government centre. Soon afterwards, however, the women of the local landowning and wealthy merchant families – families which were prominent in both local and regional politics – joined the reception day circles; since then other local middle class wives as well as the wives of some prosperous local craftsmen have been included (1974a, pp. 36-37). He notes however that the number of women involved in the reception day circles should not be exaggerated: there may be seventy-five such women altogether in a town population of five thousand. Nonetheless it is the husbands of these few women who represent '...the decision-makers of community affairs and in their hands rest the bulk of economic and political power' (1974a, p. 37).

Aswad writes at length about the discussions which characterize the reception days in the small southern Anatolian city of Antakya (pop. 60,000), where the topics '... range widely from the recent change in prices and the rates charged by various merchants, to politics, fashions and recipes' (1974, p. 20). She notes that discussion of economic conditions is 'specific and enlightened', while politics are treated in a rather more general way, which nonetheless allows '... communication of information across divisive lines which men may not cross' (1974, p. 20). Aswad also compares the women's conversation during the urban reception days with women's conversations in nearby villages and writes, the village gossip system

> was far less structured; there was no formal visiting and gossip seemed far more generalized. This difference would seem to be related both to the increase of stratification in the urban society, as well as an increase in distance between men and women in public (1974, p. 21).

To return to Benedict's account, he says the reception days are '... clear markers of inequality' (1974a, p. 37) as well as '... highly visible ways in which to show one's changing social map' (1974a, p. 39); '... the reception, because of its exclusive membership, high visibility, periodicity, and the loyalty which it commands of participants, is used as a vehicle with which to pursue certain social objectives' (1974a, p. 42). Nonetheless, Benedict also notes that,

> The social distance existing between women of this elite circle of visiting is ultimately a reflection of their husbands' status in the local society. Regardless of how well a woman manipulates her at-

73

tendance at receptions, her relative rank within the gathering is fixed and changes only as the social position of her husband declines or ascends (1974a, p.46).

It is worth noting here that for townsmen there is no comparable institution to the women's reception days, nor indeed does one seem to be required. Men have a freedom of movement and autonomy in public which is denied women. Much of a man's leisure time is spent with other men in the clubs or cafes from which townswomen are excluded. These clubs and cafes are numerous and have regular clienteles. Their atmosphere is informal and depends to an extent on quasi-joking relationships between competing family heads: men who share similar occupations, interests and levels of affluence.

Mevluds

The second type of formal women's gathering is a mevlûd, a religious celebration of the birth of the Prophet Muhammad, when the hostess hires a cantor to recite the mevlûd poem of Süleyman Celebi, perhaps the most famous poem in the Turkish language. The women's mevlûd gatherings have received no comparable attention in the literature even from authors who have written on reception days (Mansur, 1972, pp.106-08; L. and M. Fallers, 1976, pp.252; Good, 1978, pp.495-6; Kandiyoi, 1977, p.69). The unequal treatment of the two types of women's gatherings is curious for even after a very short stay in a Turkish town, it was clear to me that for most middle class townswomen, their interest and participation in the mevlud meetings is as important to them as their attendance at reception days, if not more so.

Chelebi's Mevlidi Sherif was written in 1409 in language which is simple and direct; Edmonds likens its effect to that of the first chapters of Matthew or Luke or some Christmas carols for Christians, but, as she points out, the Mevlidi Sherif is very much a poem for all seasons (Edmonds, 1969, p.1). Recitals are frequent throughout the year. Mevlûd gatherings are held separately for both men and women; men's mevlûds are most often held in the mosque, especially during major Islamic feasts, while the recitals for women are always held at home. Mevlûds ' ... are held either as a way of earning God's good will, or in order to thank him for a favour. They are always held at a death [and] for the souls of dead relatives' (Mansur, 1972, p.107).

The Mevlidi Sherif is a long poem, divided into a number of sections describing the miracles and teachings of the prophet, but its climax which comes in the middle of the recital is the description of his birth. This is told as if by the Prophet's mother, Emine Hatun, in words which are reminiscent of the Mary cult of the Roman Catholic Church. Thus, before the birth, the Prophet's mother says,

To me [the three shining heavenly fairies] said:
'Not since the world's creation

74

Hath mother had such cause for exultation.

No son like thine, such strength and grace possessing,
Hath God to earth send down, for its redressing.

Great favour has thou found, thou lovely mother,
To bear a son surpassing every other' (MacCallum, 1943, p.22).

Fallers, in a short, unpublished article, notes a tension in Turkish Islam between two conceptions or manifestations of divinity: one abstract and revealed in the Koran and Sharia, and the other highly personalized and experienced either in Sufism or as an almost cult-like relation with the Prophet Muhammed (Fallers, 1971, p.12), but the question - what roles does the idealized mother play in this personal cult? - remains to be explored. I would suggest that, at the very least, the focus on the nativity of the Prophet is likely to be an important key to the meaning of the mevlûd for women; certainly it ties up with what is already well-accepted in the Turkish literature, that, 'For a woman, the most important relationship in the family is that with her son' (Kiray, 1976, p.266).

In the provincial town of Egridir, women's mevlûd gatherings are held in private homes during the day. The gatherings are large (probably on average considerably larger than reception day gatherings there). The fifty or sixty invited women guests arrive shortly before the recital is to begin. They slip off their shoes, don lovely white embroidered prayer scarves and formally greet all the other women present as they move around the circle of seated women until they find a place to sit. The hostess sprinkles rose water on the hands of her guests who gossip quietly with women sitting next to them until the prayers begin. The recital may last for over two hours. For most of this time, the cantor (mevlûd-han), who may be either male or female but seems most often to be an imam, or prayer leader, from one of the town mosques, sings the poem alone, while the women guests remain seated, sometimes repeating the words of the poem to themselves and sometimes even weeping softly. There are however general responses which require the participation of the congregation, who may also stand and ritually act out parts of the story. When the prayers are finished, the hostess passes out sweets to all her guests; they in turn ask God's blessing for her and for each other before they depart.

I have described something of the different character of the women's reception days and mevlûd gatherings. Central to my thesis is an investigation of the extent to which these two types of gatherings need to be treated as a paired set. Something of the parallelism between them has already been suggested: their extreme formality, their frequency and the large numbers of participants they involve. They are the only two kinds of formal meetings which are, in theory, both open to all townswomen and exclusive to them (indeed it is felt that even small children should be excluded from them). In these ways, the two types of gathering differ significantly from life-cycle ceremonies and secular celebrations. In practice the same kinds of women act as hostesses at both types of gathering, while the circles of participants overlap to a considerable degree. Both kinds of gathering counteract the otherwise considerable social isolation likely to be experienced by middle class townswomen and they do provide some opportunity for women of different families to become known to each other as individuals.

But beyond these underlying similarities, there are obvious differences which also need to be explored. Thus, for example, the reception days, which are expensive to hold, operate in terms of a strict, balanced reciprocity (Aswad, 1974, p.13 ff.) and employ mechanisms which ensure that the women participants are very nearly status equals. Yet, in spite of such an egalitarian structure, the focus in the reception day gatherings in the eyes of both participants and outsiders is status differentiation (Good, 1978, p.496). Any tendency to female solidarity or support implicit in their structure is countered by the fact that the women relate to each other as adjuncts of their husbands and thus as representatives of separate, competing families. Not only are such differences between women emphasized at reception days but the institution also differentiates them as a group from those poorer women in the community who do not belong to a formal visiting circle. Indeed only wealthier women have the leisure for such activities; they can afford to hire female servants or informally command the services of poorer kinswomen to help them with domestic chores and childcare responsibilities.

By contrast, the mevlûd gatherings involve not balanced reciprocity between participants, but rather a form of generalized exchange between women of unequal status: indeed they have a redistributive function. Mevlûds are not particularly costly to hold, but they provide the hostess, herself of high status, the chance to offer the setting and opportunity for an intense, communal religious experience for a group of women who may be highly differentiated and whose ties with her may involve domestic service and other kinds of unequal reciprocity. The atmosphere at mevlûd gatherings is not in any sense competitive; rather, women as individuals appear to experience an equality before God which they share with others from all sections of the community. Mevlûd gatherings emphasize women's identity as mothers and afford them a unique opportunity to form a religious congregation exclusive of men.

Treated together, the contrasts in the structure and content of the two types of women's gatherings can be seen in relief: the structure of reception days expresses an equality among middle class women, while the actual content of the meetings differentiates them, both among themselves and from other women in the community. In both respects the women are separated from each other and identified in terms of their attachments to men. The structure of mevlûds is unequal and implicitly admits the status differentiation between families in the community; nonetheless the content of the mevlûd meetings unambiguously focuses on feminine. support, solidarity and equality.

It would seem that it is the very existence of these two types of formal women's gatherings which may prevent women from recognizing and articulating the fundamental conflict in the values and role definitions to which they subscribe. Two such areas of conflict immediately come to mind: first, the way the two roles, of mother and of wife, are constructed in provincial Turkey and, secondly, the way women are held to be uniformly subordinate to men and yet, in practice, differentiated in terms of men. Islamic orthodoxy encourages women to think of themselves as biological equals, all of whom are, for physiological reasons alone, subordinate to men. In practice the women's role as mother implicitly contradicts the notion of male domination of women: Turkish mothers are powerful, deeply loved figures and their authority over their sons is usually lifelong. And yet, women act in ways which diminish and ultimately deny this authority: they excessively indulge their sons in childhood and turn them into bullies who not only believe in their innate superiority over all women but may tyrannize women in practice. Women teach men that they have both the right and duty to control women's behaviour. Such control means that women spend much of their lives in an exclusively feminine milieu, where nonetheless they are isolated from each other and most often act out differences between them which ultimately depend on their relations with men: they become effective status demonstrators of family differentation.

The preceding examination of the women's gatherings suggests something of the way these may express and ritually condition the self-images of women. However, the full implications of the structure and function of these gatherings can only be understood in terms of their wider social setting in the provincial town [2].

The Wider Social Context of the Women's Gatherings

Anthropologists have recently noted the neglect of the study of towns compared with the now established anthropological focus on village, tribal and city populations. The distinctive character of towns has been pointed out, with reference to their role of 'brokerage' or 'articulation' between the state and rural society in matters of economics, politics, culture and development. But little has been said about the similar role many such towns must play in terms of religion, particularly in areas where world religions prevail.

In Turkey, as elsewhere in the Muslim Middle East, the town is commonly identified by the presence of a market-place, administrative offices and a religious centre, whether a shrine or Friday mosque. However, much of the Turkish countryside is better watered and more fertile than elsewhere, which may help explain the comparatively large number of market towns and their relative importance both in the past and today (cf. Benedict, 1974b). There are already a number of published monographs on small towns in Turkey; however they all focus explicitly on the political and economic aspects of town life and, as far as religious beliefs and practices or relations among women are concerned, most contain little more than a brief descriptive and theoretically pedestrian account. On small town women, Kandiyoti summarizes the position in a recent paper:

Lower middle-class women, whether they are the wives of small entrepreneurs like shopkeepers, traders and craftsmen, or of lower-ranking civil servants, are undoubtedly the most underresearched category of women in Turkey. There is good reason to believe that the wives of small entrepreneurs, some of whom can be considered as part of the traditional urban middle class, may exhibit different patterns from those married to state employed men. Thus, their being grouped under the same heading can hardly be justified on grounds other than the paucity of data. These women are literally the least 'visible' in the sense that they are the most home-bound and secluded, the most restricted in their movements and the least prominent in terms of employment (1979, p. 10).

Many of my remarks in this paper are based on observations of such middle-class women living in the small town of Egridir in southwestern Anatolia.

Egridir, with a population of nearly 10,000, is a market and administrative centre for a sub-province (ilçe) including some forty villages. It is the seat of a sub-governor (kaymakan), a professional civil servant whose main responsibility is the government of the sub-province as a whole; the municipality (belediye) itself elects local residents as mayor and councillors, and both administration and politics in the town are controlled by local people. Egridir lies on the shores of a substantial lake and has as yet unrealized potential as a tourist resort, while at present it is growing wealthy through the international export of locally grown apples. Because of its specialized economy, Egridir is more prosperous than many small towns of the region. Its success is due almost entirely to the entrepreneurial efforts of residents whose value of hard work, private enterprise and secular education is notable.

In another respect too, Egridir is unusual: the limited amount of land near the town for either cultivation or residential use has long caused emigration, particularly among the well-to-do, and often to the metropolitan centres. The Egridir population has been relatively constant in recent decades. This, coupled with the tangible wealth of the town, seems to have lent support to the view, held by all sections of the local population, that their economic aspirations can be fulfilled by their own efforts. There seems to be remarkably little political or economic disaffection in the town, which like the province has long been a Justice Party stronghold. The Turkish Army Commando School is on the outskirts of the town and it is possible that this military presence discourages potential political activity. But, if this is the case, it is nonetheless true that the townspeople themselves insist that the explanation for the lack of serious conflict in the town lies in their strong and uniform support of leading townsmen who demonstratively uphold certain Islamic and republican values. It may also be relevant to an understanding of the townspeople's self-image that many subscribe to a quite distinct myth about the purity of the water of Egridir lake; in this context the town is often spoken of as a place approaching a paradise on earth.

The town is divided into fifteen named wards, each with an elected headman and most with a mosque. Extended patriarchal families often live in the same large house or adjacent houses, but practical kinship reckoning is bilateral and spreads a net of relationships throughout the town. Kin and affinal ties are recognized in such a way that they link households of objectively unequal wealth and standing for many social activities.

Eğridir townspeople make few status distinctions among themselves. In effect they almost all see themselves as middle class, literally as town burghers or members of the petty bourgeoisie. Even from an outsider's point of view there is only a very small proletarian population. Indeed there is a severe shortage of both male and female unskilled labour. Townswomen find it difficult to hire other women as domestic servants, while the apple harvest, crucial for the town economy, is picked by itinerant workers from the east of the country. This situation is of course due to a number of different factors: the geography and demography of the town, the extensive kin networks and also the fact that lake fishing, which can be very lucrative, provides a partial income for many Eğridir families.

Though the townspeople tend to view themselves as all of the middle class, there are of course considerable variations in occupation, household incomes and life styles. I think it is analytically useful to identify families in terms of four status categories, though I would emphasize that this is very much my own model of status differentiation within the town [3].

The first status category consists of the families of professional bureaucrat-managers and senior army officers stationed nearby, families whose major source of income is from outside the town; these people are outsiders in another respect too, in that they are almost all only temporary Eğridir residents. They would certainly claim themselves to be both more sophisticated (both men and women are likely to have some education beyond the high school level) and better connected in political and economic terms than most local townsmen. However, the latter would not necessarily accept the outsiders' assumed superiority.

The families of white collar workers and teachers belong to the second status category. Men and women are likely to have had at least a high school education. Some of the people are non-local and will move to other posts after several years, but many are from local families and may own their own small apple orchards, while some also engage in commercial activities of various kinds.

The third category is almost entirely local in origin: these are the well-to-do families (including scions of the traditional class of large landowners) who own land, particularly orchards, or whose main income comes from wholesale trading, again particularly in apples. Men of this group are likely to have a high school education, though some of their wives may be functional illiterates. However the children of families of this status category are often successful competitors in university entrance exams. Many of the local notables belong to this group, including the municipal mayor and local political party representatives. Other families belonging to this category are those who have succeeded in business or commerce in the metropolitan centres and who return to live in Eğridir only during the summer months.

The fourth status category consists of the traditional bazaar merchants, shopkeepers and craftsmen among whom there is wide variation of income and wealth. Again in Eğridir many of these families may have small orchards, while the women often continue to follow traditional occupations as carpet makers, thereby increasing family income considerably. Men of this stratum cheerfully describe themselves as jacks-of-all-trades.

The Range of Religious Beliefs and Activities in Eğridir

Since 1923 and the foundation of the Turkish Republic, the state system of Turkey has been firmly secular and based on a European rather than an Islamic legal model. However the strength of the secularist lobby has varied at different points during Turkey's republican political history and, in 1949, along with other direct measures to aid the religious establishment, the government began to reintroduce religious teaching into the state schools. This process is still continuing. Turkish Islam as it has been supported by recent governments is both highly moralistic and chauvinistic. Fallers writes of its ethical, rather than ritualistic, emphasis and notes its focus on social justice and community responsibility and thus, for example, the interest in business ethics and important place of philanthropy in Turkish towns (1971, pp. 4-5). It is worth noting too the reverence with which the figure of Ataturk is treated in spite of Mustafa Kemal's indifference and sometime hostility to Islam.

It is misleading, if not worse, to begin an account of religious practice in a world religion by equating religiosity with orthodoxy and then measuring people's performance by such a standard (R. Tapper in press). However formal Islam, with its prescribed duties for believers, lends itself to such treatment, and as this notion of religiosity is an index the townspeople themselves use, it seems at least a reasonable place to begin. Thus, whatever have been the vicissitudes in relations between the religious establishment and the state, at the provincial level, townspeople seem to have remained firm in their fundamental religious convictions and active in their participation in religious rites and ceremonies. However the nature of these convictions and the types of participation they impel vary both between the four status categories I have identified and between men and women. Between status categories the main variable would seem to be the extent to which religious belief and practice are compartmentalized, while the key difference between men and women lies in the women's exclusion from the mosque and therefore from a number of associated orthodox rituals.

To take the differences between status categories first. Here the first two strata are distinguished from the second two. The former, the non-local professionals and the white collar workers, are among the least evidently religious of Egridir townspeople. As I have mentioned, these people, men and women, are the best educated adults in the town; for many of them their formal education occurred at a time when the state school system was the most unambiguously secular in its orientation, while their careers depend to a considerable degree on the extent to which they subscribe to the Kemalist ideology of statehood. Teachers, who bear the heaviest burden of educating a younger generation for citizenship, seem often particularly rigid in isolating a personal/familial religion from the republican ideology. By contrast, among both the wealthier local middle class and the petty bourgeoisie, there seems to be far less of a separation between private belief and public involvement in religious activities. It is notable among these latter categories that adherence to Islamic ideals as a guide to all areas of social life (i.e. a lack of compartmentalization) can be directly correlated with a traditional type of control of women by men. Such control is most strongly exercised by men of the petty bourgeoisie, while one important check on such control on wealthier families is their growing perception of formal education as a practical means of transforming daughters into workers in occupations with prestige in the wider community. However such differences are a matter of degree and it is members of such local middle-class families, as opposed to those depending largely on state salaries, who are most conscientious in their observance of Islamic forms.

Beyond this relation between occupational categories and religion, there remains however the dimension of gender per se. Gender qualifies religious activity regardless of family status. The great tradition of Islam prescribes various differences in men's and women's religious obligations. On the one hand, women are expected to fulfill the basic duties of the believer - the pillars of Islam: the profession of faith, prayer, fasting, alms giving and pilgrimage; but, on the other the rules for women's observance of these duties are circumscribed in certain respects because of their sexual and reproductive constitution. Hoch-Smith and Spring contend that virtually all religions define women in these terms (1978, p.2); certainly in Islamic ideology, as elsewhere, women are at once 'sacred' because of their reproductive powers and dangerous and in need of control because of the imputed nature of their sexuality. Thus, for example, there are rules relating to menstruation and childbirth which women must observe and which inhibit their participation in certain of the prescribed duties, and further there are a variety of notions about their sexuality which influence their contact with Islamic orthodoxy. But perhaps far greater than their explicit liabilities in the context of formal religious observance are the disabilities women experience because of their inferiority to and dependence on men in the domestic sphere. The strong bias in favour of males in traditional Islamic family law has a continuing impact on domestic life in provincial Turkey and thus direct consequences for the character of townswomen's religious life. Men's and women's religious participation is structured in radically different ways.

Among Egridir townspeople individual daily prayer is performed particularly by those men and women who are elderly or ill or who have suffered personal misfortune, but by few others, bar some younger men and women of the petty bourgeoisie. Men's daily prayer takes place in the mosques and this, and mosque attendance at Friday prayers, is restricted almost entirely to them, even in those mosques where there is a curtained area or gallery set apart for women. Friday prayers are attended by many local men and much larger congregations will join mosque prayers and Koran and mevlûd recitations during the celebration of the major Islamic festivals and at other times. Mosque prayers also have a nationalistic component and include prayers for the victory of the republic. Funeral prayers also take place in the mosques when again women are excluded; nor may women join funeral processions to the graveyard.

In alms-giving too there are differences between men's and women's types of activity. Each year the Turkish government defines, in terms of household income, an acceptable level of alms to be given by relatively affluent households to the families of poor non-kin from whom they expect services during the year. Beyond this however, wealthy men, rather than giving zakat alms in the prescribed manner, will often donate very substantial gifts to their local mosque - carpets, electric fans, loud-speaker systems, etc. These gifts are acknowleged and publicized by lists of donors displayed in the mosques. Such large gifts are sometimes quite calculated and may be seen as direct attempts by successful townsmen, including men who neglect most other religious observances, to convert commerical profit into religious prestige or at least respectability within the community. Women, by contrast, cannot alienate household wealth to this extent and I know of no mechanisms for women to convert wealth into prestige in this fashion. However, women of affluent families will buy smaller gifts - scarves, dress material, etc. - which they distribute as alms to poorer women on whose domestic services they depend. The traditional support system among women underlined by such gifts is also revealed in the mevlûd invitations which higher status women extend to those women who do menial work for them.

The fast during the Holy Month of Ramazan is observed by almost all families of the town, bar some of the transient professional elite, though even they may fast, rationalizing it, not in religious terms but rather as an important exercise in self-discipline and in health care. The fast is essentially a family ritual, in which, to this extent, men and women participate together. It is at once the most intense experience of the religious year and one which is particularly used to socialize children into religious faith.

Finally, both men and women can make the pilgrimage to Mecca, though in practice far more men than women go. In contrast with wealthy men who choose the vehicle of mosque gifts to gain religious prestige within the town, there seems to be a clear tendency for the more traditional and less wealthy bazaar merchants and craftsmen to gain religious prestige via pilgrimage, sometimes taking their elderly mothers with them to gain additional merit.

Beyond the obligations of the pillars of Islam, other religious activities are seen by the townspeople as 'customary' and distinct from those associated with Islamic orthodoxy and the religious establishment.

Visits to shrines and healers are one kind of customary religious activity open to both men and women, but seemingly not often resorted to by either. However members of both sexes approve of and collect a wide range of ancillary Islamic paraphernalia: good luck charms, Islamic household decorations, etc. In this sense all the townspeople are continually exposed to tangible religious symbols which are taken for granted to an extraordinary degree.

More or less covert involvement in Sufi brotherhoods (which are officially banned by the government) is also seen as a customary type of religious activity. It is one primarily open to men; however, in Eğridir, though my information is very scant, I have the impression that there is little Sufi activity, perhaps because men of all social categories have been able to find important temporal satisfactions and success in entrepreneurial activities. Other private religious meetings include most prominently <u>mevlûd</u> gatherings for both men and women.

Finally, a brief mention must be made of other rites of passage and secular festivities which complement the religious activities of Eğridir townspeople. Thus, there are some cogent arguments for including entry into co-educational primary schools at seven as a formidable rite of passage for both girls and boys. It is their first formal contact as individuals with the state. Obligatory military service is a further watershed for youths when for two years the ideals of Turkish nationalism are compellingly acted out. There is no comparable rite of citizenship for adolescent girls. However further education within the state system is highly valued by both young women and men from Eğridir and a number of them achieve some educational qualifications after high school.

National festivals occur throughout the year; they focus both on events important in recent Turkish history and on important categories of citizens: there are children's days, mothers' days, sports days for youths etc. These celebrations are primarily organized through the schools and government offices and they create a direct ritual link via songs, poems, ceremonial processions and the like, between an individual's roles within the family and the state. The values emphasized in other rites of passage also contain some nationalistic elements, but their source is primarily religious. However this religious content varies considerably. Both circumcision and marriage are family-centred rituals, whose celebrations are structurally similar in many ways. Both may include <u>mevlûd</u> recitals separately for both men and women, but otherwise the festivities are marked by an informality heightened by the very visible participation of small children. Both may take either a traditional form (in which case men and women will be segregated throughout), or they may be 'modern' (in which case men and women will participate in family groups). Rituals concerning death, on the other hand, are intensely religious and orientated towards personal salvation; as I have mentioned both men and women will participate, again separately, in <u>mevlûd</u> gatherings to commemorate family deaths.

Conclusions

It is now time to return to the women's reception days and mevlûd gatherings and try to place them in their wider social context. The direction of my concluding remarks emerges from my brief description of the social and religious organization of the town.

A paradox of men's relations with each other is contained within both secular and religious ideologies, between which there is, for men, a considerable continuity. On the one hand, men as individuals compete as heads of families, and, in terms of the resources they control, they are differentiated in many ways. On the other hand, all townsmen, as members of a gender category, are equal and superior to women.

As we have seen, individual family heads are ambitious and subscribe to an ethic of private enterprise in their competitions to achieve economic and political goals for themselves and their families. They act out these differences in the all-male settings of clubs and cafes as well as in other contexts. In religious terms too, there are individual differences between men; in particular they believe that personal salvation depends directly on personal morality. And yet, the potential equality of men is an ideal which is also expressed in both secular and religious terms. I have mentioned that though there are considerable differences in wealth and power between Eğridir families, these differences are not accorded any particular ideological importance; rather townspeople insist on the similarities between them as members of the town bourgeoisie. The general prosperity of the town and the economic opportunities it offers are themselves real factors in this social levelling. So too in terms of Islamic orthodoxy, all Muslims are equal before God. But, in local practice, some Muslims, namely the men, are more equal than others; men's mosque participation, even if only during Islamic festivals, and the general agreement among them about their right and duty to control women, are also great levellers.

What I am suggesting is that Turkish ideologies of secularism and Islam are interwoven to such a degree that men may express their equality or inequality in either secular or religious idioms. They may, with some ease, shift from one framework to the other or even operate in terms of both frames of reference simultaneously. We have seen that wealth may be spent on mosque gifts or pilgrimages to acquire religious prestige which has clear secular advantages within the community. Alternatively, family competitiveness and entrepreneurial success may be justified both in nationalist and in religious terms: as patriotism to homeland and nation or as that aspect of Muslim piety which sanctions the support of family life through honest hard work.

The same tension also exists for women: between their inequality as members of competing families and their identity as members of a gender category, whether before men or God. However, I would suggest that this contradiction between women's interests and roles is less easily disguised, or transformed, than it is for men.

Women's roles are derivative. Their prime identity as members of competing families is as wives who in both secular and religious terms are expected to be, and are, subordinate to their husbands. They have only indirect controls over family resources, whether wealth or information about their position in the wider society. Their acceptance of this subordination makes them effective status demonstrators for the family and the idiom of their competitions as wives depends heavily on the conspicuous consumption of food and manufactured domestic goods of all kinds, and on their use, in turn, of their own small children as status demonstrators. So too in practical religion, women have a second-class status which is most clearly shown in their exclusion from the mosques. Here they achieve an equality because of their uniform inferiority to men.

I would argue that women's dependence and inferiority to men in both spheres creates a marked discontinuity in their relations with each other. Men can act out and manipulate the contradictory implications of their inequality (from some perspectives) and their equality (from others) by using the ambiguous areas which exist between secular and religious ideologies. Women, because of their restricted access to secular resources and religious orthodoxy, cannot easily control or manipulate the contradictions of their position in this way. For them, the interplay between these two aspects of their roles and statuses is not fluid, but highly stylised and primarily conducted via the rituals of reception days and women's mevlûds. In their form and content, both types of gathering at once express and mask this paradox of the women's position, but in opposite ways: the structure of reception day gatherings depends on the perception of equality between participants, but their content, both in terms of gossip and in terms of the use of material symbols of domestic well-being, is about inequality between wives. Status differences between participants are revealed as are those between participants and women who do not join reception day gatherings. The structure of mevlûds, by contrast, accepts differentiation between women as wives, but their content, as intense religious experiences which focus on birth and motherhood, is about the equality of women.

In sum, the paired set of women's gatherings focuses women's attention on themselves in ways which make it difficult for them either to regulate the contradictory implications of their relations with each other or to confront the determinants of these relations that lie in their position vis-à-vis men. In effect the rituals of the formal women's gatherings reinforce the position of women vis-à-vis men; they provide no institutional support for questioning or changing the moral order, rather their main ritual function would seem to be compensatory.

A similar case of paired women's gatherings is described by Keirn (1978) who examines the participation of women of a South African township in both voluntary associations and in the isigodlo spirit possession rituals. She writes that in voluntary associations,

> women gain a heightened awareness of the hierarchical and competitive aspects of human relations associated with the role-playing required of them. These voluntary associations offer an outlet for women, but such associations are ultimately linked with the very

factors producing status ambiguity. Hence the women are not often eager to attend meetings that are in many cases characterized by undercurrents of tension and sometimes by open hostility between members who are also competitors (p.204).

The isigodlo meetings are quite different. There women

... form and reaffirm social bonds out of or removed from the general structural ambiguities and inequalities of their lives: they find a place where for a time they form a communion of individuals who share in their equal submission to the powerful beings of the spirit world and in so doing share a cathartic experience (ibid. p.204).

Keirn suggests that these two different types of experiences may be viewed as another example of an alternation between Turner's notions of communitas and structure. This is a useful key to the organization of such women's meetings; it complements my own argument about the formal gatherings of Turkish townswomen which has focused more on the way the ideological structure of gender roles is expressed in both the form and context of the gatherings. The wider question which needs an answer is - are such paired sets of formal women's gatherings common in societies where male dominance is considerable and unquestioned? If, as seems likely, they are, they will constitute an excellent area in which to test hypotheses about the relation between gender and religious belief and practice.

Notes

1. An earlier draft of this paper was presented at the Oxford University Women's Studies seminar, The Institute of Development Studies (University of Sussex) seminar on Women and Development and at the Center for Middle Eastern Studies, Harvard University. I am very grateful to members of these seminars for many helpful comments. Richard Tapper and I travelled together in Turkey in the summers of 1979 and 1980. Our joint impressions of Eğridir town are recorded here, while the idea of treating reception day gatherings and women's mevlûds as a paired set first arose in discussions we had with Dr. Akile Gürsoy; the paper owes much to both of them.

2. Both types of gathering are also found in many other parts of the Middle East (see e.g. the various articles in 'Visiting Patterns and Social Dynamics in Eastern Mediterranean Communities', Anthropological Quarterly, 1974, Vol. 47, No. 1 and R. and E. Fernea 1972, p.389). However it is difficult to be sure from the scanty literature available if these gatherings are strictly comparable to those I describe, nor do I know if they evince such complementarity in structure and function.

3. This approach is similar to that applied by Good (1978) and is intended to allow for direct comparisons between her material and that presented here.

References

Anthropological Quarterly, 1974, Visiting Patterns and Social Dynamics in Eastern Mediterranean Communities'. XLVII, 1

Antoun, R. 'On the Modesty of Women in Arab Villages', American Anthropologist, LXX, (1968), pp.672-97

Aswad, B. 'Visiting Patterns among Women of the Elite in a Small Turkish City', Anthropological Quarterly, XLVII, (1974), pp.9-27

___ 'Women, Class and Power: Examples from the Hatay, Turkey' in Beck, L. and N. Keddie (eds.), 1978

Beck, L. and N. Keddie (eds.), Women in the Muslim World. Cambridge, Mass., Harvard University Press, 1978

Benedict, P. 'The Kabul Gunu: Structured Visiting in an Anatolian Provincial Town', Anthropological Quarterly, XLVII, (1974), pp.28-47

___ 'The Changing Role of Provincial Towns: A Case Study from Southwestern Turkey', in P. Benedict, F. Mansur and E. Tümertekin (eds.), Turkey: Geographic and Social Perspectives. Leiden, Brill, 1974b

Constantinides, P. 'Ill at Ease and Sick at Heart: Symbolic Behaviour in a Sudanese Healing Cult' in I. M. Lewis (ed.), Symbols and Sentiments. London, Academic Press, 1977

___ 'Women's Spirit Possession and Urban Adaptation', in Caplan, P. and J. Bujra (eds.), Women United, Women Divided. London, Tavistock Press, 1978

Dobkin, M. 'Social Ranking in the Women's World of Purdah: a Turkish Example', Anthropological Quarterly, XL, (1967), pp.65-72

Dwyer, D. Images and Self-Images: Male and Female in Morocco. New York, Columbia University Press, 1978

Edmonds, A. 'The Mevlidi Sherif', Current Turkish Thought, No.600., Redhouse, Istanbul, 1969

Fallers, L. and M. Fallers, 'Sex roles in Edremit', in J. G. Perstiany (ed.), Mediterranean Family Structures. Cambridge, Cambridge University Press, 1976

Fallers, L. 'Turkish Islam'. Unpublished paper given at University of Chicago, March 1971, pp.1-20

Fernea, R. and E. Fernea, 'Variation in Religious Observance among Islamic Women', in N. Keddie (ed.), Scholars, Saints and Sufis. Berkeley, California University Press, 1972

Good, M. D. 'A Comparative Perspective on Women in Provincial Iran and Turkey', in Beck, L. and N. Keddie, (eds.) 1978

Hoch-Smith, J. and A. Spring, (eds.), Women in Ritual and Symbolic Roles. New York and London, Plenum Press, 1978

Kandiyoti, D. 'Sex Roles and Social Change: A Comparative Appraisal of Turkey's Women', Signs, 3 (1977), pp.57-73

___ 'Urban Change and Women's Roles'. Unpublished paper presented at the workshop on 'Processes and Consequences of Urban Change in the Middle East', State University of New York, Binghampton. July, 1979. 1-30

Keirn, S. M. 'Convivial Sisterhood, Spirit Mediumship and Client-Core Network among Black South African Women', in J. Hoch-Smith and A. Spring (eds.), 1978

Kiray, M. 'The New Role of Mothers: Changing Intra-familial Relationships in a Small Town in Turkey', in J. G. Peristiany (ed.), Mediterranean Family Structures. Cambridge University Press, 1976

Lewis, I. M. Ecstatic Religion. London, Penguin, 1971

MacCallum, F. L. The Mevlidi Sherif by Suleyman Chelebi. London, John Murray, 1943

Mansur, F. Bodrum. Leiden, Brill, 1972

Meeker, M. 'Meaning and Society in the Near East', International Journal of Middle East Studies, VII, (1976), pp. 243-70 and 383-422

Mernissi, F. Beyond the Veil. London, Wiley, 1975

Morsey, S. 'Sex Differences and Folk Illness in an Egyptian Village', in Beck, L. and N. Keddie (eds.), 1978

Nelson, C. 'Public and Private Politics: Women in the Middle Eastern World', American Ethnologist, I, 3, (1974), pp. 551-563

Papanek, H. 'Purdah: Separate Worlds and Symbolic Shelter', Comparative Studies of Society and History, XV, (1973), pp. 289-325

Peristiany, J. (ed.) Honour and Shame. London, Weidenfeld and Nicolson, 1965

Ruether, R. R. (ed.) Religion and Sexism. New York, Simon and Schuster, 1974

Sweet, L. 'Visiting Patterns and Social Dynamics in a Lebanese Druze Village', Anthropological Quarterly, XLVII (1974) pp. 112-119

Tapper, R. L. (in press), 'Holier than Thou: Islam in Three Tribal Societies' in Ahmed, A. and D. Hart (eds.) From the Atlas to the Indus, London, Routledge

Warner, M. Alone of All Her Sex: The Myth and the Cult of the Virgin Mary, London, Weidenfeld and Nicholson, 1976

6 ESSENCE AND EXISTENCE: WOMEN AND RELIGION IN ANCIENT INDIAN TEXTS

Julia Leslie

Introduction

Imagine the individual as a nut. The kernel hidden inside is the transmigrating soul or self [1], the essence or religious potential of the individual. The outer shell combines the circumstances of birth, personality, and all the existential trappings of a particular lifetime. Femaleness is evidently to do with 'existence' not 'essence'. But how far is it seen to impinge upon and even define the soul's potential in Indian religious texts?

The aims of this paper are fourfold: to draw a simplified chronological map of ancient Indian religion (see diagram); to place in that context what we know of the religious opportunities open to women; where possible, to find a female voice to put the case for women; and, finally, to investigate the tensions of 'existence' versus 'essence' in relation to women.

The story of Sulabhā illustrates the problem. She is described in India's great epic, the Mahābhārata, (XII. 321) as a woman far advanced in religious knowledge. When she hears of the great learning of Janaka, king of Mithila, she decides to find out if he is truly enlightened. Assuming the form of a beautiful woman, she goes to Janaka's court and begs him to share his knowledge. Janaka does so, and concludes his discourse with the claim that he is indeed enlightened: 'Free of all attachment, my soul fixed on the supreme truth, I regard all creatures equally.' But Sulabhā is not so easily satisfied. By means of her yogic powers, she enters his mind to test his claim for herself. Aghast, Janaka denounces her for attempting to seduce and humiliate a righteous man. 'However beautiful you are,' he declares, 'this union is unlawful. You have no right to pollute me with your touch.' Sulabhā is unabashed. 'Only one who still confuses soul and body (essence and existence) could talk like that,' she replies.

> True, our bodies should not touch, but I have not touched you with any part of my body. I rest in you like a drop of water on a lotus leaf, without permeating it in the least. How can you distinguish between souls which are in essence the same? How can you call the contact of two enlightened beings unlawful?

	I VEDIC	II CLASSICAL — A: Knowledge	II CLASSICAL — B: Action	III DEVOTION — Viṣṇu	III DEVOTION — Śiva
DATE	? 1500 – 500 B.C.	500 B.C. onwards		500 – 1000 A.D. onwards	
GEOG.	Aryans invade N.West	North, North West → South		South East → North	
KEY POINTS	1. Polytheism 2. Sacrifice, esp fire 3. Ecstasy, soma 4. Priesthood	A: Knowledge — 1. Absolutism, monism 2. Self-control, yoga, etc. 3. Esoteric knowledge 4. Indiv. outside society	B: Action — 1. Correct ritual 2. Right conduct 3. The individual within society	Devotion — 1. Monotheism 2. Relating to God 3. Use of the vernacular 4. Doctrine of grace	
LIT. OR RELIG. GROUP	Rg, Sama, Yajur and Atharva Vedas; Brahmanas; Aranyakas	Upaniṣads (Vedanta) / Buddhism, Jainism, etc.	Vedic Comm. 2 BC – 7 AD eg Jaimini Sabara / Lawbooks 7 BC – 6 AD eg Manu	6–7 Alvars; 12 Jayadeva; 16 Caitanya	4–9 Nayanars; 10 Vira-saivas
GOALS	1. Long life, wealth, progeny, etc. 2. Heaven	Release from birth and death / Enlightenment	1. Heaven, good rebirth 2. Release from birth and death	Union with God	
MEANS	Vedic education and sacrificial ritual	Knowledge of Brahman / Extinction of desire & ignorance	Rituals for 1. Gd.karma 2. No karma / 1. Conduct 2. Renunciation	Devotion to God	
TEXTS BY WOMEN	R.V. X.39,40: Ghosa; R.V. VIII.80: Apala; R.V. V.28: Visvavara	Therigatha	(Balambhatti)	6 Antal; 16 Mirabai	6 Karaikkal-ammaiyar; 12 Mahadevi
WOMEN/RELIG.	Apparent freedom	Two kinds of women / Conflicting views	Women excluded / Stridharma only	Women (and sudras) included	

(Mahabharata, Gita, Ramayana) → Epics + Puranas → Puranas

90

Sulabhā concludes that anyone so obsessed with the external fact that she is a woman cannot be enlightened.

This is precisely the problem I wish to investigate. How far is the kernel (the individual soul) defined by its outer shell (the existential fact of being a woman)? As the story of Sulabhā demonstrates, it is a problem of which Indian religious thinkers were well aware.

In order to simplify the great mass of material, I have divided mainstream Indian religion into three major periods, the primary characteristics of which are best described in diagrammatic form. Such labels are of course misleading if applied too rigidly. For example, there is a marked monotheistic strain underlying the profusion of gods and names of gods in later RgVedic hymns. Similarly, the ecstasy of soma ritual is at times counterbalanced by calmer tones that fit the label 'enstasy' better. For all its crudity, however, the diagram does display the important points we need to consider: the general religious approach of a particular period; its goals and how one was expected to reach them; the main texts written or recorded by men where we may find the characteristic attitudes towards women: and finally, the texts written by or ascribed to women.

I Vedic Religion

As my diagram indicates, Vedic religion (i.e. the beliefs and practices of the Aryan tribes in northern India, often called Brahmanism) was marked by polytheism (invoking gods for specific purposes) [3], fire sacrifices, ecstasy (perhaps involving hallucinogens such as soma), and a powerful priesthood in charge of religious knowledge and ritual. Education in the form of Vedic studies was the necessary preliminary to any kind of religious activity. But were women initiated into Vedic studies? The little evidence available suggests that they were. There are many references to female scholars, poets and seers, to women taking the rite of initiation and wearing the sacred thread, the mark of the initiated. Once embarked on the religious life, then, were women allowed to act as priests? Were they permitted to invoke the gods on their own behalf or for others, to chant sacred texts and formulae, to offer fire and soma sacrifices? Again, the rather sparse evidence suggests that they were.

Several hymns of the RgVeda (abbreviated RV) are ascribed to female seers, some of them describing the priestly activities of the women concerned. In RV.X.39, for example, Ghosā invokes the twin sun gods on behalf of the people with the stirring words:

As 'twere the name of father, easy to invoke, we all assembled here invoke this Car of yours,
O Aśvins ...
Awake all pleasant strains and let the hymns flow forth ...
O Aśvins, bestow on us a glorious heritage, and give our princes treasure fair as Soma is ... (v.1-2)

In RV.VIII.80, Apālā describes how she herself plucks the sacred

<u>soma</u>, presses it, and offers it with invocations to the god, Indra, saying:

> Drink thou this Soma pressed with teeth, accompanied with grain and curds, with cake of meal and song of praise. (v.2)

In RV.V.28, Viśvavārā invokes and offers sacrifice to Agni, god of fire. She conducts the ceremony herself, pouring oil with the sacrificial ladle, and declaring:

> Thy glory, Agni, I adore, kindled, exalted in thy strength. (v.4)

There is no suggestion in any of these examples that being a woman might disqualify one from ritual acts.

However, both Ghoṣā and Apālā are described as having some skin disease, possibly leprosy. This might have placed them in a different category from the other women of their time. It is also impossible to prove the historicity of any of these seers, male or female. Nonetheless, the little evidence we have does suggest that women could both receive religious education and conduct ritual sacrifice. In view of later developments, this is important.

II The Classical Period

A: *The pursuit of knowledge*

The Classical period marks a radical change in the Indian religious approach. The worship of many gods was replaced by an increasing tendency to reduce everything to one ultimate truth; external sacrifice by the inner ritual of self-control (yoga, meditation etc); ecstasy by the pursuit of esoteric knowledge ('seeing things as they really are'); the emphasis on the priesthood reinforcing the social hierarchy by that on the individual outside society's demands. Although the Upaniṣads are strictly speaking Vedic texts and the two great Upaniṣads probably older than the Buddha, it is likely that they are records of the same spiritual turmoil from which Buddhism and Jainism arose.

1. *The Upaniṣads*

For the Upaniṣads, esoteric knowledge means the knowledge of Brahman which alone can release the individual from the endless cycle of births and deaths. Our concern here is to discover whether women were both considered capable of attaining this knowledge and allowed to pursue it. Once again, the literature available provides markedly little evidence for the religious involvement of women. What there is, however, suggests that religious pursuits were not yet barred to them.

The story of the sage, Yājñavalkya, and his two wives demonstrates that, from the religious point of view, there were two kinds of women. Kātyāyanī is described as 'possessing only a woman's knowledge'. Maitreyī, however, is 'one who discourses on (the knowledge of) Brahman'. When Yājñavalkya decides to renounce the life of the householder and become a forest hermit, he offers to divide his wealth between his two wives. Kātyāyanī agrees. The Bṛhadāraṇyaka Upaniṣad continues:

> But Maitreyī said: "If, sir, this whole earth, filled as it is with riches, where to belong to me, would I be immortal thereby? "
> 'No,' said Yājñavalkya. 'As is the life of the rich, so would your life be. For there is no hope of immortality in riches.'
> And Maitreyī said: 'What should I do with something that does not bring me immortality? Tell me, good sir, what you know. (Br. Up. II.4.2-3.)

Without a second thought, Yājñavalkya complies.

The story of Gārgī is even more persuasive (Br. Up. III.6,8). In a public debate in which she is the only woman mentioned, Gārgī repeatedly questions the great Yājñavalkya. Her persistence and perspicacity finally elicit from him one of the finest definitions of Reality that we have (Br. Up. III.8.11). We may conclude that Gārgī was sufficiently learned in religious matters to be taken seriously, and that such learned women were permitted to display their knowledge and debating skills in a predominantly male public gathering.

Yājñavalkya does not question either Maitreyī's or Gārgī's capacity to understand religious truth, nor does he deny their right to pursue it, either in private or in public. But it must be added that the epithet applied to Kātyāyanī indicates the apparently equally current notion that religious knowledge is somehow not the property of women. It is this idea that takes increasing precedence in later Hindu literature.

2. Buddhism

With the advent of Buddhism, we at last find plenty of material on the religious potential of women. According to the threefold reality of Buddhism, all is suffering, all is impermanent, and there is no 'essence' or 'soul'. Strictly speaking, then, my metaphor of the nut with its kernel/shell, 'essence'/'existence' distinction is inappropriate here. For Buddhism allows for no 'kernel', no 'soul' at all. Life itself is only one of the twenty-two faculties that make up a person: selfhood the illusion they create. Sex thus makes no more than a schematic difference, merely 'to show on what account that selfhood is called "woman" or "man"' (Visuddhimagga XVI.1-9). In practical Buddhism, however, and in the majority of stories and teachings, the strict 'no-soul' doctrine is not emphasised [4]. It is, therefore, still appropriate to ask: were women as well as men considered capable of attaining enlightenment? Were they too able to extinguish the impediments of ignorance and desire?

I shall divide the evidence into three main viewpoints: first, the general tendency to take social norms as evidence of the spiritual inferiority of women; secondly, the Buddha's apparent ambivalence on the subject; and finally, the wholly positive views of the Buddhist nuns themselves.

There is ample material to support the first view. The Aṅguttara Nikāya states it plainly:

> It is impossible ... that a woman should be an Arahant who is a fully Enlightened One. But ... it is quite possible for a man to be one. (I.27.15)

The Saddharma-puṇḍarīka-sūtra supplies the usual reason:

> ... the body of a woman is filthy and not a vessel of the Law ... Moreover, a woman by her body still has five hindrances; she cannot become first, king of the Brahma-heaven; second, Śakra; third, a Māra-king; fourth, a holy emperor; and fifth, a buddha. (XI)

The story of Sumedha, a previous incarnation of the Buddha, proves it. When he makes his vow to become a Buddha in a future life, he lists the eight things he will need to achieve this aim. The first is human existence, the second the attainment of the male sex; while the other six include such things as seeing a teacher, embarking on the ascetic life, and so on (Buddhavaṃsa II.A.v.59). The Commentary adds that 'a bodhisattva (one who is to become a Buddha) who makes such a vow will never be reborn as a woman' (Cariyāpiṭaka 330). Finally, a graphic Buddhist myth spells the message out. A pious woman, seeing a starving mother about to devour her child, cuts off her own breasts to feed her. When questioned by Indra, she declares that she did it not to challenge his power but 'to tame the untamed'; and by that truth she asks to become a man. She is instantly transformed into a man and everyone rejoices. We must conclude, it seems, that the truly religious woman not only destroys the outward signs of femaleness (by cutting off her breasts) but she in fact becomes a man. Elsewhere, she need only become 'like' a man, 'abandoning a woman's thoughts and cultivating the thoughts of a man' (Dialogue II.271-2). For according to this view, a woman's presumably 'untamed' nature is inherently unfit for the religious path.

The Buddha's ambivalence on the matter is equally well-documented. His extreme reluctance to allow women to join the Order is accompanied in textual accounts by some undoubtedly negative, if cryptic, remarks. The Order was to have lasted a thousand years, he is given to say, but now that women have joined it will survive only five hundred. For just as a house with many women and few men is easily burgled, so any religion that allows women to follow the homeless life cannot last long. Other images ascribed to the Buddha compare the admission of women into the previously all-male Order to 'mildew falling on a field of fine rice', or 'blight on a field of sugarcane' (Cullavagga X.1.6). Yet elsewhere the Buddha is recorded as

94

making equally categorical statements about the irrelevance of one's sex to religious aspiration. In the Majjhima Nikāya, for example, he declares at some length that both men and women can utterly destroy 'the five fetters', thereby attaining enlightenment, never again to be reborn (I.465-8). Such apparent incongruities make sense only when we realise that for the Buddha the problem is one of 'existence' not 'essence'. He is in fact facing a tricky strategic problem: he preaches salvation for all, yet does not wish to be accused of undermining social norms.

A glance at the account of the admission of women into the Order soon makes this clear. When Mahāpajāpatī (the Buddha's aunt and fostermother) first asks the Buddha if women may also renounce their homes and become ascetics, she is refused. Moved by her dist- ress, Ānanda repeats the same request on her behalf three times, and three times he too is refused. Ānanda then deliberately rephrases the question, asking the Buddha instead:

> Are women, Lord, capable - when they have gone forth from the household life and entered the homeless state, under the doctrine and discipline of the Blessed One - are they capable of realising the fruit of conversion, or of the second Path, or the third Path, or of Arahantship? (Cullavagga X.I.3., my italics).

The Buddha admits that they are, and at last gives his permission for an Order of nuns to be formed. Clearly what is at issue here is not the capacity of women to pursue the religious life, but the pro- priety of their doing so.

When the Buddha finally gives his permission, the same reasons of propriety compel him to lay down the Eight Rules for nuns. For the most important of the four rules hitherto laid down for monks was that deference should be paid to those who had been in the Order longest. It was a kind of gerontocracy, the opinions of novices being formed in accordance with those of their elders. When men of differ- ent castes became monks, the rule still held: higher-caste novices were required to show deference to lower-caste elders. But it was apparently inconceivable that the same rule should hold for women too. On this point, the Budda seems adamant:

> You are not, O monks, to bow down before women, to rise up in their presence, to stretch out your joined hands towards them, nor to perform towards them those duties that are proper (from an inferior to a superior) (Cullavagga) X.3.1).

All Eight Rules for nuns contradict the monastic norm of geron- tocracy, conforming instead to the social norm of female inferiority. For each rule in turn stresses the dependence of nuns on monks, regardless of their religious experience. For example, the first rule reads that a nun even of one hundred years' standing must show def- erence to a monk even if he has just been initiated. The practical result is that nuns, whatever their years in the Order, are consis- tently treated as novices [5].

The procession organised by the wealthy layman Citta, recorded in the Dhammapada Commentary, makes the order of priority quite clear: monks are followed by nuns, then laymen, and lastly laywomen. Religious life takes precedence over the world (to the extent that laymen bow to nuns) but monks always take precedence over nuns. We may conclude perhaps that although the Buddha did not go out of his way to denounce the distinctions of either caste or sex as seen in the world, he nonetheless regarded neither as a barrier to salvation [6].

For the views of Buddhist nuns, I shall turn to the Therīgāthā, the 'songs' or 'psalms' of the female Elders. On the question of the historicity of these women, I shall say only that the existence of many of them is supported by frequent references to them in other texts. The question of authorship is more difficult. Some of the 'songs' seem to be genuine compositions by the nuns they are ascribed to. Others are merely associated with certain names: often, for example, verses are linked with a particular nun not because she invented them (sometimes she is the recipient), but because she used to recite them. Others again are evidently literary compositions. Many describe how women became nuns in the first place: often not for 'essential' reasons, but in order to escape the hardships of their external existence as women. Some were unable to find husbands, or were widowed. Other took up the homeless life after a series of misfortunes, or to escape the 'five woes of women': having to leave one's parents' home when young to live with strangers; menstruation; pregnancy; giving birth; and having to wait on a man whether father, husband or son. But perhaps as many songs detail the spiritual heights attained by individual women. Sujātā, for example, becomes enlightened while still a laywoman (145-50). Sumedhā realises the six branches of insight (448-522 and Comm.). Dhammadinnā is described as a great preacher who cuts every question as one might a lotus stalk with a knife (Comm. on 12). Nanduttarā is an impressive religious debater (Comm. on 87-91). Sundarī is famous for her many conversions (312-37 and Comm.). And so on. For these women, the religious life is far more than a refuge from a harsh world: it is the proper environment for those intent upon the highest spiritual goals.

I have selected two 'songs' in particular to put the case for women. First, Somā describes her encounter with Māra (the god of Death and the Buddhist equivalent of Satan). In an effort to tempt Soma back to the world, Mara derides her religious commitment, maintaining that enlightenment is impossible for a woman with 'two-finger intelligence'. Undeterred, Somā asks him what difference being a woman could possibly make to one who has real insight (60-1). In another version, she adds significantly:

> To one for whom the question arises, 'Am I woman in these matters or am I a man?' to such a one is Māra fit to talk. (Saṃyutta Nik-āya V.2)

For Māra is associated with worldly not spiritual things, with the outer shell and not the aspirations within. Subhā puts the thought into action. She describes how a 'rogue' inveigles her into the forest and tries to seduce her. Subhā responds by preaching the Doctrine to him. But the 'rogue' sees only the beauty of her eyes, and ignores her lofty words. So, to demonstrate the irrelevance of both beauty and sex to the inner life, Subhā plucks out one of those lovely eyes and offers it to him. He is converted at once. For the 'rogue' conditioned by social norms, her existence as a woman had, until that moment, superseded all else. For Subhā, her essence as a religious aspirant was untouched by the social and sexual implications of being a woman (Therīgāthā 366-99 and Comm.).

B: Right action

The upsurge of Buddhism and other ascetic sects [7] provoked a counter-reaction on the part of orthodox brahmanism. The importance of knowledge is replaced by that of action: either correct ritual action as laid down by the Vedic Commentators, or appropriate human action within society as ordained by cosmic law (dharma) and interpreted for men by the lawgivers. The religious goals for both approaches are the same: release from the cycle of births and deaths: or, failing that, heaven and a good rebirth in the next life. But were both these goals considered attainable by women as well as by men?

1. The Vedic Commentators and Ritual Action

In an effort to stem 'heretical' thought, the Vedic Commentators (by which I mean primarily the Mīmāṃsā school of Vedic exegesis) devoted themselves to resuscitating the ancient traditions and ideals of the already distant Vedic past. In relation to women, however, their concern was not merely to turn back the clock. The religious education and opportunities left open to women in Vedic times are repeatedly curtailed, and Vedic references to them redefined. For example, references to women wearing the sacred thread are now interpreted as referring to the bride wearing her saree over her left shoulder 'like' a sacred thread (Comm. on Gobhila-gṛhya-sūtra II.1.19). References to a 'learned' man are taken to mean religious learning; but the same word applied to a woman, as in the prayer for the birth of a 'learned' daughter, is taken to refer to domestic skills (Saṃkara's Comm. on Br.Up.VI.4.17). The Upaniṣadic suggestion that religious knowledge is not 'normal' for women seems to have taken root.

A woman's right to perform sacrifice is abolished altogether. Three main reasons are given. The first is a parallel argument to that against the offering of sacrifices by the lowest of the four 'classes' [8] of men, the śūdras. Since Vedic injunctions specifically mention only the three higher classes, śūdras must by implication be excluded (Jaiminīya-sūtra VI.1.25-8). Similarly, Vedic injunctions refer specifically only to men, and therefore by implication women must also be excluded. The truth is, of course, that injunctions are merely given in the masculine form. The question remains whether this masculine form is to be understood as inclusive (he and/or she) or exclusive (he and not she). How, for example, is the injunction, 'He who desires heaven should offer sacrifice' to be interpreted? According to Jaimini (VI.1.6-20), the masculine form is inclusive: for psychological or 'essential' reasons (i.e. that religious aspiration is as strong in women as in men); and for purely grammatical reasons. Śabara's Commentary denies the former and redefines the latter.

It is this latter grammatical point that constitutes the second major argument against the offering of sacrifices by women. For early grammarians such as Patañjali (2nd century B.C.), gender is listed as one of the types of modification that may operate in a sentence. Other modifications include that of noun, number, and so on. The modification of gender, however, means precisely what Jaimini claims it does: that the masculine form may be 'modified' to give the feminine meaning as an alternative. Śabara simply denies this rule. Later grammarians follow suit until we find the 17th century author Nāgeśa (in his commentary on Patañjali) defining linga not as 'gender' but as 'noun-stem'. In other realms too, the male is increasingly taken as the paradigm. Instructions concerning meditations on the body, ritual ablutions and so on invariably refer to the male body. In theory, the modification of gender may be invoked. In practice, it is ignored: the information is evidently intended for the male.

The third major argument for the exclusion of women from sacrifices is related to the rights of women to own property. In order to qualify as a performer of sacrifice, one must own property. According to Jaimini women can become the owners of property either through a marriage settlement, or as a result of their own earnings by such activities as spinning. But according to Śabara, a woman can own nothing: what is hers belongs either to her father or to her husband; indeed she herself is the property of either father or husband. He bases this view on the Vedic description of a marriage ceremony in which the father gives his daughter away in exchange for a cow and a bull; an exchange which Śabara takes to be a sale of property. Jaimini argues reasonably that this constitutes only one form of marriage; and that it is anyway not a sale but a formal gift, as is proved by the fact that the 'price' does not fluctuate according to the value of the 'goods' (VI.1.10-12).

Even the rights of the wife taking part in the joint sacrifice with her husband, a tradition much in evidence in Vedic literature, are whittled away. In both Vedic and epic times, the wife's participation in the joint sacrifice is a religious necessity. According both to the grammarian, Pānini (IV.1.33), and to Jaimini (VI.1.17-21), patnī (the word used to refer to the chief wife of equal caste) means 'female owner', and thus one who is qualified to take an equal share in the joint sacrifice. But later commentators insist first, that all injunctions for joint sacrifice expressed in the masculine form refer to the husband alone; and secondly, that those expressed in the feminine form should be reinterpreted according to what is considered 'proper' for women. For example, the invocation of blessings often ascribed to the wife involves Vedic mantras; but women are now redefined as unworthy of Vedic education. In relation to women, therefore, such references must be reinterpreted to mean 'bathing' or some equally unimportant activity (Jaiminīya-sūtra VI.1.24; Śabarabhāṣya). The wife's religious role even in the joint sacrifice thus becomes increasingly passive and insignificant, covering such things as looking after the implements her husband alone can use. We have come a long way from the female seers of the RgVeda.

2. The Lawbooks and Human Conduct

The lawbooks take this trend even further. Religious education and ritual are categorically denied to women. No sacramental rite with sacred texts may be performed for women for they are weak, impure, and have no knowledge of Vedic literature (Manusmṛti IX.18). No sacrifice, no vow and no fast may be performed by a woman independently of her husband (V.155), or she will go to hell (XI.36).

The emphasis has changed from knowledge and ritual to conduct: the concepts of dharma and svadharma. Dharma is the law of the cosmos, the principle underlying all creation. It is both descriptive and prescriptive: what is and what ought to be. Svadharma (own dharma) is this same cosmic law reflected in human existence. This too is both descriptive and prescriptive: what is (i.e. the duties and functions ordained by one's birth and circumstances) and what ought to be. Hence one's religious duty is to fulfil the obligations of one's current existence. Svadharma, the religious duty of every individual is also referred to as varnāśramadharma, the duty of one's class (varna) and stage (āśrama) in life.

The theory of class is briefly detailed in, for example, the Baudhayāna Dharmasūtra. Brahmins are expected to study the Vedas, teach, and perform sacrifices. The warrior class should study the Vedas, perform sacrifices and carry arms. The merchant or artisan class should study the Vedas, perform sacrifices, cultivate the soil, tend cattle and do business. The lowest class (śūdras) are required merely to serve the three higher classes.

It is often assumed that this hierarchy is applicable to both sexes. But a glance at the religious literature on the subject of class in relation to women soon reveals that it is not. Women of whatever class are increasingly relegated to the inferior status of śūdras. In Vedic literature, the four-class hierarchy is mentioned only once, right at the end of the RgVedic period (RV.X.90). In the Upaniṣads, the four classes are mentioned but do not yet form a rigid system. The oft-repeated question of the Upaniṣadic era is rather: Who is the real brahmin? The answer is unambiguous: he who sees things as they really are. In matters of religious truth, both class and sex are irrelevant. Buddhist literature shows the beginning of the downward trend: while the hierarchy of class is overruled by monastic values, that of sex is not. For the Vedic Commentators, however, both class and sex are crucial: śūdras and women are excluded from all religious ritual. From now on, women are openly grouped together with the lowest class. The lawbooks make this fact quite plain: the three higher classes are defined as having the right to study the Vedas and offer sacrifice; women, regardless of the class they are born into, are forbidden to do either. For example, Manu's instructions on the ritual purification of the body read that the three higher classes should sip water three times and wipe their mouths once; but that a woman and a śūdra should perform each action only once (V.139).

The theory of the four stages of life are equally clear-cut and equally inappropriate for women. The first stage is that of the student of the Vedas, a long and intense period of religious instruction with a teacher. This is followed by marriage and the assumption of the duties of the householder. The birth of one's first grandson heralds the third stage, that of the forest hermit. The fourth begins when the renunciate performs his own funeral rites while still alive to indicate his total rejection of the world.

Once again, we must ask how far this admittedly idealised hierarchy was seen to be applicable to women. As we have seen, the first stage of religious education was apparently open to women in Vedic times, but closed to them by the later commentators and lawgivers. With the gradual extension of the study period to 12-16 years [9], and the simultaneous drop in the age of marriage for girls [10], it became impossible for women to do both. Perhaps for a while there were two kinds of women (like Maitreyī and Kātyāyanī in the Upaniṣads), but it seems that marriage became increasingly crucial. The religious education of women was dropped. By the time of Manu, a girl's wedding ceremony is described as equivalent in religious terms to the boy's rite of initiation; hence the way a married woman wears her saree draped across her left shoulder may be likened to the wearing of the sacred thread. The service of wife to husband is seen to parallel the boy's period of study and service with his teacher. Domestic duties incumbent on the wife correspond to the sacrificial ritual required of the male householder in the second stage.

The last two stages of hermit and renunciate are gradually barred to women. There are frequent epic references to women hermits such as Sulabha, who are described as possessing great knowledge and yogic powers. The Mahābhārata even mentions special hermitages for women ascetics. But Manu in his section on forest hermits tells us only that a man becoming a hermit may either commit his wife to his son's keeping or take her with him (VI.3). There is no suggestion that she may take up this stage on her own behalf. For Manu, no woman may ever leave her home to take up the ascetic life (V.149). She must always be controlled by a man: by her father in childhood, by her husband after marriage, by her son after her husband's death (V.148). This is undoubtedly the kind of prejudice the Buddha faced when he was considering the admission of women into his monastic order. In this context, his reluctance is hardly surprising. Even more important perhaps, from the orthodox male point of view, 'female ascetic' is simply a contradiction in terms. For women are wholly identified with the social, familial and sexual world that the (male) ascetic must renounce.

For the ancient lawgivers, then, religious goals and means vary according to the status of the individual. Release may be attained only by male brahmins who fulfil the duties of class and stage and whose lives therefore culminate in the purity of renunciation. Heaven and a good rebirth in the next life may be attained by all other men who fulfil their ordained functions. Women, of whatever class, now constitute an entirely separate category. They may attain heaven and a good rebirth (as a man perhaps) if they fulfil not the dharma of class and stage but the dharma of women. This is to be found in the male-related roles of daughter, wife, mother and widow, and all the obligations that these entail.

The role of wife is of paramount importance. The Viṣṇusmṛti intones:

Obedience to her Lord is the only way for a woman to obtain bliss in heaven. (XXV.15)

This all-important role is perhaps best symbolised by the epic heroine, Sītā, for whom her husband is the incarnation of supreme law in her life, the definition of her religious duty, a god to be appeased (Rāmāyaṇa). The role of mother comes a close second, and is as emotively described. For women must provide their husbands with sons to perform the necessary funeral rites [11]. Without these regular offerings, one's ancestors (literally 'fathers') suffer pangs of hunger in the interim 'world of the fathers' [12]. As social requirements crystallise into religious duty, women become totally dependent on their menfolk for salvation.

If we return once more to the image of the nut with which we began, we find that the outer shell protecting the kernel is now, for women, in two halves. The dark half is the polluted and inherently evil nature of women. For according to Manu, women are naturally lustful, heartless, disloyal, malicious, and so on. These accusations are seen to be proved by the fact of menstruation, a powerful symbol of guilt and pollution thoughout Indian literature. If a woman indulges this half of her existential self (i.e. is disobedient etc.), she will go to hell. The bright half of the outer shell is provided by the idealised female roles prescribed by the dharma of women. A woman's religious progress is measured by the degree of her success in these male-related roles; that is, by the existence and continued health of her husband and sons, and by her devotion to them. The propaganda to this effect is persuasive: the truly religious (i.e. virtuous) woman may in this life wield astounding powers [13], and in the next enjoy the rewards of heaven [14].

Before moving on to the final section in my diagram, I must add that I searched in vain for a lawbook written by a woman to constitute the woman's voice in these negative times [15]. Apart from several medieval commentaries inspired by royal patronesses, the text that most nearly fits the bill is the Bālaṃbhaṭṭī, (ca. 1800) ascribed to a woman named Lakṣmīdevī. Female authorship is at least arguable on the grounds that, wherever possible, lenient views on women are expressed and the most generous interpretations of a ruling given.

For example, the order of succession not only places sisters after brothers and half-sisters after half-brothers, but includes daughters-in-law as well. Widows are allowed to adopt without the express authority of their deceased husbands; and so on. However, the Bālaṃbhaṭṭi is not rated highly even today: if cited in legal cases, it is usually overruled. Its tolerant views are only accepted as law if supported by other authorities. The work is anyway probably written by Lakṣmīdevī's son and merely ascribed to her, perhaps precisely because of those lenient views. All I can suggest is that it may at least show the influence of a woman in the realm of sacred law.

III Devotional Religion

My third general phase of Indian religion is radically different from and opposed to the preceding ones. For devotional religion (bhakti) entails neither correct ritual practice nor esoteric knowledge, nor even the fulfilment of the obligations of one's birth and station. It requires only an intense personal relationship with a single supreme God, usually Viṣṇu or Śiva. As long as this relationship is direct, constant and deeply emotional, the exact form it takes is less important. Rāvaṇa, for example, retains to the end a fierce hatred of and opposition to Rāma (an incarnation of Viṣṇu), yet this very ferocity related to God takes him to heaven. Love, however, is the most appropriate emotion. This may be interpreted in any number of ways: the love of a mother for her child (as in the worship of the baby Kṛṣṇa, another incarnation of Viṣṇu), of a child for his parent, of a servant for his master or mistress, of brothers (as in Lakṣmaṇa's love for his brother, Rāma), and so on. The only kind of relationship that is consistently ruled out as a form of worship is devotion to the Goddess on the part of a male devotee identifying himself as her lover or husband. But the most intense and therefore most effective love of all is that of a woman for a man. For in devotional terms, both men and women are spiritually female and God is the only male. While one of the (male) Vaiṣṇavite Ālvārs describes his languishing soul as 'a beautiful maiden', Mahādevī praises Śiva as one 'for whom men, all men, are but women, wives'. For though men and women are now equal in the eyes of God, the male-female hierarchy remains. In the devotional ideal of the agony and ecstasy of love, the soul of the devotee (whether male or female) must burn for God as a lovelorn woman burns for her man.

Unlike the bhakti of the Bhagavad Gītā which is strictly controlled and virtually synonymous with yoga, bhakti proper (such as in the 9th century Bhāgavata Purāṇa) is a religion of the heart and passions. The intellectual bias of Classical religion is swept away: the study of the Vedas and Sanskrit is replaced by hymns and poems in the vernacular to be sung by all regardless of education or status. The social hierarchies of class, caste and sex are ignored by the doctrine of the grace of God. Salvation in the form of union with God is now open to all, even women and śūdras, through the practice of whole-hearted, often abject, devotion. I shall limit my account

to two particularly striking forms, one each from Vaiṣṇava and Śaiva
devotionalism.

1. *Devotion to Viṣṇu*

The devotional worship of Viṣṇu is perhaps best exemplified by the
erotic passion of the gopīs (female cowherds) for Kṛṣṇa in the form
of an amorous and mischievous young man [16]. The gopīs represent
the amoral intoxication of devotional love: all married women, they
abandon husbands, homes and children without a backward glance in
order to seek out their God. This overpowering devotion takes two
main forms. For Caitanya, the devotee identifies himself with Radha,
Kṛṣṇa's favourite gopī, and longs to experience union with Kṛṣṇa as
she did. For Jayadeva, the devotee identifies himself with the other
less fortunate gopīs, longing instead to witness that glorious union.
Either way, male devotees must divest themselves of their masculinity, and think and act like women. The 19th century saint, Rāmakrishna, for example, spent six months in systematic devotion as a woman to Kṛṣṇa. He dressed as a woman (wearing ornaments, false
hair, etc.) and used feminine gestures with such effect that village
women accepted him as one of themselves. Following the tradition of
Caitanya, Rāmakrishna identified himself with Rādhā, but with such
intensity that he saw a vision of her merging with his own body.
When he later had a vision of Kṛṣṇa uniting with his Rādhā-body,
Rāmakrishna's devotional goal was achieved. This form of worship on
the part of the male devotee may be extreme but it is not new. The
14th century theologian, Vedānta Désika, was similarly renowned. In
an annual festival in South India today, his image is still dressed as
a woman and placed facing an image of Kṛṣṇa for the purposes of
joint worship [17].

It becomes the earliest woman saint in this tradition, however, is probably
Antāl [18] (6th century A.D.), the only woman among the twelve
Alvārs. Her fervent Tamil poems depict the gopīs' total surrender to
Kṛṣṇa as bridegroom, while her Song Divine is still sung daily in
Vaiṣṇava shrines. But perhaps Mīrābāī (16th century A.D.) [19] is
the most famous woman poet-saint of the tradition. Widowed early,
her life of devotion repeatedly obstructed by in-laws more concerned
with the orthodox ideals of strīdharma, Mīrābāī's early poems sing
only of the pain of separation from her Lord Kṛṣṇa. Later, when her
devotion bears fruit, she sings of union and joy: 'My Beloved lives
in my heart!' Ostracised at first for her refusal to immolate herself
on her husband's pyre in accordance with Rajput custom, Mīrābāī is
at last regarded as a saint.

It becomes clear from the literature that, for the female devotee,
the Vaiṣṇava path of devotion often takes shape as an uneasy combination of bhakti and strīdharma. The gopī model is followed only in
part: externally, social conventions are kept; internally, they are
broken by the 'illicit' love of God. Bahiṇabāī, the 17th century Ma-
hārāstrian brahmin saint flouts caste rules by accepting a śūdra as
her teacher; yet she discourses in a most orthodox manner on the

duties of a woman to obey her husband, control her sexual appetite, and perform her household duties. The example of the gopis seems to be more a metaphor than a genuine goal. Yet many saintly women are recorded as having resisted the contrary demands of strīdharma. Mīrābāī refuses to let herself be burned, the only acceptable widowhood in her community. In one legend, a Kerala saint, determined to resist her family's plans for an arranged marriage, is saved by the intervention of her God who steps out of the image she worships so fervently. Another Kerala saint, rebuked for reciting the Lord's name when she is menstruating, replies unabashed that life may desert her at any moment, even during her period, and she wishes at all costs to be prepared. In yet another tale, a 19th century Andhra saint refuses to shave her head when her husband dies: when the priests shave her by force, her luxuriant hair, symbol of uncensored femaleness, grows back at once. Such stories as these demonstrate that the unimpeded passion of the gopis in their pursuit of God had to come to terms in one way or another with the orthodox demands of strīdharma in real life.

2. Devotion to Śiva

Śaiva devotionalism, unlike the gopī model, is more applicable to the saint-ascetic outside society. Perhaps the earliest female mystic in this tradition is Kāraikkālammaiyār (6th century A.D.), one of the sixty-three Nāyanārs. She left three Tamil treatises expressing a profound love for God as 'Father' or 'Lord'. Although married, she was so intoxicated by her love for Śiva, so totally absorbed in Him, that she was held to be possessed.

In Vīraśaiva devotionalism in particular, the relationship with God, though equally important, is at the same time often less personal, less emotional and more abstract than in the Vaiṣṇava version. While importance is given to the teacher and the community of saints, their model and ideal is the wandering ascetic mystic. Within this framework, the hierarchies of class, caste and sex are accepted as social facts but are never regarded as barriers to religious progress. Dēvara Dāsimayya, a renowned male Virasaiva mystic, demands in one of his poems:

Did the breath of the mistress
have breasts and long hair?

Or did the master's breath
wear sacred thread?

Did the outcaste, last in line,
hold with his outgoing breath
the stick of his tribe?

What do the fools of this world know
of the snares you set,

O Rāmanātha? [20]

For, as he explains elsewhere,

> If they see
> breasts and long hair coming
> they call it woman,
>
> if beard and whiskers
> they call it man:
>
> but, look, the self that hovers
> in between
> is neither man
> nor woman
>
> O Rāmanātha.

Here at last the distinction between the kernel and the outer shell is clear.

The woman's voice is provided by Mahādevī (12th century A.D.). Married against her will to a powerful and worldly man, Mahādevī endeavours to combine the dharma of women with devotion to God. But when her husband jealously obstructs her worship of Śiva, she leaves him to become a wandering ascetic. Whereas the gopis' love for Kṛṣna is seen as illicit and that owed their husbands as lawful, Mahādevī regards Śiva as her true husband. She exclaims contemptuously in one of her poems:

> Take these husbands who die,
> decay, and feed them
> to your kitchen fires!

For her only goal is Śiva. Since for this end being a woman is irrelevant, Mahādevī breaks all the rules laid down by strīdharma. One poem describes how she must escape the 'traps' set by her in-laws to guard her, all the social conventions that prevent her from following her God. She casts even her clothes aside, wandering naked through the forest. She explains:

> To the shameless girl
> wearing the White Jasmine Lord's
> light of morning,
> you fool,
> where's the need for cover and jewel?

When men molest her in the forest, she speaks movingly of their futile obsession with the physical:

> O brothers, why do you talk
> to this woman,

hair loose,
face withered,
body shrunk?

O fathers, why do you bother
with this woman?
She has no strength of limb,
has lost the world,
lost power of will,
turned devotee,

she has lain down
with the Lord, white as jasmine,
and has lost caste.

Mahādevī reaches the great community of saints, is cross-examined by their teacher, then accepted among them. Before long, intoxicated by devotion, she wanders off again in search of Śiva's holy mountain. At last, she finds it, and Him, and dies. She is in her early twenties.

I shall conclude by moving away from the more extreme examples of such as Mahādevī towards a more representative female point of view. This is persuasively supplied by the story of Cūḍālā, taken from the Yoga Vāsiṣṭha (ca. 1300). Queen Cūḍālā conscientiously performs all the duties entailed by having a husband, a household and a kingdom. But even as she does so, she realises the pointlessness of worldly things. She sees the Truth and becomes enlightened. But when she seeks to share this knowledge with her pleasure-loving husband, he commands her to be silent. Recognising that he will never learn from her, Cūḍālā asks the court brahmins to preach to him instead. At last, their words prevail and the king too sees the futility of pleasures. Unlike his wife, however, he renounces everything to become a hermit in the forest. Cūḍālā does not try to stop him. Instead, she uses her yogic powers to watch over him in secret. She sees that he is now as attached to his hermit existence as he had been to his throne, and that he is as far from enlightenment as ever. She knows he needs guidance but realises that he still cannot accept it from her. So she assumes the body of a young monk (thus demonstrating the irrelevance of her external form), goes to him in the forest, and eventually brings him to an understanding of the Truth. The king attains liberation and returns to his kingdom. There the enlightened couple rule together perfectly for thousands of years. The story ends with the appropriate accolades both to Cūḍālā's wifely devotion (according to the dharma of women) and to her wise spirituality. This is the ideal Indian compromise between outer and inner, between kernel and shell.

Notes

1. The doctrine of transmigration does not, in fact, appear until the Upaniṣads, that is, until the Classical Period.

2. The problem of dating Indian religious literature is a complex one. For we are dealing with what is essentially an oral tradition: generations of scholar–priests, each trained to word-perfect recall of his own discipline. References to writing in the work of the early grammarian, Pāṇini, suggest that it was already in use before 350 B.C. Indeed, the earliest inscription discovered so far can be dated at around the third century B.C. But it is clear that the written word was not held in high regard in religious matters. Studying from written texts was frowned upon, recitation and repetition invariably preferred. One phonetic treatise includes the scholar who reads aloud from a written text among the six vilest types of reciter. We may thus safely assume that religious texts were not recorded in writing until long after the invention and use of scripts. Even when they were recorded, the harshness of the Indian climate and the perishable nature of the materials used meant that little early writing has survived. We are left with manuscripts the contents of which are far earlier than the materials on which they have been recorded. The dates tentatively supplied in my diagram represent, therefore, the probable period of the composition of the verses or treatises concerned.

3. The Indian pantheon is not so much polytheistic in the Greek sense as henotheistic: that is, the characteristics of the supreme are attributed to whichever deity is being invoked.

4. For a detailed discussion of the doctrine of no soul and for the fact that it is 'insisted on only in a certain specific kind of conceptually sophisticated theoretical context', see S. Collins 1979 pp. 97 ff.

5. It is interesting to note that in Sri Lanka today there are strictly speaking no nuns (i.e. those who have taken the higher ordination, and live according to the 227 monastic rules); but only novices who live according to the Ten Precepts. There are no references to nuns at all after about A.D. 1000. Nowadays, however, the question of whether female novices should take the higher ordination is being raised again.

6. I am reminded here of Marina Warner's description of the attitudes to women in the Catholic Church, in which 'the oscillation between regarding them as equal in God's eyes (endowed with an immortal soul) and yet subject and inferior to the male in the order of creation and society ... has never ceased'. (See Marina Warner: 1976, p. xxiv.) Apart from the concept of an immortal soul, there is a remarkable similarity between the two traditions.

7. Jainism was the other major non-orthodox sect that flourished at the time of the Buddha. In contrast to the Buddhist case, there seems to have been no problem here concerning the admission of women into the monastic life. While the Buddhist order of nuns was formed only with extreme reluctance (prompted perhaps by the Jain example) and then only lasted in India for a few centuries, nuns are in the majority among the Śvetāmbaras, the largest of the Jain sects.

According to the 1977 census, the Śvetāmbara sect included 1,200 monks and 3,400 nuns (mostly widows, a fact yet to be examined from a sociological perspective). On the question of whether a woman can attain liberation, there is a clear doctrinal split between the majority Śvetāmbara and the extremist Digambara sects. According to the former, a woman can attain liberation; and the 19th Tīrthankara ('ford-maker', i.e. great Teacher) was in fact a woman, Mallī. According to the latter, a woman cannot attain liberation until first reborn as a man. But a closer look reveals that the split is based not on real doctrinal differences but on the social implications arising from the issue of nudity. For the Śvetāmbaras, nudity is not essential for the attainment of liberation. For the Digambaras, it is. In theory, nudity is open to both men and women but, since it is socially unacceptable for women to go around naked (on the grounds of modesty in general and menstruation in particular), they must wait to be reborn as men. Only one 13th century Digambara author has recorded his approval of administering the vows of nudity to a woman; and then only on her deathbed.

It is perhaps also worth remarking that, in the Śvetāmbara case, the Tīrthankara Mallī's birth as a woman is put down to misdeeds when she was a male ascetic in a previous life. Having agreed with her colleagues to observe a particular number of fasts, he/she apparently cheated in order to outdo them. Such vices as cheating, greed, cunning and so on are traditional causes for rebirth as a woman for both Śvetāmbara and Digambara sects.

8. I deliberately avoid using the word 'caste' here. 'Caste' is the correct translation, not of varṇa, but of jāti. The latter term covers the innumerable subdivisions within the four-fold hierarchy of 'class' (varṇa).

9. As time passed, the spoken language developed further and further away from the language of the Vedas. This, together with the belief that the slightest mistake in or mispronunciation of a Vedic text would bring distaster, led to an insistence on longer and longer periods of study.

10. Several reasons are given for this. Perhaps the most powerful is the belief that a woman's 'season' (the 4th to 16th days after menstruation) is a divine call to motherhood not to be ignored. It is thus a father's sacred duty to get his daughter married before her first menstrual period. For this and other reasons, see Julia Leslie 1980 pp.65 ff.; note 65.

11. It is interesting to note that if a man dies without sons then, for religious purposes, his daughter may be 'reclassified' as a son. As an 'appointed daughter', she may perform the necessary funeral rites for her own father. But a girl who does so is automatically disqualified from the religious duties required of a wife: her son performs the funeral sacrifice not for his own father but for his maternal grandfather. Manu therefore warns men never to marry such a girl.

12. According to the rules of Sanskrit grammar, the masculine of coordinate pairs of relations can be used alone in the dual so as to include the female. Thus pitarau means either 'two fathers' or 'father

and mother'; hence 'fathers' or ancestors.

13. For hyperbolic descriptions of the power accruing to the virtuous woman see Julia Leslie 1980, p.80. Sītā enters the fire unharmed; Sāvitrī wrests her husband from the grip of Death; Gāndhārī exterminates an entire race; and so on.

14. Among the rewards awaiting the devoted wife in heaven is the opportunity to rejoin her husband so that she may continue to serve him.

15. Even works on women written by men are rare. Apart from several works containing sections on women, I have found only one major Sanskrit text devoted to women. The Strīdharmapaddhati, (A Guide to the Religious Duties of Women) (ca. 1720) is ascribed to the chief minister at the court of King Sāhajī of Thanjavur. A unique, if somewhat depressing document, it forms the basis of my current research.

16. For a detailed discussion of emotional Krsna worship, see F. Hardy 1976.

17. Cf. Milton Singer 1966 p.133.

18. Cf. F. Hardy, 1976, pp.487-502. Hardy argues convincingly that Āntāl, being herself a woman, establishes for the first time a direct analogy between the mystic's 'I': the poetic symbol of the girl in love, the mythical gopī, and the actual poet-singer. For her, this is no mere poetic device. The girl Āntāl depicts so passionately is her own 'I': mystic, poet, gopī and, encompassing all these, the deeply physical woman who longs for Krsna to touch 'her soft large breasts and splendid abdomen'.

19. Cf. A. J. Alston 1980.

20. The following quotations are taken from A. K. Ramanujan: 1973: pp.105, 110, 134, 129, 135.

Postcript

An article in Kesarī, a Marathi daily newspaper on 6 November 1981 describes a meeting between a Vedic scholar from Germany and the highly revered religious leader, Sankaracārya Candrasekharendra Sarasvatī of the Kancī Kāmakoti Pīth. On being informed that she was learning to recite the Vedas, the Sankaracārya ruled that as a woman she had no right to do so: only Hindu men who had undergone initiation had that right.

References

Abbott, J. E. (tr.) Bahiṇā Bāī, A Translation of her Autobiography and Verses. Poona, Scottish Mission Industries Co. Ltd, 1929

Alston, A. J. (tr.) The Devotional Poems of Mīrābāī. Delhi, Motilal Banarsidass, 1980

Altekar, A. S. The Position of Women in Hindu Civilisation. Delhi, Motilal Banarsidass, 2nd edition 1959, 3rd reprint 1978

Atharva Veda. See Bloomfield, M. 1897

Basham, A. L. The Wonder that was India. 2nd edition 1967, London, Fontana, 1974

Baudhāyana dharmasūtra. See Bühler, G. 1882

Bhagavata Gita. See Zaehner, R. C., 1966

Bhagavata Purāṇa. See Burnouf, E., 1800; Sanyal, J. M., 1952

Bloomfield, M. (tr.) Hymns of the Atharva Veda, together with Extracts from the Ritual Books and Commentaries. 1897. Delhi, Motilal Banarsidass, 1978

Buddhism. See Horner, I. B., 1930, 1954-59, 1975; Warren H. C., 1896; Rhys Davids, T. W., 1881, 1885; Rhys Davids, Mrs., 1917-30, 1909, 1913; Norman, K. R., 1969, 1971; Woodward, F. E., 1932-36; Kern, H., 1909; Cowell, E. B., 1894

Bühler, G. (tr.) The Laws of Manu, translated with extracts from Seven Commentaries. 1886. Delhi, Motilal Banarsidass, 1979
___ (tr.) The Sacred Laws of the Āryas, as taught in the Schools of Apastamba, Gautama, Vāsishtha and Baudhāyana. Part I 1879, Part II 1882. Delhi, Motilal Banarsidass. Part I 1975, Part II 1965

Burnouf, E. (ed. and tr.) Le Bhagavata Purāna ou L'Histoire Poétique de Krichna. 5 vols. Paris, 1840-98 (Vol V. tr. M. Hauvette-Besnault and Le P. Roussel.)

Chatterji, K. C. (Sanskrit text and tr.) Patanjali's Mahābhāsya: paspasahnika (introductory chapter). Calcutta, A. Mukherji, 1957

Collins, S. Personal Continuity in Theravada Buddhism. Oxford University D.Phil. thesis, 1979

Cowell, E. B. and others (tr.). Buddhist Mahayana Texts. 1894. New York, Dover, 1969

Filliozat, P. (Sanskrit text and tr.) Le Mahābhāsya de Patañjali avec le Pradīpa de Kaiyaṭa et L'Uddyota de Nāgeśa, Adhyaya I, Pāda I, Āhnika 1-4. Pondechery, Publications de L'Institut Français d'Indologie No 54, 1, 1975

Gobhila-grhya-sūtra. See Oldenberg, H., 1892

Griffith, R. T. H. (tr.) The Hymns of the RgVeda. 1889. Revised 2nd edition, Delhi, Motilal Banarsidass, 1973

Hardy, F. Emotional Krsna Bhakti. Oxford University D.Phil. thesis, 1976

Horner, I. B. Women Under Primitive Buddhism. London, George Routledge and Sons, 1930
___ (tr.) The Collection of the Middle Length Sayings (Majjhima-Nikāya). 3 vols. London, Pali Text Society, 1954-59
___ (tr.) The Book of the Discipline (Vinaya-Piṭaka) Vol. V (Cullavagga). London, Lurzac and Co. Ltd., 1952

Jacobson, D. 'The Chaste Wife' in S. Vatuk (ed.) American Studies in the Anthropology of India. Delhi, 1978

Jaiminīya-sūtra. See Sandal, M. L., 1923-25; Jha, G., 1942

Jaini, P. S. The Jaina Path of Purification. Berkeley etc, University of California Press, 1979

Jayal, S. The Status of Women in the Epics. Delhi, Motilal Banarsidass, 1966

Jha, G. Purva-Mīmāṃsā in its Sources. Benares, Benares Hindu
    University. 1942
Jolly, J. (tr.) The Institute of Vishnu. 1880. Delhi, Motilal Banar-
    sidass, 1977
___ (tr.) The Minor Lawbooks. 1889. Delhi, Motilal Banarsidass,
    1965
Kane, P. V. History of Dharmaśastra (Ancient and Mediaeval Religi-
    ous and Civil Law in India), 5 vols. 1930-62. 2nd edition,
    Poona, Bhandarkar Oriental Research Institute, 1968-77
Kern, H. (tr.) The Lotus of the True Law. (Saddharmapuṇḍarīka-
    sūtra). 1909
Law, B. C. (tr.) The Minor Anthologies of the Pali Canon Part I.
    (Buddhavamsa and Caryapiṭaka). London, Oxford University
    Press, 1938
Leslie, I. J. The Religious Role of Women in Ancient India. Oxford
    University M.Phil. thesis, 1980
Madhavananda, Swami and Majumdar, R. C. (eds.) Great Women of
    India. Almora, Advaita Ashrama, 1953
Mahābhārata. See van Buitenen, J. A. B., 1973-78; Roy, P. C.
    1919-35; Narasimhan, C. V., 1964
Manusmṛti. See Buhler, G., 1886
Mīrābāī. See Alston, A. J., 1980
Monier-Williams, Sir Monier. A Sanskrit-English Dictionary, etymo-
    logically and philologically arranged with special reference to
    cognate Indo-European Languages. 1899. Oxford, Oxford Uni-
    versity Press, 1976
Narasimhan, C. V. The Mahābhārata, an English version based on
    selected verses. New York etc, Columbia University Press, 1965
Nikhilananda, Swami (tr.) The Gospel of Sri Ramakrishna. 1942.
    New York, Ramakrishna-Vivekananda Center, 1973
Norman, K. R. (tr.) The Elders' Verses. Vol. I, Theragāthā, Lon-
    don, Pali Text Society, 1969; Vol. II, Therigāthā, London, Pali
    Text Society, 1971
O'Flaherty, W. D. (tr.) The Rig Veda, an anthology. Harmonds-
    worth, Penguin, 1981
Oldenberg, H. (tr.) The Grihya-Sūtras, Rules of Vedic Domestic
    Ceremonies. Vol. I, 1886; Vol. II, 1892. Delhi, Motilal Banar-
    sidass, 1967
Patañjali. See Chatterji, K.C., 1957; Filliozat, P., 1975
Panini. See Vasu, S. C., 1891
Radhakrishnan, S. (Sanskrit text and tr.) The Principal Upaniṣads.
    1953. London, George Allen and Unwin Ltd., 1974
Ramanujan, A. K. (tr.) Speaking of Śiva. 1973. Harmondsworth,
    Penguin, 1979
Rāmāyaṇa. See Shastri, H. P., 1953-59
RgVeda. See Griffith, R. T. H., 1889; O'Flaherty, W. D., 1981;
    Shastri, S. R., 1952; Upadhyaya, B. S., 1974
Rhys Davids, Mrs. (tr.) The Book of the Kindred Sayings (Saṃ-
    yutta Nikāya) or Grouped Suttas. 5 vols. London, Pali Text
    Society, 1917-30. (Vols IV and V translated by F. L.
    Woodward)

___ (ed. and tr.) The Minor Anthologies of the Pali Canon Part I (Dharmapada etc.) London, Oxford University Press, 1931

___ (tr.) Psalms of the Early Buddhists. London, Pali Text Society, Vol. I Psalms of the Sisters 1909, Vol. II Psalms of the Brethren 1913

Rhys Davids, T. W. Buddhist Suttas. 1881. New York, Dover, 1969

Roy, M. Bengali Women. Chicago etc., University of Chicago Press, 1975

Roy, P. C. The Mahabharata of Krishna Dwaipayana Vyasa. 12 vols. 2nd edition (Revised by E. H. Haldar), Calcutta, Oriental Publishing Co., (undated)

Sabarabhāṣya. See Sandal, M. L., 1923-25; Jha, G., 1942

Sandal, M. L. The Mīmāmsā Sūtras of Jaimini. (text, tr. and comm. of Chapters I-XII.) Allahabad, 1923-25. New York reprint, 1974

Sanyal, J. M. The Srimad Bhagabatam of Krishna-Dwaipayana Vyasa. 5 vols. 2nd edition, Calcutta, D. N. Bose, 1952

Shastri, H. P. (tr.) The World Within the Mind (Yoga-Vasishta.) 1937. 5th edition, London, Shanti Sadan, 1971

___ (tr.) The Ramayana of Valmiki. 3 Vols. London, Shanti Sadan, 1953-59

Shastri, S. R. Women in the Vedic Age. Bombay, 1952

Siegel, L. Sacred and Profane Dimensions of Love in Indian Traditions as Exemplified in the Gitagovinda of Jayadeva. Delhi etc., Oxford University Press, 1978

Singer, M. (ed.) Krishna: Myths, Rites and Attitudes. 1966 Chicago and London, University of Chicago Press, Phoenix edition 1968, 1971 reprint

Therīgāthā. See Norman, R. R., 1971; Rhys Davids, Mrs., 1909

Upadhyaya, B. S. Women in ṚgVeda. 1933. 3rd edition, Delhi, S. Chand and Co. (Pvt.) Ltd., 1974

Upaniṣads. See Zaehner, R. C., 1966; Radhakrishnan, S., 1953

van Buitenen, J. A. B. (tr.) The Mahābhārata. Vols 1-3 (incomplete). 1973-78 Chicago and London, University of Chicago Press, Phoenix edition 1980-81 (2 vols.)

Vasu, S. C. (tr.) The Ashṭādhyāyī of Pāṇini. 2 vols. 1891. Delhi, Motilal Banarsidass, 1977

Viṣṇusmṛti. See Jolly, J., 1880

Warner, M. Alone of All Her Sex: The Myth and the Cult of the Virgin Mary. 1976. London etc., Quartet Books, 1978

Warren, H. C. (tr.) Buddhism in Translations: Passages Selected from the Buddhist Sacred Books and Translated from the original Pali into English. 1896. New York, Atheneum, 1977

Woodward, F. L. The Book of the Gradual Sayings (Anguttara Nikāya) or More-numbered Suttas. 5 vols. London, Pali Text Society, 1932-36. Vols. 3, 4 by E. M. Hare

Yoga Vasistha. See Shastri, H. P., 1971

Zaehner, R. C. (tr.) Hindu Scriptures. 1938. 2nd edition 1966. London and Toronto, J. M. Dent and Sons Ltd., 1977

7 WOMEN, FERTILITY AND THE WORSHIP OF GODS IN A HINDU VILLAGE

Catherine Thompson

Introduction

Viewed from a distance participation in the worship of the gods in a Hindu village seems determined by the degree of purity ascribed to individuals. Thus the Brahmin priest is more pure than other men and worships the gods in the temple on behalf of other villagers. Men and women must purify themselves before worshipping gods in shrines and temples. Low castes may not worship in temples of high castes because they are considered impure.

Women's role in particular seems to be determined by criteria of purity. Wadley notes that 'Hindu mythology explicitly relates to the low ritual status of women to (a) her monthly periods, (b) her ability to bear children' (Wadley, 1977, p.137). In village terms this is clear during menstruation and childbirth. During her menstrual period a woman becomes impure. She may not touch others and above all she may not worship in temples. If she does she is thought to anger the gods and misfortune will result for her and her family members. At childbirth she suffers the same restrictions and these last for one and a quarter months after the birth of the child. All women seem to adhere to these restrictions and women in a household will keep a check and if they observe tell-tale signs that a woman is performing forbidden activities they will criticize her sharply however slight the misdemeanour.

Despite these restrictions, if one counts the number of occasions when gods are worshipped in the village, the number of occasions when women worship seems to outnumber those performed by men. Other writers have also noted this (see Luschinsky, 1962; Ray, 1975; Fruzetti, 1975). Recent discussions of Hindu religion have suggested that in many analyses the significance of purity and impurity has been over emphasized. It has been suggested that certain powers are associated with certain categories of people and it is these powers which make it appropriate for these people to worship on certain occasions and not on others (Das and Singh, 1971, p.38).

To explore this idea it is necessary to understand certain features of the Hindu pantheon and the precise nature of the role of a worshipper in relation to this pantheon. The Hindu pantheon contains many deities some of which are gods all the time and some of which are only gods for specified periods. The usual situation in a North Indian village is described by Wadley:

> ... human beings can be and often are deities in Karimpur as well as plows, snakes, bullocks, wheat seedlings and the normally recognized 'pantheon'. The basic rule seems thus: any being which you consider more powerful than yourself is a potential object of worship (Wadley, 1976, p.154).

Occasions of worship are often about establishing a particular kind of relationship between worshipper and deity so that the power of the deity may be invoked. The way in which women worship, and the deities which they worship therefore indicate powers that are important to women. Moreover they indicate the powers with which women themselves are associated. Das suggests:

> ... it is the ambiguity of sacrifice which makes any contact between the sacred and the profane possible and it is in this that Hubert and Mauss saw the very source of life. In a similar way special powers are bestowed in Hindu belief on the holders of the statuses of Brahmin, king and ascetic. These combine in themselves the opposite forces of the profane and the sacred, the social and the cosmic. The Brahmin as Hubert and Mauss argued stands on the threshold of the sacred and the profane and represents them at one and the same time. He is referred to as Bhūdevatā a deity on earth who links the cosmic and the social. Similarly the king is said to have a portion of Viṣṇu in him and the ascetic controls the social and cosmic through his tapa ... (Das, 1976, p.261-2).

Das does not discuss the role of women but their role in relation to the sacred can be understood in terms of an affinity between the powers of women themselves and the powers they try to invoke in worship.

In this paper I shall focus on the kind of religious activities women are involved in. Although physiological processes connected with reproduction exclude women from worship of the gods at certain times; at other times their reproductive powers seem to take on a different dimension - a dimension which enables them to become mediators between gods and men. It is this aspect of women's powers that I describe and analyse below.

Background

The material on which this analysis is based was gathered during fieldwork in a Central Indian village in the Malwa region of the Madhya Pradesh State. I lived in the village for just over a year. The village is Hindu in a region where Moslems are relatively scarce. It has a population of 1,400 and although it is only seven miles from

Indore the largest city in Madhya Pradesh most villagers are involved in agricultural work within the village. A mixture of cash and subsistence crops are grown and the atmosphere of the village is that of a traditional rural community.

There are differences in wealth within the village, the bigger landholders own forty or fifty acres and can afford to build concrete houses and run motor scooters, while the smaller landholders and wage labourers can only manage a bicycle and the traditional mud hut. However differences of wealth are not as great as elsewhere in India. One indication of this is that nearly every woman works in the fields, either in her own family's or as a wage labourer in someone else's. The few who do not are women from the tailor and tanner castes who are involved in their families' traditional crafts.

The village has eighteen different subcastes [1], although four of these subcastes make up 75% of the total village population. About half of the village are Harijans, that is members of the untouchable low castes. The rest are upper and middle caste. Despite the divisions of caste and wealth, religious practice is broadly similar among all sections so the account that follows applies to all sections of the village.

Descent is reckoned patrilineally. Women must marry within their own subcaste but the subcastes are divided into patrilineal clans known as gotra. These are exogamous. Village exogamy is also practised and so at marriage women change clan and village [2]. Although women's labour is important to the village, women do not generally inherit land or own property. They are not usually involved in trading and play little part in the public life of the village. Their concerns are thus usually limited to the domestic sphere.

The Status of Women's Ritual Activities

Worship of the gods occurs on three types of occasion; when a festival in the lunar-solar calendar is being marked, at personal life crisis rites, and on other occasions brought about by illnesses, personal desires, astrological and meteorological conditions (cf. Jacobson, 1970, p.385). Women may worship on any or all of these kinds of occasions. When they do worship what is noticeable is that generally they have their own special role.

Nowhere is this more obvious than in the role of women in life crisis rites, - particularly weddings. The role of the Brahmin priest in a wedding is constructed according to the sacred texts of the Vedas (the earliest and most authoritative of the Hindu scriptures). Only Brahmin men are allowed to use the Vedas in approaching the gods (Wadley, 1977, p.126). However, in addition to the rituals conducted by the Brahmins, women conduct rites which involve the worship and invocation of ancestral and other deities, the worship of the bride and groom who are thought of as gods for this period, and the anointing of bride and groom with turmeric. Villagers are adamant that the rituals conducted by women are as important as those conducted by the Brahmin. Without the women's rituals, they say, it would not be a proper marriage, and without the application of turmeric there would be no children.

The importance of women's rituals in a wedding is not confined to this region of India. Fruzetti describes a similar situation in Bengal. She suggests that in Bengal women's activities religious or otherwise form:

> ... a social domain separable and understandable in its own terms ... this domain is not defined by morphology alone (i.e. separate sex role activities) but also through symbols which define and reinterpret a woman's society in relation to society at large. Women's domain is rendered visible, systematic and coherent and is controlled as well as exposed by rituals that can be performed by women alone (Fruzetti, 1975, p.335. The emphasis is mine).

What Fruzetti's use of the concept 'domain' makes clear is that in understanding women's roles we must take into account not only whether they have more or less power than men, or how far they are separated from men, but also how far the kinds of powers women have are different from those of men. Below I shall refer to the concept 'ritual domain' again and it is essentially Fruzetti's usage I am following.

Dharma

When questioned as to why village women perform certain rituals and not others people generally say that it is their dharma. Dharma can be translated as moral duty but this does not do justice to what is a very complicated concept in Hinduism. The complexity of the concept becomes evident when it is realized that villagers, in common with other Hindus, believe that all objects and beings, inanimate and animate, have dharma. Pandey and Weightman (1978) have discussed the different ways dharma can be translated and these include duty, character and religion. They argue that the different nuances centre round a core meaning which can be viewed as 'moral duty' arising from one's very substance.

It is a Brahmin's dharma to be a priest. Weightman describes the role of the Brahmin as follows:

> Brahmins are the purest of men. Purity is the prime requisite for the worship of the gods. Brahmins are therefore the people most suited to act as priests, that is as intermediaries between a man and his deities (1978, p.53).

It is the purity of his substance that leads his dharma to be that of a priest. The question that must then be answered is what is it about women and their dharma which makes it particularly appropriate for them to act as intermediaries between men and the supernatural world on particular occasions. It does not seem to be their physical powers per se as on occasions these powers exclude them from worship of the gods.

This can be illustrated by the changes that occur in a woman's dharma at menarche. A woman's dharma changes when she reaches menarche – the sign of her physical maturity. When her dharma changes so does her ritual domain. However the ritual domain of an adult woman is not simply or even wholly dependent on her physical maturity. As an unmarried girl who has not menstruated a girl is known as kumari or colloquially as larki. She has her own distinctive domain of ritual activity and her dharma is distinct. Ideally she is married before menarche and after marriage (whether the marriage has been consummated or not) her dharma becomes that of a stri (a woman) [3]. Her ritual domain changes at the same time as her dharma and she can take part in the worship of adult women. This makes it appear that the change in dharma and ritual domain is contingent only upon marriage but this is not so. If by chance a girl reaches menarche before marriage then her dharma is also referred to as being that of stri (a woman) for physical maturity also changes a woman's dharma. However although in this case her ritual domain changes in the sense that she may no longer worship with kumari, in addition she is thought to be inauspicious and may not worship with married women until she herself is married. Her ritual domain is not yet that of a married woman because although biological growth has brought about certain substantive changes, the substantive changes that enable her to worship gods with married women have not occurred because she herself is not married. The implication of this is that the worship of the gods by married women is related to physical maturity because their ritual domain does not exclude it as the kumari's does. However, it is at marriage that the relevant substantive changes are accomplished.

Women at Weddings

The substantive change that takes place at weddings can best be understood by looking at the role of married women in weddings for these are women who have been through the transformation and are now in their turn creating a transformation in bride and groom.

Marriage rituals within the village are complex. They take place over a period of a fortnight and consist of many different and separate rituals culminating in the couple taking seven steps round the sacred fire in the presence of the Brahmin and this solemnizes their union [4]. The rites are multidimensional for many different changes take place at weddings. The bride is transferred from one kin group to another. She and her husband are joined together in a union which for many purposes gives them a single social personality, and an alliance is made between two kin groups. What I propose to focus upon here is the aspect of the marriage rites which Van Gennep has referred to as 'social puberty' (Van Gennep, 1960, p.65) [5].

Van Gennep suggests that rites of 'social puberty' are those that concern the 'separation from the asexual world and they are followed by rites of incorporation into the world of sexuality (Van Gennep, 1960 ibid. p.65). Thus the aspects of the wedding rituals that I wish to concentrate on are those in which women take part and those that have as their theme mature sexuality. This involves the movement of the bride and the groom from immaturity to maturity; what should be noted is that these changes are concerned with 'social' maturity not simply physical maturity. There are a series of rituals which involve women, and the bride and the groom. The theme of these rituals is the rebirth of bride and groom [6]. What is significant about them is that while actual physical birth is regarded as something polluting which must be concealed, in a wedding the 'birth' that takes place is performed in public, and rather than <u>excluding</u> women from worship of the gods as physical birth does it <u>involves</u> women in worshipping the gods.

On the first day of the wedding ceremonies the god Ganesh is worshipped by women and put into the lap of the mother of the spouse. Later on the same day the spouse is worshipped with his or her mother touching his/her shoulder. This lap is often used as a symbol of the filial relationship between mother and child and of a woman's fecundity. The underlying structural message seems to be 1) The mother has a god in her lap. 2) Her son/daughter is then worshipped as a deity in her presence. 3) Therefore the woman has given birth to a deity. Women sing songs which compare the spouse to Ganesh. One runs 'Oh Ganesh, lord, come into the grooms clothes'.

Another ritual involving the theme of birth is when a mother draws a thread in vermilion powder on her son's body. In classical Hinduism members of the upper castes are known as 'the twice born'. Before a boy marries a ceremony known as <u>Upanayana</u> takes place when the boy is invested with a sacred thread which marks his second birth (e.g. Basham, 1971, p.162 f.). Only two castes in the village actually perform this ceremony (even out of those who consider themselves twice born). But the imitative ceremony performed in the wedding is indicative. The 'thread' made of vermilion is known as <u>janoo</u> the colloquial name for the thread worn by the twice born. In the wedding the mother of the spouse, not the Brahmin, worships the gods and invests the spouse with the 'thread'. This taken in conjunction with other evidence suggests that women have a role in the 'birth' that takes place at marriage that is distinct from their role as genetrix. It is a second birth and an appropriate symbol for the substantive change that occurs at marriage.

In another context and for another continent, Gudeman has shown how the godparent-child relationship, while analogous with a biological pattern is used to portray man as having a spiritual existence in addition to his existence as a biological being (Gudeman 1971). It is possible that the 'birth' that women are involved in at marriage has parallels with this process. For our purposes what should be noticed is that the rituals in which this 'second birth' take place are performed without a Brahmin and are considered absolutely necessary for the marriage to take place. Thus ritual birth is linked to physical birth by its imagery and yet is distinct from it. These

118

rituals imply female powers that (unlike the powers of physical reproduction) are not polluting or dirty and do not exclude women from the worship of the gods. They are part of the domain of married women for only married women may perform them.

The mother who gives birth to the child in these ceremonies need not in fact be a real mother but she must be a married woman with a husband [7]; and only a woman who is not in a state of pollution may take the role. If a woman is widowed, or menstruating, someone else will step in. Unlike the physical relationships, the social relationships can be manipulated. The roles reflect physical relationships but are not dependent on them, suggesting that a substantive change that parallels certain kinds of physical change is taking place.

The physical change reflected in the rituals described so far is that of birth. Other rites bring us closer to the idea of 'social puberty' by emphasizing the fertility, not just of women performing the ritual, but of the bride and groom themselves. Very soon after bride and groom have been worshipped for the first time, both bride and groom are bathed daily in turmeric paste. This continues until the climax of the marriage. As mentioned above turmeric is seen as essential if the marriage is to be blessed with children. Turmeric is also rubbed on the bride and groom at the consummation ceremony as if to emphasize this. Other writers have also drawn attention to the association between turmeric and fertility (e.g. Selwyn, 1979, p.685).

The categories of women who may not rub turmeric on the bride and groom are also significant. Kumari may not rub turmeric on the spouse or on themselves. They are not associated with physical maturity nor are they associated with the ritual domain of married women. Unmarried girls who have reached menarche should not take part since they are also not associated with the ritual domain of married women. The 'mother of the spouse' may not rub turmeric on the spouse and this seems to be linked to the idea that an adult should never display evidence of his or her mature sexuality in front of his or her parents.

Since there is a link between turmeric and physical fertility and the ritual domain of married women the question remains as to the nature of the association between turmeric and physical fertility, and in consequence the nature of the relationship between physical fertility and the ritual domain of married women. Turmeric has certain properties that distinguish it from mature physical sexuality per se. Firstly although villagers believe that turmeric is necessary for the marriage to produce children they readily acknowledge that children may be produced outside wedlock, and they do not ascribe any physical part to it in the process of reproduction rather it is seen as preventing the dosh (misfortune) of barrenness through its powers to ensure fertility. Secondly physical sexuality is associated with impurity. (Men and women should purify themselves after sexual intercourse and childbirth and menstruation are impure). Turmeric in contrast is purifying. Hence it is associated with consecration and the invocation of gods who are by their nature associated with purity. During the turmeric baths the women sing songs stressing the god like qualities of the bride and groom. One such runs:

My groom is like Ram he is taking a bath in turmeric.
My groom has come to the house of Ram,
Women are bathing him in oil.

Turmeric is associated with the crucial ceremony just before the couple walk round the sacred fire when the couple's clothes are tied together in front of an image of the gotra (clan) deities. The ends of the groom's loin cloth and the bride's sari are dyed in turmeric. An impure substance would be inappropriate at this point. It is possible that these aspects of the power associated with turmeric indicate the way in which it is symbolic of a kind of 'meta-fertility'. It is like physical fertility and yet at the same time it is unlike physical fertility. Human sexuality is spoken of and experienced as hot. Turmeric is spoken of as hot and the games and rowdiness that accompany its application have been seen by more than one writer as expressing the heat and disorder associated with human fertility (Selwyn, 1979, p.658). Yet villagers and analysts alike say the turmeric is cooling as well (Selwyn, 1979, p.697). It has facets which protect and 'cool' the power of evil spirits and protective threads tied round the wrists of bride and groom are died in turmeric. Menstruation and childbirth expose women and men to the dangers of evil spirits and the heat of human sexuality seems to have dangers which are not mirrored in the power of turmeric.

Thus at weddings women not only take part in the meta-birth of the bride and groom but also, in so far as they seem to endow them with a kind of meta-fertility, they are instrumental in the social puberty of bride and groom. In both instances the threatening and impure aspects of physiological birth and puberty are absent. The participation of women in weddings suggests that women have powers that parallel physical processes but are without their dangers. These are the powers which make women appropriate mediators between gods and men on particular occasions [8].

The Division of Ritual Labour

Within the context of wedding this idea can be illustrated with reference to the roles of men, women and Brahmins. The rituals within a wedding can be divided as follows:

1) Women can perform the ritual alone
2) Men can perform the ritual alone
3) Women can perform the ritual with a Brahmin or other ritual specialist
4) Men can perform the ritual with a Brahmin or other ritual specialist (eg. the Barber is important in weddings)
5) Men and women can perform the rituals together both worshipping the deity
6) Women can perform the ritual with a man (the groom) as the

only male participant

7) Men and women can worship deities in the presence of a Brahmin

This ritual division of labour applies in calendrical rituals and other life crisis rites.

This division of labour becomes more comprehensible if an explanatory model is used in which the ritual division of labour is organised so that worship is done by those who are best suited to mediate with the deities conceconcerned not solely on grounds of purity but because they have certain attributes that are related to the attributes of the deity they are invoking. The rituals where women predominate (i.e. categories 1, 3 and 6,) concern the second birth and social puberty of bride and groom and the milieu where this new found maturity will find full expression (i.e. the household). In contrast the rituals where men predominate seem more concerned with creation of alliances and links between kin groups. The Brahmin priest is involved where Sanskrit texts are used and purity is the major criteria. Metaphorically one might say that male rituals emphasize the structural framework or skeleton of caste and kinship groupings while women's ceremonies stress women's contributions in nurturing this framework – that is in putting flesh on the skeleton [9]. Brahmin rituals set these activities in the context of received written traditions and higher values which stand outside and encompass the concerns of individuals and individual families (see below) [10].

There are also some rites when neither sex can be said to dominate. In the worship of the gotra deities, women prepare and cook food and then both sexes are involved in the worship of the deities and the offering of the food. Here this combination is appropriate because the clan is patrilineal and men are the living representatives of the continuance of the clan. The woman's presence and especially her preparation of the food is appropriate for although the gotra is patrilineal it cannot continue without women coming in from outside. In this instance male and female ritual domains are complementary [11].

The kind of ritual division of labour that occurs in wedding rituals recurs in calendrical rituals. However in the rituals which women perform alone which account for some twenty-four out of forty-five annual festivals the theme is not so much fecundity per se but the health and welfare of particular family members. These members are usually the women's children, husbands or brothers. In the Hindu month of Bhadon there are eleven festivals of this nature most of which involve fasting and all of which centre round this theme. In the calendrical rituals men worship the gods for the general prosperity of the household as a whole. They may also make occasional offerings to the gods in respect of particular vows. However, it is only women who worship regularly to obtain favours specifically for these named individuals in the household. The myths that accompany these festivals show the great benefits that can accrue to the family of the woman who observes these fasts and the dangers that may occur if she does not. In the marriage rituals it is fecundity in the sense of giving birth and having the power to have children that is celebrated. In these calendrical rituals it seems to be women's association with a force, which seems to give them the power to prolong life, that makes them appropriate mediators between men and their gods. At marriage their physical fertility is paralleled by their role in the metabirth of bride and groom. On other occasions their part in the creation of physical life seems to link them with the metaphysical powers of the gods to promote well being.

Woman as a Mediator

To review, women are associated with a life-giving auspicious power which makes them appropriate intermediaries between the gods and men when such powers are being invoked. This power is associated with physical sexuality in that it seems to borrow some images from it but it is not identical with physiological processes and is not presented as polluting as sexual intercourse, child birth and menstruation are. Moreover childbirth and menstruation expose women to attacks from malicious, inauspicious spirits which are very far removed from the auspicious powers that a woman invokes at other periods in her life. The question remains – how are these two aspects of female power related, and since they possess two seemingly contradictory attributes how are they reconciled?

Wadley in her study of women and the Hindu tradition which includes analysis of figures in mythology as well as ethnographic materials suggests that:

As Power and Nature, and controlling her own sexuality the female is potentially destructive and malevolent ... With the control of her sexuality transferred to men the female is fertile and benevolent (Wadley, 1977, p.119).

To an extent this is born out by my own data. A woman's mature sexuality is only made auspicious once she becomes a wife. As a wife she is under the control of a man. However the problem remains that even as wives women are at times impure and inauspicious – (i.e. at childbirth and menstruation), while at other times they seem to have benevolent, auspicious powers which are related to life-giving forces, of which childbirth and menstruation could be seen to be a physical aspect. In addition, on many of the occasions where women invoke beneficial powers, they do so without the aid of men. Wadley suggests that in the pantheon, the mother goddess is both a 'bestower' and sometimes a 'destroyer!' In human forms a wife, who is a mother, is also both [12].

In the remaining section of this paper I want to suggest that women themselves mediate between contradictory forces as it were 'socializing' their own sexuality. This is why at times they are excluded from worship of the gods by virtue of their role in the reproductive process while at other times this role seems to justify their participation. Das suggests that in general the sacred:

> separates out the domain of religious discourse from other types of discourse and bestows society with an axiomatic 'taken-for-granted' cognitive quality. The historically crucial part of religion in legitimizing the particular institutions in society as axiomatic, is best explained in terms of its unique capacity to 'locate' human phenomena in a cosmic frame of reference. This process of cosmosization bestows inherently precarious and transitory constructions of human activity with security durability and permanence, which takes on an axiomatic character (Das, 1976, p.246).

She goes on to suggest that in every 'frame of reference' marginalities occur which threaten to destroy the system of classification and so there are mechanisms for dealing with these marginalities. In Hinduism she argues that:

> ... impurity marks off those liminal situations where the paradigm is provided by birth and death when the individual experiences his social world as separated off from the cosmic and has to be brought back to an earlier reality enabling him to see society and the cosmos as an intergrated whole (Das 1976, p.248).

Das points out that liminality 'may often symbolize a creative transcendence of given categories of a system' (Das, 1976, p.261). It is this latter idea which may provide a clue to women's religious function in relation to their seemingly inauspicious physical sexuality. For women in their impurity are the creators of the lifesource that presents confusion to the 'frame of reference'.

Women both threaten the structure and yet are necessary for its continued existence. The contrast between women being excluded from the worship of the gods at childbirth and menstruation and yet at other times being seen as the most appropriate intermediaries, when the power of the gods is needed to make these events auspicious and unthreatening, can be seen as a function of women integrating polluting and potentially threatening, but necessary, forces into an ordered social world. For the world of the gods with its connotations of purity is, if one follows Das 'the symbolism for dealing with the cosmic when it is experienced integrated with the social ...' (Das 1976, p.248). Women are more appropriate than Brahmins or men in this particular respect because they are associated with the powers that need to be socialised in a way that men are not. The social construction of their physiology makes them straddle both kinds of force; the source of confusion to the system and the system itself [13].

Birth

This interpretation of women's religious roles throws light on one of the most puzzling contradictions in an understanding of a woman's sexuality; fertility and fecundity are highly valued, a mother has a high status and yet women are considered polluting after birth. The issues are too complex to develop here but it should be noted that a woman ends her 1¼ month period of pollution after birth not simply by washing herself (nearly all pollution caused by bodily impurities can be removed in this way), but in addition she worships the 'water mother' by placing offerings at the well and then brings water to her father-in-law. Crooke writes that 'In India ... water is the prime source of fertility' (Crooke, 1926, p.4). But water is also a purifying substance that can mediate between the impurity associated with fertility and the purity required for normal social contact and contact with the gods in worship. A woman should not only purify herself after birth but should also worship the means of her purification and then symbolically bring this means into her household and present it to the household's head. This suggests that aside from the physical aspect of fertility, which is impure, a woman is closely associated with a different kind of life giving power which enables her to integrate these forces into daily social life and gives her a special role with respect to the gods.

The Muting of Women's Religious Role

If, as I have suggested women's power to mediate between polluting asocial life forces and the purer ordered world of gods and mortals is so significant the question remains as to why the Brahmin priest has so much prestige and importance and why women's role is not recognized more explicitly. This question can be answered at a number of different levels, some more concerned with values in Hinduism in general and others with the social structure. The levels of explanation may be interrelated but this interrelation cannot be examined in depth here [14].

At the level of articulated values the role of women conflicts and challenges the dominant ascetic theme in Hindu religion. The ultimate spiritual aim of a Hindu is to gain release from the cycle of rebirth by dissociating him or herself as far as possible from the ties of the physical and social life. O'Flaherty writes of what she calls the complexity of the relationship between 'eroticism' and 'asceticism'. For a man, in theory, marriage is the beginning of just one of a number of stages that a man should pass through during his lifetime. At marriage he passes from being a chaste student to being a house-holder; later when he has had a son and brought his son up he should pass on first to being a vanaprastha, a man who dwells in the forest with or without his wife, and then to being a sannyasi, an ascetic who renounces everything (O'Flaherty, 1969, p.128). O'Flaherty looking at the mythology of Shiva suggests that there is a certain tension between the qualities of eroticism and asceticism in Indian thought. Shiva overcomes the tension between these two qualities by combining them within himself and alternating between expressing one or other aspect of his dual nature. In the lives of mortal men O'Flaherty argues this tension is expressed in the seemingly contradictory aims in the various stages of a man's life cycle.

As a householder a man is very much involved in the physical world. He is allowed to be sexually active because his 'erotic' existence is used for the perpetuation of ordered human existence. Once he has fulfilled his dharma in this respect the next stage is for him to renounce the world in which he has been so actively involved. The tension lies in the paradox that a man cannot effectively renounce the world unless he has been actively involved with it. Thus though eroticism and worldly involvement are both subjugated under the higher goal of asceticism and renunciation nevertheless renunciation is dependent upon worldly involvement.

A woman, however, cannot become an ascetic. Theoretically she must be born as a man to gain release. Her association with life forces is thus different from a man's. The qualities of eroticism and asceticism are not expressed in the same way in a woman's lifecycle. A man can gain spiritual strength through seminal retention. A woman cannot control her menstrual or other secretions in the same way. Thus the relation between eroticism and asceticism in respect of a woman's bodily functions represents a different set of conceptual problems. In her worship of the gods her emphasis is on ordering these forces in the ordered social world of living men.

In terms of the division of religious labour, Brahmins, as we have seen, are primarily associated with purity. Men are more frequently involved with worship which stresses the continuity of the patrilineal group beyond death in their worship of the ancestors and it is women who are more concerned with the immediate social world. Thus while their contribution is vital to daily life it conflicts with some of the expressed fundamental values of Hinduism. Outside the confines of home and village, where much of written Hindu tradition has been formulated women's acts of worship lose significance and since women themselves are more often illiterate and are less likely to make a home outside these arenas their role in the religious life becomes invisible and the view from a distance that is commonly held about village Hinduism becomes the only view.

Other factors that militate against a woman's role being given more significance concern the way that access to wealth is limited. Ultimately men have control over the key resources of land and are the major deciding influences in public life. In part, as Sharma (1978) and others have noted, this structure is maintained by women being divided among themselves. Women have split loyalties between natal and conjugal homes and not only between husbands and brothers but also between their own mothers and sisters and their husbands' mothers and sisters. Hostility is more often openly expressed between groups of women than between women and men [15]. They do not have a strong sense of collective identity which might otherwise foster their sense of importance in the worship of the gods.

In addition the beliefs surrounding women's worship of the gods emphasize their importance for individuals such as their children, brothers, husbands etc. but their significance is rarely thought of outside the context of the welfare of individuals within the family and household group. It may be that women realize their own importance for the welfare of their families but it is men and Brahmin priests who deal with larger groups that seem more powerful and have higher status [16]. There may be other reasons for the muting of women's religious roles but these at least seem the most significant.

Conclusion

Social anthropologists writing about women have been able to throw much light on the position of women by concentrating on the qualitative aspects of women's powers as well as whether they have more or less power. This has been a major theme underlying this paper. For as Weiner in her book on women in Trobriand religion writes:

> Given that women control some kinds of cultural resources defined as their own it follows that they maintain some degree of power that differs from male power. Therefore if we begin to understand the social and cultural dimensions of power in its own right rather than focusing on power in its political phase we not only learn about women we also learn about men (Weiner, 1976, p.12).

Thus in discussing women's religious roles in this paper I hope that I have been able to explore some issues that touch on the totality of the worship of the gods in a Hindu village as well as those that specifically concern women.

I have been highly selective in the evidence presented, in order to develop a particular theme about the relation of women's fertility to the worship of the gods. While I have moved away from the stereotype of purity being the all important criteria in the worship of the gods, I have not discussed all aspects of the role of women in the worship of the gods. However it is my hope that the evidence presented does shed some light on the importance and frequency of women's participation in worship of the gods in a Hindu village and how seeming contradictions in women's powers are reconciled. The social construction of women's biology and how it affects her access to the sacred differs from culture to culture but is an important component of how 'femineity' (Ardener, 1977, pp.46-8) is constructed. This then is a case study of the perceptions of women's powers in one culture which may lead to more general discussion about women and religion when compared with the perceptions of other cultures.

Acknowledgements

The fieldwork on which this paper was based was conducted between 1978 and 1979. Financial support was obtained from the SSRC, the University of London Central Research Fund and a Mary Ewart Travel Scholarship from Newnham College Cambridge. I am particularly grateful to all those who assisted me in the field especially to Miss

Neeta Tiagi my research assistant, Miss Sunalini Nayudu and the villagers themselves. I am also grateful for the help received from Professor Mayer and others in the social anthropology department at SOAS University of London, and members of the Women's Social Anthropology Group at Oxford for the ideas and comments they provided during the time I was trying to analyse my fieldwork material. This paper is one product of that period.

Notes

1. I am using the term 'subcaste' to refer to a group often referred to by other writers as caste. My usage follows Mayer who discusses the implications of the usage of this term in his introduction to a study of caste and kinship of another village in the Malwa region (Mayer 1973, p.3).

2. For a more detailed discussion of the kinship system see Mayer (op. cit.) and for a consideration of how it effects women in particular see Jacobson, 1970.

3. This is important for the consummation of a marriage never occurs until after the menarche and it is always postponed for at least a year even if menarche has not occurred. Villagers feel that 'it looks bad' if consummation follows marriage too closely. Apart from what this implies about the relation of marriage and sex in the minds of the villagers it means that the change that occurs to a woman during marriage does <u>not</u> centre round the loss of her virginity. No where is virginity emphasized and unlike other areas in north India even at the consummation ceremony there is no parading of blood stained sheets.

4. Mayer provides a summary of events at weddings in the Malwa region (Mayer, 1973, pp.227-35) however, he has to omit much detail for the sake of space. The detailed descriptions of weddings in Fruzetti, 1975, Luschinsky, 1962 and Gupta, 1974 provide a better idea of the extent and elaboration of rituals at weddings.

5. Aside from the social maturity specifically concerned with legitimating mature sexuality there is other evidence which suggests that marriage marks the incorporation of a man and woman into the adult world. (cf Mayer, 1973, p.277). Villagers believe that marriage is a necessary stage in the life of all. In the village the only unmarried adult was a very severely crippled girl. Many villagers believe that if a person dies before marriage, that person should be buried and not cremated. Small children are always buried, as are <u>sannyasin</u> (renouncers). These are both categories of individuals who are not fully integrated into normal social life. The implication of the burial of older <u>unmarried</u> men and women is that they too have not been fully integrated into adult social life.

6. Interestingly Hershman suggests that images of birth also figure largely in Punjabi ritual (Hershman, 1977, p.287 ff).

7. This can be explained by the fact that at marriage a woman's social persona becomes incorporated into that of her husband. A woman is only permitted to undergo marriage in the full form once

127

although it is accepted by most castes that she can perform a kind of secondary marriage if she wishes. If her husband dies she must cease to wear suhag a collective term for the ornaments and decorations of a married woman with a living husband. If he dies that aspect of her husband dies too. If she dies and her husband remarries (men are allowed to have the full marriage rites more than once) then his second wife must wear a small medal known as a sok (literally a co-wife) and perform a small ritual before it every day. The sok represents the husband's first wife. The woman who marries a widower seems also to marry the dead wife since the dead wife has been incorporated in the social persons of the husband. A widow cannot be the 'mother' of the spouse at a wedding because in some sense she is socially dead.

8. I am aware that my arguments here have resonances with the nature – culture debate which has characterised much social anthropological discussion about women and others (see for example Wadley 1977 on Indian woman). There are difficulties in using the idea 'nature' which is why I have tried to use the more neutral word 'physical' because, as MacCormack points out, ' ... ideas about culture and nature are not value free' (MacCormack, 1980, p.6). A further difficulty is that involvment in this debate among structuralists at least has obscured the role of women as mediators between different sets of forces (see MacCormack, 1980, p.129). Since I am concerned specifically with the way that women do have powers that integrate physical forces into the realm of gods and men and are therefore mediators I have avoided a consideration of how far these physical forces are identical to a concept of nature. This is a question that may need answering.

9. This is comparable to the metaphor often used in India about the contribution of a man and a woman to the process of reproduction. A man is compared to the seed while a woman is compared to the field. (see Dube, 1978).

10. This paper concentrating as it does on the powers which make it appropriate for women to worship the gods pays scant attention to the powers which make it appropriate for men and Brahmins to worship the gods. Das (1976) has considered this in terms of the role of certain men such as Brahmin, Kings and ascetics, and Kaushik (1976) has looked at the role of religious specialists in funerals. Similar material is not available for the powers which make it appropriate for other men to worship the gods on other occasions so the characterization of their role given here may be a little simplistic.

11. Fruzetti argues that complementarity characterizes the relations between men and women in India in contrast to the contradictory or oppositional relations between the sexes that may exist elsewhere (Fruzetti, 1975, p.56).

12. Wadley also notes 'the relationship between female biology (pollution/purity) and perceptions of the female in Hinduism' (Wadley, 1977, p.137, n.31) but since her analysis concerns females in mythology, at that point she leaves the relationship unexamined.

13. This interpretation is one that I arrived at before reading MacCormack's critique of the nature culture debate and was gratified to find that her comments concerning women as 'mediators' which seems to some extent to reflect certain attributes of Hindu women's religious role as I describe it here. 'If we took an extreme position of defining women but not men socializer, cultivators, cooks - as mediators between nature and culture - and if we viewed them in the structure of kinship as mediators between exogamous social groups, then we must look more closely at the attributes structuralists confer upon mediators. Because they can merge and reconcile opposites, mediators are deity or messiah and at the same time clown and trickster' (MacCormack, 1980, p.9). Note however I am not saying that women alone mediate or that women mediate between 'nature' and 'culture' rather that they do seem to mediate between different types of force.

14. For a more detailed discussion of the way in which women's models become muted see articles by Shirley and Edwin Ardener and others in Ardener, 1977.

15. This aspect of relations between the sexes has been noted by other writers on India including Kakar (1978, p.59).

16. The opportunity that women have to become aware of the significance of their religious role may be related to the amount of co-operation that can occur between women in the public sphere. In Africa, Hoffer (1974) and others have described the existence of women's secret societies. Hoffer in particular describes how Mende and Shebro women's societies elaborate and stress the significance of woman's ability to give birth, in the public rituals they perform. This is done to such an extent that the women chiefs of these societies can use their power to initiate women as a political weapon in struggles with male chiefs. The point is that women are allowed to move freely in public and thus they have succeeded in transforming birth from a private, relatively insignificant 'woman's affair' into an event that is elaborated and stressed by women themselves in public.

References

Ardener, S. (ed.). Perceiving Women. London, Dent Halsted Press, 1977

Basham, A. L. The Wonder that was India. Calcutta, Fontana and Rupa, 1971

Bennet, L. 'The Wives of the Rishis. An Analysis of the Tij-Rishi Panchami Women's Festival'. Kailash 2 (1976), 185-207.

Das, V. 'The Uses of Liminality: Society and Cosmos in Hinduism'. Contributions to Indian Sociology (NS) 10, 2 (1976), 245-263.

Das, V. and Singh, J. S. 'The Elementary Structure of Caste'. Contributions to Indian Sociology (NS) 5 (1971), 33-43.

Dube, L. 'The Seed and the Field. The Symbolism of Biological Reproduction in India'. Paper given at the tenth international congress of anthropological and ethnological sciences, New

Delhi, 1978

Fruzetti, L. 'Conch Shells, Bangles, Iron Bangles. An Analysis of Ritual in Bengali Society'. Unpublished PhD. thesis, University of Minnesota, Minnesota, 1975

Gudeman, S. 'The Compadrazgo as a Reflection of the Natural and Spiritual Person'. Proceedings of the RAI (1971) 45-67.

Gupta, G. R. Marriage, Religion and Society, Patterns of Change in an Indian Village. London and Dublin, Curzon Press, 1974

Hershman, P. 'Virgin and Mother' in Lewis, I. M. (ed.), Symbols and Sentiments. London and New York, Academic Press, 1977

Hoffer, C. P. 'Madame Yoko, Ruler of the Kpa Mende Confederacy'. in Rosaldo, M. Z. and Lamphere, L. (eds.), Woman, Culture, and Society. Stanford, Stanford University Press, 1974

Jacobson, D. 'Hidden Faces: Hindu and Muslim Purdah in a Central Indian Village'. Unpublished PhD. thesis, University of Columbia, Columbia, 1970

Kakar, S. The Inner World: A Psychoanalytic Study of Childhood and Society in India. Delhi, Oxford University Press, 1978

Kaushik, M. 'The Symbolic Representation of Death'. Contributions to Indian Sociology (NS) 10, 2 (1976)

Luschinsky, M. S. 'The Life of Women in a Village in Northern India. A Study in Role and Status'. Unpublished PhD. thesis, Cornell University, Cornell, 1962

MacCormack, C. P. 'Nature, Culture and Gender: A Critique'. in MacCormack, C. P. and Strathern, M. (eds.), Nature, Culture and Gender. Cambridge, Cambridge University Press, 1980

Mayer, A. C. Caste and Kinship in Central India: A Village and its Region. Berkeley and Los Angeles, University of California Press (Paperback), 1973

O'Flaherty, W. D. 'Asceticism and Sexuality in the Mythology of Siva'. History of Religions, (1969) Part 1 in Vol. 8, 3, 300-37. Part 2 in Vol. 9, 1, 1-141.

Pandey and Weightman, S. Paper in Derret and O'Flaherty, (eds.), The Concept of Duty in South Asia. London, Vikas and the School of Oriental and African Studies, 1978

Ray, M. Bengali Women. Chicago, University of Chicago Press, 1975

Selwyn, T. 'Images of Reproduction: An Analysis of a Hindu Marriage Ceremony'. Man (NS) 14 (1979), 684-9.

Sharma, U. 'Segregation and its Consequences in India'. in Caplan, P. and Bujra, J. M. (eds.), Women United Women Divided. London, Tavistock, 1978

Van Gennep, A. Rites of Passage. London, Routledge and Kegan Paul, 1960

Wadley, S. 'Brothers, Husbands and Sometimes Sons: Kinsmen in North Indian Ritual'. Eastern Anthropologist 29 (1976), 149-170.

_____ 'Women and the Hindu Tradition'. in Wadley, S. and Jacobson, D. (eds.), Women in India Two Perspectives. Delhi, Manohar, 1977

Weightman, S. Hinduism in the Village Setting. Milton Keynes, Open

University Press, 1978

Weiner, A. Women of Value, Men of Renown. New Perspectives in Trobriand Exchange. Austin, Texas, University of Texas Press, 1976

8 WOMAN IN JUDAISM: THE FACT AND THE FICTION

Rabbi Julia Neuberger

Let me begin by dispelling a few myths. Judaism has often been accused of subjugating women to their husbands and of giving them a legal status inferior to that of men. Both of those statements are only partially true, and certainly at the time of the consolidation of the greater part of Jewish law, running parallel with the first centuries of Christianity, the position of Jewish women often compared favourably with that of women of other societies. That said, it must also be made clear that the problems experienced by many modern orthodox Jewish women now are the direct result of that old position, for Jewish law has changed very little, and slowly, over the last fifteen hundred years.

The problem lies in finding out where all this begins. Of course one can begin with the Bible. The women in the Bible can be divided up roughly into three categories. There are the tough, powerful women who achieve what they want through sheer strength of personality, women such as Sarah, who persuaded Abraham to send Hagar, her handmaid who was also his concubine, into the wilderness with her son Ishmael. They took with them nothing but some food and a leather bottle of water – and the cruelty, to our way of thinking, is appalling. Yet God instructs Abraham to do what Sarah says:

> Do not be vexed on account of the boy and the slave-girl. Do what Sarah says, because you shall have descendants through Isaac. I will make a great nation of the slave-girl's son too, because he is your own child (Gen. 21:12).

And the comment made on this by Rashi, the famous 11th century commentator on the Bible, is that this proves that Sarah was superior to Abraham in prophecy, for he had to listen to her voice. There was Deborah, too, one of the judges, and Jael who killed Sisera. But there were also the schemers – Rebecca, who gets her younger son, her favourite, Jacob, to impersonate the elder, Esau, and steal his birthright:

> Now Rebecca was listening as Isaac talked to his son Esau. When Esau when off into the country to find some venison and bring it

132

home, she said to her son Jacob, 'I heard your father talking to your brother Esau, and he said "Bring me some venison and make it into a savoury dish so that I may eat it and bless you in the presence of the LORD before I die." Listen to me, my son, and do what I tell you. Go to the flock and pick me out two fine young kids, and I will make them in to your dish for your father, of the kind he likes. Then take them to your father, and he will eat them so that he may bless you before he dies.' (Jacob said to his mother Rebecca) 'But my brother Esau is a hairy man, and my skin is smooth. Suppose my father feels me, he will know I am tricking him and I shall bring a curse upon myself instead of a blessing. (His mother answered him.) Let the curse fall on me, my son, but do as I say; go and bring me the kids' (Gen. 27:5-13).

Or there was Naomi, usually considered such a very 'nice' woman, who in her schemes to get Ruth her daughter-in-law, married off to Boaz a distant cousin, sends her at dead of night to sleep at Boaz's feet. Not, perhaps, the behaviour one might expect of a mother-in-law (Ruth 3:1-4).

Finally, in these categories, we have the nice quiet types – the sweet and gentle women who have been upheld as the image of the right-minded woman. But there are few of these – Hannah is perhaps the best example, for she is sweet and gentle and weeps in the Temple because she is childless and her rival wife Peninah has been taunting her. There is Rachel, too, a quiet lady, and Ruth whose gentleness makes her a marked contrast with her mother-in-law. But these quiet women are in the minority in the Bible, and certainly women in the Biblical period are portrayed as having a considerable amount of character, holding their opinions very strongly – they are real people and not the oppressed women so often described by historians of Judaism. Of course they had disabilities – in all but a few contemporary societies women were considered infinitely inferior to men – but their position was <u>within</u> society. They were seen and heard – they could voice their opinions and they could act as judges and prophetesses. They could even inherit property, as witnessed in the famous story of the daughters of Zelophehad, provided the inheritance remained within the tribe (Numbers 36:1-12).

Naturally this is oversimplified, and were we to examine every single woman in the Old Testament, there would, of course, be several who fit into none of these categories. But there are two women who do not fit into the categories who deserve further study – the 'ideal woman' of the author of the Book of Proverbs, and Eve, wife of Adam.

This perfect woman of Proverbs is a fascinating character – she has more hours at her disposal than there are during the day, she lives a life of constant labour, she has no name and no opinions.

> Who can find a capable wife?
> Her worth is far beyond coral.
> Her husband's whole trust is in her,

and children are not lacking.
She repays him with good, not evil,
all her life long.
She chooses wool and flax
and toils at her work (Proverbs 31:10ff).

This is the passage read traditionally by every Jewish husband to his wife at the beginning of the Sabbath. This is the song of praise to the home-maker, the paean of praise of domesticity. Yet one wonders whether it should indeed be read like this. For the Hebrew reads <u>eshet chayil mi yimtza</u> - a woman of valour who can find? And indeed perhaps the sense is sarcastic - a woman of valour who <u>can</u> find - for she does not exist, she is only a figment of the author's imagination. Certainly Jewish husbands through the ages have meant it seriously, but that does not necessarily suggest that the author meant it as praise. And certainly when it is compared with other passages in the Book of Proverbs, such as: 'Endless dripping on a rainy day, that is what a nagging wife is like' (Proverbs 27:15), or passages describing the enticements of harlots, such as the one that follows, one is dubious, to say the least, about the author's intentions.

I glanced out of the window of my house,
I looked down through the lattice,
and I saw among simple youths,
there amongst the boys I noticed
a lad, a foolish lad,
passing along the street, at the corner,
stepping out in the direction of her house
at twilight, as the day faded,
at dusk as the night grew dark;
suddenly a woman came to meet him,
dressed like a prostitute, full of wiles,
flighty and inconstant,
a woman never content to stay at home,
lying in wait at every corner,
now in the street, now in the public squares.
She caught hold of him and kissed him;
brazenly she accosted him...
Come! Let us drown ourselves in pleasure,
let us spend a whole night of love;
for the man of the house is away,
he has gone on a long journey,
he has taken a bag of silver with him;
until the moon is full he will not be home (Proverbs 7:6-13, 18-19).

But no passage so far quoted has caused anything like as much trouble as the story of Eve. For Jews, the story of Adam and Eve is not the story of the Fall of Man. We do not view it in that light. Nevertheless, Eve is made to feel that, through her, women in the future will suffer pain in childbirth, because she listened to the serpent:

And to the woman he said:

> I will increase your labour and your groaning,
> and in labour you shall bear children.
> You shall be eager for your husband,
> <u>and</u> he shall be your master (Genesis 3:16).

This may indeed be an early legend to explain the pain of childbirth – or it may be an explanation for women as to why they should obey their husbands. Whatever its origin, this story has caused untold misery to generations of women, more amongst Christians than amongst Jews, because Paul took the passage and elaborated upon it:

> It is my desire, therefore, that everywhere prayers be said by the men of the congregation, who shall lift up their hands with a pure intention, excluding angry or quarrelsome thoughts. Women again must dress in becoming manner, modestly and soberly, not with elaborate hair-styles, not decked out with gold or pearls, or expensive clothes, but with good deeds, as befits women who claim to be religious. A woman must be a learner, listening quietly and with due submission. I do not permit a woman to be a teacher, nor must woman dominate over man; she should be quiet. For Adam was created first, and Eve afterwards; and it was not Adam who was deceived; it was the woman who, yielding to deception, fell into sin. Yet she will be saved through motherhood – if only women continue in faith, love, and holiness, with a sober mind (1 Timothy 2:8-15).

And from this and other similar passages comes the belief of the early church in the value of the silence of women, a view which many Christians have argued derives from contemporary Jewish thinking. Indeed, Paul may have been strongly influenced by contemporary Jewish attitudes. For from roughly this period dates the well-known passage from the Mishnah, from the Ethics of the Fathers, which reads:

> Engage not in much gossip with women. This applies even to one's own wife. How much more so to the wife of one's neighbour. For he who engages in much gossip with women will bring evil upon himself, neglects the Torah, and will in the end inherit Gehinnom (Avot. 1:5).

But one has to accept that by the period of the Mishnah women had become far <u>less</u> educated, far <u>less</u> important in the structure of society, than they had been in the Biblical period – and this came about presumably as a result of Hellenistic influence on Jewish society. The real problem that emerges from that attitude to women – although it was by no means universal in any case – is that it is from precisely this period that much of Jewish law dates, and it is because women were less in the public eye and less educated that, presumably, their legal status was so much lower than that of men. One can make no apology for this - but one <u>can</u> explain it. In a society where women received little education and were gradually excluded from public life, it was hardly surprising that in the great period of the formation of Jewish law, they should have received a lower legal status than that of men. What is much more surprising is that that status was not as low as the status of women in other contemporary societies, particularly the Hellenistic, and that at no stage was the status of Jewish women as low as that for instance of Christian women under mediaeval canon law. Women in Judaism were never chattels. They always had specific rights. However, many fundamental rights were denied to them - a wife could not divorce her husband whilst a man could divorce a woman relatively easily, originally, as far as we can tell from the book of Deuteronomy, by writing her a bill of divorce and simply sending her away. However, the rabbis did protect women to a certain extent. Although divorce was always unilateral [1] - and within orthodox Judaism it still is - there was a considerable amount of legislation laying down financial settlements to be paid to the divorced wife out of the husband's estate. There was also an opportunity for a wife to institute divorce proceedings - although she could never actually divorce her husband - by complaining to the <u>Beth Din</u>, the court, about any matrimonial offences, whereupon the court would bring considerable pressure to bear, amounting almost to coercion, upon the husband to divorce his wife. As well as that, by a <u>takkanah</u>, a legal decree valid not for eternity but for a set period - usually 1000 years - traditionally attributed to Rabbi Gershom of Mainz but probably a little later, from the 12th century, - a husband could no longer divorce his wife (unless she was guilty of a matrimonial offence) without her consent. This was, in fact, a considerable protection for women - nevertheless, even now the <u>get</u>, the religious divorce, can be abused very easily and it is not uncommon for a husband to refuse to give a <u>get</u> to his wife already divorced by civil law or for a wife to refuse to accept it - both these situations usually arise out of the acute ill-feeling held by one towards the other, but the net result is that it is impossible for the wife to remarry according to Jewish law - she is still a married woman. And this situation can cause considerable distress.

Within the area of matrimonial law generally, women do suffer considerable disabilities. There are two specialised cases which have caused some controversy, those of the <u>agunah</u> and the <u>yebamah</u>. The <u>agunah</u>, first, is the forsaken wife - the wife whose husband has simply gone missing without trace, very often the wife whose husband would be described in our terminology as 'missing, presumed dead', and who would be regarded as a widow after some time had elapsed. In Jewish law an <u>agunah</u> is not free to remarry unless a witness can be brought to testify to the death of her husband - and although the rabbis were as lenient as the general framework of Jewish law would allow them to be - accepting the testimony, for instance, of women, minors, slaves and non-Jews in this matter, ultimately if no evidence of any kind could be brought, the woman was trapped. This had tragic repercussions at times of persecution when all the men from a certain village or town were taken away and killed – and there were no witnesses left to tell the tale. During the holocaust period once again the witnesses to the deaths of so many Jews themselves did not survive – and the widows were left trapped, unable to marry ever again [2]. Hence an increasingly common custom amongst orthodox Israelis on going to war of divorcing their wives before leaving and remarrying them on their return – just to ensure that the women should not be trapped by the laws relating to <u>agunot</u>.

The other important example of this kind is the case of the <u>yebamah</u>. The <u>yebamah</u> is a widow whose husband has died leaving her childless, without an heir to inherit his estate. The deceased husband's brother or nearest male relative (and in Europe it must be an unmarried male relative) is the <u>yabem</u> – the redeemer who is obliged to marry the widow; and their first male child will bear the name of the deceased and inherit his estate – and if the brother-in-law or nearest male relative does not wish to act as redeemer there is a rather degrading ceremony in which the widow spits in a shoe and throws it at him, which effectively releases him from the obligation and means that she does <u>not</u> have to marry her deceased husband's brother. But what has developed is a considerable unfairness in this whole area, with the brother-in-law or male relative making financial and other conditions in order to go through the ceremony – since if the ceremony is not performed and the woman <u>not</u> released, she is, of course, not able to remarry. What is, perhaps, most distressing about this is that it was designed originally for the protection of women, so that there was no doubt that they belonged to a household and to a family – and the ceremony was presumably made degrading in order to encourage the brother-in-law to do 'the decent thing'. Now, of course, a widow would rarely wish to marry her brother-in-law (and in European Jewry in fact it is now not usually allowed, so that the ceremony of <u>chalitzah</u> becomes essential) and the protection of name and estate has little attraction. Both cases, that of the <u>agunah</u> and that of the <u>yebamah</u> can still cause considerable distress amongst orthodox Jews.

Women are not only under a disadvantage in matrimonial law. They are generally accorded a lower legal status than that of men – they cannot give evidence, act as judges, form part of the necessary number for a full service in the synagogue (a <u>minyan</u> is required, a group of ten men), and quite apart from all these, the gravest disability is not a prohibition but an exemption. For according to Jewish law women are exempt from any positive commandment – <u>mitzvah</u> – for which there is a fixed time [3]. They are exempt, apparently, because they have other duties with home and children – but the exemption means that they are not obliged to take part in synagogue services, that they are not obliged to wear phylacteries, and that they are not obliged to take part in the religious activities of the community. They are not <u>obliged</u> to do any of these things – yet at no stage was it suggested that they might not do them, that they

137

were not <u>allowed</u> to do them - and it was over the course of the centuries that that exemption became an exclusion and women were kept apart and discouraged from playing an active part in the community. On one level the reasoning was sound, if unattractive - women were busy with caring for children, with constant childbirth, and with household chores. Yet even at the time of the rabbinic legislation, from about 100-500 C.E. (A.D.), women would have had large parts of their lives when they had no children - either because they were too young or because their children had grown up and left home - and at that stage there was no justification for their exclusion from communal activity. But on another and more serious level, the exemption which became an exclusion was a grave disability for women. Effectively, it limited the religious life of women to the area of the home, to the observance of dietary laws, and to special duties which did indeed give the woman great honour, such as lighting of the Sabbath candles. What it did not do was to make her feel a religious equal with her husband, and despite all the apologetics of orthodox men, and women, it does seem that although women felt they reigned supreme within the home, they often felt slighted in the community outside.

One can gain this impression only very slightly from the available texts - there are, for instance, texts which date from the 11th - 12th centuries discussing whether or not women should be called to the reading of the scrolls of the Law. The answer given is that it was permissible, but that it should not be done out of respect for the congregation - presumably because it might shame some of the men who could not read fluently [4]. There is too a debate about whether or not women can blow the <u>shofar,</u> the ram's horn used to bring in the New Year and new moon - and then a debate as to whether they were obliged to hear it. And although the decision was that women <u>might</u> blow the shofar and should hear it, one feels that again petty decisions were being taken, petty restrictions imposed. The classic example of the petty restriction is the gradual introduction in the early mediaeval period of the <u>mehitzah,</u> the division between men and women in the synagogue, which was probably merely a division in the seating originally but which led to women sitting up in a gallery, or behind a curtain, or even in some Eastern communities in a separate room or outside the building altogether. And these disadvantages, coupled with non-participation in services, a general lack of education, and a lack of incentive to take part in religious activities, led to a spiritually deprived section of the community - its women. One can only imagine what women must have felt on hearing their menfolk say in the morning service: 'Blessed art thou, O Lord, Our God, King of the Universe, who has not made me a woman,' whilst they said 'Blessed art thou...who has made me according to they will'. Even the most talented apologists find that difficult to deal with, and despite all arguments to the effect that it refers to men's gratitude for the ability to perform all the <u>mitzvot,</u> religious duties, it is hardly satisfactory!

And the result of the exemption, and the lack of involvement in the performance of the <u>mitzvot</u> and particularly in the <u>mitzvah</u> of Talmud

Torah, the study and teaching of Torah, was that women received less and less education, to the extent that in the nineteenth century special translations of Bible stories into Yiddish were done for the benefit of the Jewish women of Russia and Poland, who could no longer read Hebrew.

The curious thing about all this is that at the same time as the legal status of women was getting lower and lower, much of what was written about them was highly complimentary and the attitude to them within the family was good by comparison with surrounding cultures. Women lit the candles to welcome the Sabbath. Women had most of the responsibility for children - and they were held in respect and love by husbands and children - the honouring of parents included mothers as well as fathers. And the stereotype of the 'yiddishe mama' with her bowl of chicken soup as a cure for all ills, her family thoroughly under her control and a little world revolving round her at home - that stereotype has its origin in fact. There were women like that - and there still are - and there is no doubt that many women found this a satisfactory role. They were cared for by their families, respected, supported financially, and had a considerable amount of independence within the home. And for many it was a happy life, such as for Glueckel of Hameln who wrote her fascinating journal [5].

The problems arose in a variety of ways. There must always have been women who felt spiritually starved, and excluded from the religion. The best example we have of this is the extraordinary group of women Chasidim (the Chasidic movement was a mystical movement which spread over Russia and Poland in the eighteenth and nineteenth centuries led by Hannah Rachel Werbermacher, the maid of Ludomir); these were women who practised their religion and performed all the religious duties from which women were exempt, from the putting on of phylacteries to the wearing of the tallit, the prayershawl. And for a short time they had many followers and it was a successful movement (Twersky, 1949) Soon, however, they seem to have returned home and become absorbed once again in the usual run of Jewish life. But to them we owe one genre of literature, the techinot, the prayers of women in childbirth written by women for women - and that is a genre of literature which has survived.

But the lack of expression of religious sentiment for women is clearly something which has bothered the apologists for Jewish law as well - they argue, and Moshe Meiselman argues most strongly along these lines in his book entitled Jewish Women in Jewish Law, (1978) - that men and women are essentially different and that when God created woman, he took one aspect of man's personality and developed it to a much greater magnitude in women - this quality is tseniut - usually translated humility, as in the famous verse from Micah:

'And now, O man, what is it that the Lord your God requires of you, but to do justly, love mercy and walk humbly with your God.' (Micah. 6:8) - humbly, humility ... Meiselman and others who agree with him tend to translate it as 'privacy' - that women have a much more personal and private relationship with God than men, that

they do not need the community in the same way – and they quote
Rashi in his commentary of Genesis 18 when the angels at Mamre ask
Abraham where Sarah is and he replies 'In the tent' – Rashi comments
that this teaches us that Sarah was a very private – or humble! –
person. In fact the verse merely shows us that the tent is where she
happened to be, and in any case we know from the end of chapter
that she was standing in the doorway listening eagerly to what was
going on. But even if she had been a very private person, and even
if some women do not need the community, this is no argument for
saying that others do not. Within orthodox Judaism, men have the
choice as to whether or not they participate. Women do not – they
cannot take an active part in the public life of the community
(Meiselman, 1975).

And so one of the first reasons for reform in Judaism was
precisely the issue of the emancipation of women. In his sermon at
the consecration of the West London Synagogue in 1842 D.W. Marks
poured scorn on the education of women presently available and
promised to make the education of girls equal with that of boys [6].
At the Frankfurt Conference of Reform Jews in 1845 a committee was
set up to investigate the religious rights of women. In 1846 the
Breslau conference recommended equal status for women – but the
delegates had not time to discuss it! And by the 1870's most of the
disabilities had been removed, men and women sat together and girls
and boys were educated together. But as early as 1817 girls had
been confirmed in Berlin and amongst the earliest salon ladies in
Germany were two Jewish women, Henritla Herz and Rachel Levin –
later Varnhagen – who probably had had more education than many of
their Christian counterparts (Arnot, 1957).

But with all the changes made by the Reform movement and with all
its acceptance of women as equal with men in the community, women
rabbis and all the other equalisations, it is undoubtedly true that the
majority of Jewish women still suffer considerable disabilities. And
what is tragic about this is that the suffering is quite unnecessary.
For what they see as exclusions are only exemptions, and even within the framework of the law which they, as orthodox Jews, accept,
they are entitled to a much more active religious life than they now
have. But two things have conspired to prevent it; one is the
distressing lack of interest on the part of women themselves, for
having been taught that it is not their area, they now, unsurpri-
singly, believe that it is not, and hence exert remarkably little
pressure in order to get any change. The other contributing factor is
that, like many other religious groups, orthodox Judaism is becoming
even more conservative at the moment and anything which smacks
even slightly of radicalism is highly suspect. And so, with the
exception of the Reform and Liberal communities in this country, and
the Reform and Conservative movements in the U.S.A., there has
been little change. But there is room for a considerable amount of
change and the need for the application of pressure is very great:
there are many Jewish women's groups in the U.S.A., but most of
them are in the Reform or Conservative camp where women's equality
is more or less accepted. There are very few pressure groups within

orthodoxy - and the passivity which exists is a cause of concern because it goes along with occasional complaints about lack of religious opportunity for women.

Personally, of course, I am within the Liberal group who assert that women are entirely equal with men; indeed, one of the founders of Liberal Judaism in this country was a woman. As a result I have been allowed to do anything a man might do, and no obstacles have been put in my way. Nevertheless, despite the fact that it does not affect me directly, I am increasingly worried by the position of women in orthodox Judaism - not so much the legal side, but by the acceptance of their lower status by so many women, even though, within their own terms, they could play a much fuller role. And until orthodox women want to play a more public religious role, and want to be part of the community, Judaism as a whole will suffer from being rather lop-sided, rather male-orientated, and will give little in the way of invitation to participation to its daughters. Jewish women have been treated as inferiors. That need no longer be true - but it is in no small part the fault of Jewish women that it is so.

Notes

1. A woman could never divorce her husband, but in certain circumstances she could approach the beth din (court) with a valid claim against her husband, so that the court would then order the husband to initiate proceedings. If he refused, the court could sentence him to be beaten until he consented. (Talmud B. Gitten, passim; Maimonides Yad Hilchot Gerushin 2:20).

2. A variety of methods of getting around this problem legally have been suggested over the ages, and the debate continues still, particularly in the U.S.A. and Israel. For a complete summary, see M. Meiselman, Jewish Women in Jewish Law (1978), pp.103-115.

3. Mishnah Kiddushin 1:7. 4. B. Megilah 23a.

4. There is an enormous amount of literature on this subject. A summary of the 'feminist' issue can be found in S. Berman, 'The Status of Women in Halakhic Judaism', in: E. Koltun (ed.) The Jewish Woman: New Perspectives, 1976. A classic of the apologist school, dealing with the whole issue of the study of Torah by women particularly well, is: M. Meiselman, Jewish Woman in Jewish Law (1978) (especially pp.34-42).

5. Memoirs of Glueckl of Hameln, transl. M. Lowenthal.

6. D.W. Marks: Sermons preached on various occasions. Introductory Discourse, pp.18-19.

References

Arnot, H. Robert Varnhagen - the Life of a Jewess. London, 1957
Berman, S. 'The Status of Women in Halathic Judaism', in: E. Koltun
   (ed.) The Jewish Woman. New Perspectives, New York, 1976
Feldman, D. Birth Control in Jewish Law. New York, 1968

___ 'Women's Role and Jewish Law', in <u>Conservative Judaism</u> 26, 4, 1972

Hyman, P. 'The Other Half: Woman in Jewish Tradition', in E. Koltun, (ed.) 1976

Koltun, E. (ed.) <u>The Jewish Woman: New Perspectives</u>, New York, 1976

Marks, D.W. <u>Sermons</u> Vol. 1, London, 1851

Meiselman, M. <u>Jewish Woman in Jewish Law</u>, New York, 1978

___ 'Women and Judaism: A Rejoinder', <u>Tradition</u>, 3, 1975

Priesand, S. <u>Judaism and the New Woman</u>, New York, 1975

Twersky, Y. <u>Ha-betulah mi-Ludomir</u>, Jerusalem, 1949

9   BETWEEN LAW AND CUSTOM: WOMEN'S EXPERIENCE OF JUDAISM

Jonathan Webber

Introduction

In theory, men and women experience Judaism quite differently. Traditional Judaism, both in its earliest, biblical formulation and also as interpreted in contemporary Orthodoxy, sharply distinguishes the rights and duties of women from those of men, and in effect presupposes a woman's role as being essentially no more than that of a home-maker. Men and women are considered spiritually equal before God, but the rules governing their respective life-cycles and daily concerns are clearly intended to place them in separate domains; men and women are expected to follow different routes in the pursuit of the ideal life that God has prescribed for them.

Traditional Jewish practice by and large confirms this prescription. There is today a strong and well-argued feminist critique of Judaism which draws attention to the thoroughness of the sexual division of roles: Jewish women have traditionally been excluded from positions of political and religious authority, from active participation in public ritual, and even from institutional scholarly study of the rules themselves. So perfect, indeed, is the elaboration of the idea that males and females have separate domains that Judaism is in practice a male religion, a male culture, a male-dominated social system; the effective confining of women to the home, so the argument runs, represents a particularly specious interpretation of spiritual equality, for it can barely compensate for the lack of access to the real heartland of Judaism, in practice occupied by males alone. In short, spiritual equality ought to confer an equality of rights and duties as well; the premise of separate domains is not an aid but an obstacle to the furtherance of the ideal Jewish life and Jewish social justice. Certainly it is not difficult to perceive the alien, remote source of traditional Judaism in the patriarchal civilisations of the Ancient Near East when it is contrasted with the modern Western values of sexual equality, and in this sense it is perhaps hardly surprising that reformers who yearn for a contemporary Liberal Judaism based on these values have established communities of their own that have removed the premise of separateness altogether and have granted a total equality of rights and duties. A new, feminist-inspired definition of the ideal Jewish life has been brought into being.

Not all Jewish women have become feminists; nor do all Jewish feminists espouse the same goals. But the feminist critique of Judaism, in its various manifestations, and the distance between Liberal and traditional Judaism on the whole question of a sexual division of roles, raises some central questions. Some of these questions are questions of fact: is it true (to give one example) that the traditional ideal of a Jewish woman is that of a toiling housewife whose religious accomplishments can extend little further than providing the context for her husband's religious career? Other questions are evaluative: is the separateness of women from men in the traditional system a form of equality (in that men are excluded from the domain of women), or is it really a form of inferiority (in that the home is not at all the evaluative equal of the male domain, even in traditional theory, let alone as measured by the frustration experienced and articulated by a sector of modern Jewish women)? Is the avoidance behaviour practised during menstruation an indicator of male disgust and fear of female biology (as claimed by some feminists), or is a system of abstinence alternating with conjugality designed to sanctify and spiritualise marital sex relations that can thus renew a marriage through a kind of monthly honeymoon (as claimed by those in support of traditional values)?

In addition to such questions, perhaps closely paralleled in other religious systems, the feminist approach raises other questions, which can be treated here as methodological in character. Is it appropriate to distinguish between fact and evaluation of fact? Is a feminist Liberal Judaism 'Judaism' in the same sense as traditional Judaism? If Judaism supposedly preaches equality but in practice generates apparent inequality, how are we to interpret the contradiction? To study the experience and position of women in Judaism, what should be considered as the most reliable evidence - theory or practice? If some women today feel inferior or frustrated, does this mean that they are poorly socialised into the values of the system, or does it mean that they have - at last - correctly interpreted what the system is all about?

Underlying the difficulties implicit in these questions is the fact that Judaism is not a religion in the same sense as Christianity is a religion. The 'ism' of Judaism suggests a system, a system of law, philosophy and ethics - but the Jews are a people and a nation, not simply a voluntary group of believers in a religious creed. There are thus two types of evidence in any case - the legal, jurisprudential, or normative, on the one hand, and the ethnographic, sociological, or behavioural, on the other. Nor are the two supposed to match each other. What is taken as defining the Jewish people is not the succession of adaptations to the numerous social and cultural environments in the various lands in which they have lived, but rather a notional adherence to the legal system (halacha) that theoretically remains completely aloof from these environments. The halacha consists of detailed rules and regulations, presupposed as divine commands in the holy books of the Bible, in turn expanded exegetically as legal commentaries on the Bible (that are technically its oral traditions) by the contributors to the Talmud and later rabbinical works. The purpose of halacha is to specify how a divinely-prescribed guide to life can infuse spirituality, ever more widely and intensely, into day-to-day practical concerns. Thus the rules are supposed to generate behaviour; it is quite contrary to the theory of this system (blasphemous even, for some) to suppose that it is behaviour that is responsible for the rules. To say that the halacha effectively codifies - or should codify - Jewish social realities existing at a particular moment in historical time is open to any sociologically-minded cultural historian, but it is not a traditional mode of explanation, which sees biblical commands as timeless and eternally valid. No matter how many Jews eat pork (to cite a simple example to il-lustrate the point), pork is still forbidden; even if an entire Jewish community contained not a single Jew who abstained from eating pork or censured others for so doing, pork would still be forbidden. A sociologist would be justified in claiming in the latter case that pork had in some sense become permitted; members of the community in question would probably put it somewhat differently - that the law, though embodying authentic Jewish tradition, was ¹out of touch with reality¹. Either way, however, Jewish behaviour and practice is ulti-mately incapable of being treated as truly normative, whatever the realities on the ground; halacha remains permanently lurking in the wings. Recent changes in the status of women in Judaism, insofar as they conflict with the details of halacha, can genuinely be dismissed as non-events by those who claim the right and indeed the duty to look the other way.

It is thus no easy matter to decide whether evidence for the posi-tion of women in Judaism should best be drawn from halachic theory or ethnographic practice. Modern secularised Jewish society - in its major population centres of North America, the Soviet Union, Israel and Western Europe - has moved far enough away from traditional halachic Judaism to make a straightforward choice between these two levels of analysis look like a choice between two quite incompatible sets of descriptions. Not that such contradictions cannot be made to serve a useful purpose: Jewish feminist writers, in the attempt to provide halachic justifications and historical precedents for a more active female role in Jewish ceremonial and public life, often take as their starting-point the obvious contrast between the apparently nega-tive attitude of the halacha towards women with Jewish ethnographic practice of a distinctly more positive character. But strictly speak-ing, a selective, ad hoc presentation of material from both sources in this way is methodologically unsound; however even if this were not to be the case, the fact is that the conclusions that can be drawn from following such a technique do not point in just one direction. If the two sources are taken together indiscriminately, the total evidence turns out to be sufficiently equivocal to permit a great variety of interpretations, including both a feminist justification for the desira-bility and appropriateness of fundamental change and also apologetic arguments for maintenance of the status quo. But the truth remains that no real inference regarding practice or custom can properly be drawn from analysis of the halacha alone, nor can the halacha be inferred from study of actual Jewish social life. Certainly there are numerous examples from Jewish history of folk-ways (including legends and superstitions) and sociological norms (including forbidden or discouraged activities) being adopted without ever becoming acknowledged, codified or sanctioned by the halacha. On the other hand, despite the obvious disadvantages of a rigid and immobile legal code the paradoxical implication is that because changes in Jewish social behaviour will rarely come to be registered by the traditional scholars, the mass of the Jewish population is thus given considerable freedom of manoeuvre in its behaviour. It is as if the very distance of halacha from the real world actually encourages the consolidation of folk interpretation. For halacha remains the law, whether or not it commands hordes of devout practitioners. But the process works both ways: if, from the point of view of halacha, social change is an illusion, Jewish culture is on the other hand free to develop its own dynamic beyond the reach of the purist scholar.

And yet the dichotomy, necessary though it is for an understanding of Judaism, is almost certainly an analytic over-simplification of the facts: Judaism has evolved over several thousand years as a result of interaction in both directions. Obviously the halacha must depend on some sort of social consensus, and indeed it has changed over the centuries in response to social change, despite the belief in its intrinsic changelessness (the law, it would be said, is merely being amplified and translated into the prevailing categories); moreover a return to halacha also characterises many Jewish reform movements, despite their frustration at the concomitant loss of some freedom (done, it would be said, in the name of the unity of the Jewish people). Midway between theory and practice there thus exists a working model of Judaism, seldom legitimated as such but ethnographically quite real, and indeed fairly common in scholarly as well as popular expositions of Jewish life: namely halacha used as an explanation of social behaviour, or, to put it the other way round, social reality described by articulate laymen in categories ostensibly belonging to halacha but using halachic categories that may well be either distorted or else poorly comprehended. Strictly speaking such expositions rest on a confusion of models, but halachic categories seem in the last resort to be the only truly 'Jewish' categories, even when it is customary practice that is being described. But the technique is intelligible, and widespread at that; after all, native social explanation usually exists on several levels simultaneously, and in the Jewish case it is precisely through a filter of both halacha and indigenous folk explanation that Jews adapt to and make sense of the world in which they live. Social life is constantly explicated by reference to halachic categories, however dimly or inaccurately these may be grasped.

The foregoing issues are of particular importance in the case of the position of women. The halacha itself is a male world. Jewish women have traditionally enjoyed no direct access to Talmudic law, whether in the study or in the making of halacha. The folk explanations I have been referring to may thus even be seen as typically female (though not exclusively so); in any case women are in no position to rely on halachic categories alone to describe their experi-

146

ence of Judaism. Yet they have no alternative except to use them if their experience is to appear as authentically Jewish, and legitimate moreover to their menfolk. The first point, then, that needs to be made here is that women's very perception of their Jewish identity is one that seems only barely authentic to the traditionally-educated male: it is concerned with the domestic world, rather than the more obviously 'Jewish' ceremonial world in which the male moves; it seems primitive and uneducated, compared with the male's belief in his knowledge of and attachment to the world of learning, to which he is regularly (and ritually) exposed; it introduces strange and perhaps even alien interpretations, emphases and preoccupations that cannot be derived from the male's ideas about valid categories of explanation. The cognitive bifurcation of male and female within Judaism is, in short, as complete as their physical separation during the daily round. But even this statement requires careful qualification, as we shall see.

Jewish Law and Jewish Women

The difficulty is that halachic Judaism is not 'about' these men's worlds and women's worlds at all. The mere fact that these empirical and cognitive worlds exist cannot of itself put any claims on the categories according to which halachic Judaism is organised, for the latter operates exclusively on the basis of a set of principles originally laid down in the Hebrew Bible. It is these principles alone, not any subsequent ethnographic facts, that decide what is and what is not a category or subject of interest intrinsically worthy of philosophical and legal speculation within its own frame of reference. Questions regarding the observance of the Sabbath or of the dietary laws are examples of typical halachic problems based on original biblical laws; the details of dividing up the physical and spiritual world between the Sabbath and the weekday, or between the holy and the profane, or between kosher food and non-kosher food, are examples of typical halachic distinctions also based on biblical cosmology. But the experience of being a man, or the experience of being a woman, are examples of something which is not a halachic preoccupation. That is not to say that the halacha expresses no interest in these matters; on the contrary, inasmuch as the whole world is to be 'full of the glory of God', scholars have the duty to interpret all things in the light of halacha – but the distinction must be made between categories or problems generated within the system, and other areas, not belonging to its a priori categories, that are defined and illuminated by principles elaborated elsewhere, i.e. within the former group of traditional core interests of the halacha.

There is a substantial difference, therefore, between traditional questions on the one hand, and other questions, that are decided not on their own merits or within their own frame of reference, on the other. The mere fact that the halacha presumes to legislate on all things should not allow the observer to ignore this important difference in method and conceptualisation. Now it is not a traditional halachic question to ask about the general status of women in Judaism, any more than it would be to ask about the position of men. 'Women' do not form a self-evident, self-contained halachic category in opposition to 'men'; it is even very doubtful whether they form a halachic category at all. The assumption that the halacha does possess such a category - or that it ought to - leads either to misunderstanding, or alternatively to the attempt to impose one onto the evidence. For what such an assumption would overlook is the fact that although there are clearly a number of traditional questions which directly involve women as women (regarding matrimonial and family law, for example), nevertheless these collocate with other traditional questions (the law of contract, for example, marriage and divorce being contracts in Judaism, rather than sacraments); they are not intended to provide elements for such a non-traditional subject as 'the status of women' in general, nor indeed is the Talmud so arranged.

The fact that one of the six 'orders' or parts of the vast Talmud consists of seven tractates collectively entitled Women is an interesting case in point. The seven Talmudic tractates deal syntagmatically but also paradigmatically with certain subjects that involve women, such as marriage and divorce; hence they deal neither exclusively nor exhaustively with the position of women. The Talmudic tractate concerned with menstruation, for example, is to be found not in Women but in the part entitled Ritual Purity. Scanning the halachic literature for cases where women are mentioned is thus an endeavour which would not correspond with nor reproduce the halachic technique; and in practice it would probably even distort halachic categories, since it would not distinguish the technical legal features, not specific to women, that pertain to the particular issues discussed in which women just happen to be involved.

If one wished, therefore, to find an adequate comprehensive survey of the halachic assessment of women, traditional halachic literature is not the place to look [1]. Perhaps the only way of undertaking such a task would be to sift through the material and then re-arrange it under the following four headings:

a) where women are not significantly differentiated from men;
b) where women seem to be granted privileges;
c) where women seem to be discriminated against;
d) where the halacha provides specifically female-oriented ritual.

In the space allotted here a few random examples of each must suffice.

a) Jewish women are not distinguished from men in the right to acquire, inherit and bequeath property; like men they have the duty to observe all religious prohibitions and to accept martyrdom if necessary.
b) Women are not invariably obliged to defend their chastity to the death, nor to marry (whereas a man is obligated to marry, and he is not permitted - even on pain of death - to engage in any forbidden sexual relations). A married woman is entitled to receive

from her husband food, clothing and sexual gratification (the latter, interestingly, also beyond menopause; the male's sexual life is generally not so favourably described) [2]. Women are granted exemption from sundry demands of the law, such as fasting, when consideration is shown for the exigencies of pregnancy, breast-feeding or the onset of menstruation. Women are exempt from virtually all ritual, liturgical and other ceremonial duties prescribed by law to take place at a particular time (daily prayer, for example) - on the ground that they cannot be expected to abandon such domestic duties as they may have; if they have none they still remain exempt, but there is no discouragement whatever of their private and voluntary implementation of such rituals.

c) Exemption from obligation, as just cited, is taken as implying exclusion from actively participating in or conducting the ceremonies of men, who are obligated; thus women cannot be counted in for the quorum needed for certain synagogue prayers, nor can they lead men in prayer, nor accept ritual honours in the synagogue when men are present (but all of these are possible when men are not present). Women cannot formally initiate marriage or divorce contracts; nor can they bequeath property during the period they are married without their husband's consent.

d) Laws of ritual purity, which in the biblical period were treated as affecting men also, have now by and large come to be restricted to women (chiefly during menstruation and child-birth), who are thus given the main opportunity (or the honour) of preserving this element or idiom of religious holiness [3].

It will be evident from the foregoing that a single, formal legal characterisation of the whole range of halacha affecting women cannot easily be generated from within the system, even though of course a modern observer may draw his or her own conclusions about this or that particular element. A number of underlying principles can however be suggested, if this is of any help:

1. Equality before the law exists in certain specified areas, indicating (and articulating) the general Jewish religious principle that men and women are potentially spiritually equal before God.
2. Men and women are considered to have different daily preoccupations and physiologies; their physical apartness must therefore be matched by complementary sets of (effectively) mutually exclusive ritual rights and duties. However the effect of this is to create manifest disabilities for women.
3. This seems to entail an unnecessary and possibly dysfunctional cosmic imbalance, rectified to some extent by the ritual purity privileges. At any rate, the need for making concessions to women is recognised (by the arrangements exemplified under heading b above).

Even though these three suggested underlying principles do appear to account for and explain a good part of the regulations governing women's conduct, they only represent a structuralist rationalisation:

equality versus inequality, mediated by the notion of making 'concessions'. It is quite possible that Jewish customary practice in fact leans on a tendency to preserve a structural balance of just this kind; that is, when perceptions of inequalities increase, cultural energies will obviously come to be directed to making 'concessions' - so long as the desire remains to keep the overall model intact. But that is quite a different level of analysis from making the claim that there exists a traditional halachic category that subsumes all the relevant rules within a single frame of reference, within which the constituent elements have semantic relationships with each other. On the contrary, halachic ideology is not based on rationalisations of ethnographic practice, nor is there, on the question of women, any attempt to draw up a balance-sheet of the kind suggested above. What happens in any one area involving women does not have any necessary effect on what is the halacha in any other area involving women. From a halachic point of view the very idea that the life of women is to be separately considered as such is in any case contrary to the notion of the ultimate equality of the sexes, even though it is a halachic truism that different ritual behaviour is expected of men and women.

The halacha concerning women has in fact changed over time (the examples listed above represent the current state of Jewish law), but when for example 'concessions' are made they are traditionally made on points of detail, not with reference to the 'problem of women' perceived globally. This is why it is not difficult to find the distinct awareness, among the rabbis of the Talmud and the later responsa literature, that the system created a certain measure of unnecessary and inappropriate injustice for women, for instance the interference with a wife's freedom of action to dispose of her own property during marriage. Nor was the Jewish law of divorce ever thought to be quite satisfactory: its basic requirement, that a valid divorce simply consists of the witnessed delivery of a letter of divorce by a husband to his wife, did not prevent women being divorced against their will, and moreover was not always possible to arrange in practice (during periods of persecution, to take an extreme but common case). The problem of abandoned wives, unable to remarry without such a letter or else witnessed proof of their husbands' death, has been especially marked during the present century, as a result of the mass deportation and murder of Jews in the Second World War. Now rabbinic attempts to make 'concessions' and in effect to protect women's rights in these matters - even though often notably unsuccessful - do recur as a constant theme in the halachic literature. Apart from the introduction of a ban on forcible divorce in the 11th century, perhaps the most important example is the final ban in Europe on polygamy at around the same time; the latter drew its justification in part on monogamous Jewish custom that had been of very long standing (cf. Abrahams, 1932, pp.129 ff; Falk, 1966, pp.1-34; see also Kahana, 1966).

But in these and other such cases the halachic issue was not to structure or restructure the general position of women in Judaism, even though this may have been the effect. Rather the rabbis were here responding to particular, ad hoc issues (probably of a political or demographic nature) that happened to affect women, it is true, but which they dealt with in the classic halachic manner of applying legal principles derived from elsewhere in the halacha to these cases in which women just happened to be involved. If 'women' did constitute a halachic category, problems would be generated internally, by the system working upon itself; inferences, analogies and other conceptual and empirical refinements would be constantly infused (as in the case of Sabbath or dietary observance, for example). But nowhere is there any evidence that the ban on forcible divorce or polygamy specifically led to other 'improvements' in the position of women in the Middle Ages; no halachic inferences could be drawn from these cases, just because the system does not contain a global mode of perception to generate and justify them.

Popular Theories Regarding the Status of Women in Judaism

Women's experience of Judaism, and men's beliefs about women's experience of Judaism, cannot normally be expressed except through the idiom of the halacha. But the difficulty is, as we have seen, that the halacha does not possess a single, unambiguous, and coherent position on the subject. A fragmentary approach is therefore the only way in which the halacha is apprehended in practice, even though its categories may be distorted in the process. Thus if someone were to pick out at random a few halachic rulings and describe their social implications, in order (for example) to characterise this area of halacha as 'positive' or 'negative', such a method would belong to a decidedly non-halachic frame of discourse, typical (so the scholar would think) of a primitive, unlettered (woman's) view of the technical considerations that generated the rulings in the first place. But it is ethnographically the case that one principal characteristic of the technical halachic literature is precisely its capacity to generate its own meta-discussion and myths about itself; in this sense the substantial scope for a popular presentation of the halachic approach to women is but one example out of many. Correcting or eliminating 'superstitions' or folk interpretations of the halacha by the rabbi pontificating ex cathedra to his congregation (or, at the family level, by the husband to his wife) is indeed almost an ethnographic genre, and a variety of institutional devices exists in the Jewish calendar and popular Jewish literature precisely for this purpose – though cognitively the effect is doubtless to restate the existence of the gap rather than to bridge it or remove it altogether. At any rate the ordinary person and, in particular, the ordinary Jewish woman, is constantly reminded of the intellectual chasm on the other side of which lies the domain of the learned and, in particular, that of men. Halacha is entirely a man's world: in medieval Jewish society learning was open to all male comers, but women were seldom taught Talmud at all, nor indeed were they expected even to be literate in Hebrew or Aramaic (and so, as a 'concession', the vernacular was introduced into the synagogue liturgy for their benefit; Abrahams, 1932, pp. 369-371). This historical legacy from what are (as far as Jewish historiography is concerned) comparatively recent times has made it difficult today for educated Jewish women to write authoritatively on matters of halacha, and the serious shortcomings of female halachic interpretation in the works of Jewish feminists are an easy target for traditional male scholars [4].

But the fact remains that Jews do retain a great number of popular theories to explain the nature of their society, whatever the halachic purist may say about them. Why, it may be asked, should there be so many theories? Part of the answer to this question can undoubtedly be sought in the nature of Jewish social circumstances: traditionally living as members of a minority culture, Jews are not uniformly socialised into their own classical world-view, and so differ amongst themselves on the degree to which random categories and explanations deriving from the wider Gentile society in which they move are introduced into their understanding of their own life as Jews. The modern assumption that the halacha has a position of some sort on the subject of women, be it 'positive' or 'negative', can probably be attributed to this source. But in addition the halachic literature itself seems highly equivocal: passages in support of sexual equality and sexual inequality, together with the 'concessionary' responsa, all add up to a wide array of primary material enough to feed innumerable folk controversies. It is not difficult, for example, to find biblical or Talmudic aphorisms pointing in all three directions. Jewish liturgy, likewise, contains passages that are unmistakably male chauvinist, but it also includes long tracts in praise of women. It is often thought that the Bible represents the deity as male (as Father or King, etc.), but another view is possible also: Trible (1965a, 1965b) has usefully documented the predominance of female imagery in a significant number of divine attributes, such as mercy (cognate with the word for womb, and symbolically interchangeable with it also), and even in one of the names for God (shaddai, a term related to that for the female breast). Moreover the idea that Judaism conceptualises itself in male-dominated terms alone can also be challenged: the mystical, kabbalah tradition in Judaism, with which liturgy, popular literature and folk custom is deeply permeated, treats the all-pervasive Divine Presence as feminine in character (and for example urges a perception of the Sabbath as a bride), a theme which evokes the often-reiterated biblical image of a courtship and (incidentally monogamous) marriage relationship between God and the Jewish people. There is, then, enough of a supply of diverse source-material from the halacha and its secondary literature to encourage heated folk controversy; plenty of scope is available for Jews to disagree with each other on what their religion has to say about women. Nor is there any particular reason why popular understanding of the halacha should take full cognizance of all the apparently contradictory facts. At best, there can only be the intuitive, somewhat mystified feeling that the halacha, for reasons best known to the scholars, looks both ways.

The working model with which Jews thus collectively perceive the problem is probably in essence a compound of views. In their extreme form they can conveniently be described as feminist (at one end) or apologetic (at the other), though until quite recently it was not the practice for the ordinary Jew to articulate the matter in such terms at all. Although the halacha has always projected itself as expounding the one right way for Jews, the ordinary person traditionally regarded it as a set of norms rather than as a body of doctrinal practice to be accepted or rejected in toto. Over the past two centuries however Jews have gradually begun to adopt and articulate relatively fixed positions to describe their relation to the halacha, using such labels as 'orthodox' and 'reform'. Jewish feminism is today usually associated with reform and tends to regard the halacha as 'wrong', negative, and contrary to its own ideals with regard to women; its 'concessions' are seen as condescending, designed only to ensure the smooth operation of the unequivocally male-dominated status quo. Feminist writers have also paid a good deal of attention to criticism of the Jewish 'Sunday school myth' that some women have historically risen to positions of power and authority, namely the well-attested and apparently anomalous cases of certain educated female scholars during the mediaeval period, as well as such biblical figures as Miriam, Deborah and the like who even came to be leaders of the Jewish people. Given their unequivocal interpretation of classical halacha the feminist labelling of these individuals as 'exceptional women' is hardly surprising – but far from undermining the model, however, 'exceptional women' are shown to provide evidence for it: they are 'token' women, part of the self-deceptive, tokenist male attitude to women which is thus really the underlying principle of the halacha in any case. It has been suggested, alternatively, that 'exceptional women' are known of only during periods when the community was in danger; in such circumstances women could become socially redefined as 'men', but once the crisis had passed women were relegated to becoming 'women' again. Jewish feminists today can therefore point to the precedent, as well as to the urgency of their claims: the community is in danger of extinction as a result of widespread assimilation, and so it should re-use this ancient device, instead of being dismissive of half its population (equal to half its resources). Quite apart, in other words, from the attack on halacha as morally or spiritually outrageous to the modern Jew for its attitude to women, feminists do occasionally rely on what they see as halachic precedents in their attempt to encourage women to renounce their second-class status. The halacha is in effect shown to contain its own justification for a feminist revolution [5].

Rather a different construction is put by the orthodox apologist on the status of the 'exceptional women'. For such a person the halacha unequivocally holds all Jewish women in high esteem, offering them honours and privileges denied to men and moreover advantageously exempting them – perfectly legitimately and compassionately – from the burden of the law as far as possible. Women are to be ritually differentiated from men inasmuch as Jews are to be ritually differentiated from Gentiles. These and other sets of differentiations reflect and articulate the divine will (as revealed in the Bible) that human beings should do no more than live out their own particular social destinies. These destinies are complementary to each other, in that they collectively amount to an inclusive spiritual scheme for the whole world that God created. Religious law and ritual are thus intended to provide the individual not with some sort of ego-trip (which would justify any form of personalised devotion), but with the opportunity - and indeed the duty - to participate directly in the cosmic order of things. It is thus meaningless to propose that halacha looks at women 'negatively'. On the contrary, all its provisions are by definition 'positive', and to argue that women should - on some supposed 'moral' grounds or for the sake of a religious ego-trip - share equally in the rights and duties allotted by God to men would make no more sense than a proposal that Jews should henceforth conduct their religious affairs on the model offered by Gentiles. Moreover the existence of what some call 'exceptional women' clearly shows that the halacha is perfectly capable of generating not simply the pious, retiring, submissive, ignorant and socially inactive woman, which seems to constitute the stereotype of womankind for the reformist detractors of halachic Judaism; assertive, educated women are equally the products of the halachic system, and indeed there is no reason to suppose that Jewish communities should not foster this latter as the ideal type should social circumstances permit [6]. 'Exceptional women' do not, therefore, belong to an anomalous category - they merely reflect the intrinsic flexibility of the halacha to deal with social change creatively.

It will be apparent to the reader that the two 'extreme' positions just considered are both viable interpretations of the halacha, which seems to contain such a variety of conflicting evidence. But perhaps one reason why the 'extreme' positions have been less typical of Jewish attitudes is that they erroneously imply that Judaism possesses such as thing as a halachic category concerning the 'status of women' as such. Far more typical is the popular awareness that there is something to be said for both 'extreme' positions, that Judaism has both its good points and its bad points in its treatment of women, that women hold a very low position in certain matters but an esteemed position in others. Whatever may be felt to be the final judgment of the halacha, however, the way is clearly left open for individual Jews to practise their own interpretations, and for individual Jewish communities to experiment differently and creatively in their social organisation. Some comments must therefore be added on the social and ethnographic implications of the issues so far discussed.

The Position of Women in Modern Jewish Life

The traditional male's failure to perceive the authenticity and the reality of the modern woman's quest for an understanding (whether popular or scholarly) of her halachic identity perhaps constitutes one of the most interesting contemporary examples of the remoteness of the world of halacha from ethnographic explanation. It is not simply that halacha does not purport to be a rationalisation of Jewish social life; it is rather that halacha does not necessarily perceive empirical social realities at all, and, in the particular case of the question of women, it therefore constitutes a 'male' view of the world in more ways than one. No amount of study of the halacha, whether in its popular or its scholarly recensions, would yield the inference that the position of women in Judaism has in fact changed most dramatically over the last 150 years or so - even though at the ideological level this change has hardly come to be registered at all (and so for very many Jews, both male and female, it is as if no change has taken place).

Leaving aside, therefore, the ideological developments in modern Jewish intellectual history such as the emancipation and reform movements, perhaps the single most critical trigger of this change has been the steady disappearance, during this period, of Jewish social and political disabilities. Membership of the Jewish community in Western countries is today entirely voluntary, instead of being imposed by the state. In theory at least, Jews are perfectly free to join or not to join their local synagogue, to accept or not to accept the authority of their local rabbinical court (Beth Din); in other words they are free to develop their own social mechanisms for expressing group solidarity and perceptions of identity without being compelled to accept interference on these matters from the outside. Although a preoccupation with the ethnic stereotyping of Jews by Gentiles (both the search for esteem and the fear of antisemitism, whether real or imagined) is still a distinctive feature of the sometimes tortuous process of Jewish self-definition, it is clear that from a sociological point of view Jewish society is today constituted very differently from the mode of social organisation that prevailed when Jews lived an autonomous existence and the halacha was the principal source of civil law. Halacha today belongs ethnographically to Jewish culture and Jewish history, rather than, as formerly, to the realm of rabbinic political authority.

Indeed one of the principal mechanisms through which Jewish society has reconstituted itself under these new conditions is to fragment traditional ritual behaviour and halachic preoccupations into a substantial number of different, not always overlapping, forms of social activity, each of which offers its voluntary members a sense of participation in the Jewish world now broadly defined. From the point of view of halacha this amounts to 'secularisation' - a road that begins with 'acculturation' and leads eventually to 'assimilation'. Ethnographic analysis of the modern diaspora Jewish community, say in Britain, is thus a complex subject (surprisingly little-researched), requiring new sets of conceptual paradigms. For the consequences that flow from the decision to be 'Jewish' are many and varied: the centrality of the synagogue, rabbi and Talmudical school has waned (though not without resistance) in favour of Jewish sporting and recreational clubs, Zionist associations, committees for the defence of oppressed Jews in other lands, Jewish historical, learned and other societies, and so on; restaurants now exist to serve 'Jewish' rather than kosher food; and the Jewish newspaper has tended to supersede the Talmudical scholar for the presentation and dissemination of matters of importance affecting Jews. In a phrase, Judaism is no longer explicable through the male world of the halacha alone. The opportunity now exists for a greatly increased scope in expressing Jewish identity, and indeed the new, public participation of women in the new Judaism is virtually a direct ethnographic reflection of the effective dethronement of halachic authoritarianism.

It cannot really be taken for granted today that Jews continue to regard themselves as Jews. But it has been made possible for atheist and agnostic Jews to be very active in Jewish communities should they so wish and indeed to see nothing particularly unusual about such participation despite their lack of religious commitment. The basis for the recruitment of membership has thus in effect been considerably broadened - hence the profound and widespread institutional diversification, even including informal and non-institutionalised associational patterns as a valid context for the individual's self-realisation as a Jew. Women fit into this structure without any difficulty and can thus come to be redefined as full members of the community, albeit in this quite new sense. Apart from the prestige accorded to their own philanthropic and cultural organisations, women's experience of Judaism seems to be undergoing a revolutionary sociological shift, towards a participation and contribution apparently differing very little from that of men.

And yet - paradoxically perhaps - there is some substance in the perception that nothing has really changed at all. For inasmuch as women's experience of Judaism was seldom accepted by men as valid in its own terms, women were always given the opportunity to diversify their social and cultural life because - by definition - it did not encroach on the male preserve. From the male point of view there was no real difference between women gossiping on street corners with the local East European Gentile peasantry, and then to return home, their minds filled with senseless superstitions and other baseless knowledge - and women going to university to obtain the best education in the humanities. Whatever form it took, a sophisticated knowledge of the Gentile world was something difficult for the male breadwinner to acquire; he may not always have valued it highly, but this did not necessarily mean that it was inappropriate for women. On the contrary, women from the most traditionally 'orthodox' backgrounds have often been cultured (in a Gentile sense) and have otherwise attempted to gain a secular education, such as was available in the immediate environment. There are plenty of well-attested historical cases: that women were encouraged to develop musical talents is known from the medieval period, for example (Abrahams, 1932, p. 367). But the circumstances of the 20th-century West make a female Jewish interest in, and exposure to, the outside world a much more comprehensive affair. Women today are still far less likely than men to have had a good Jewish education, but on the other hand when it comes to a secular education the reverse is true. In inter-war Poland Jewish women were disproportionately well-represented as students in the humanities departments of the universities, taking advantage of the numerus clausus or quota system that discriminated against Jews, and particularly against male Jewish students seeking to study professional subjects such as law or medicine. It is true, therefore, that there are a few external considerations that can be cited to explain the presence of secular knowledge amongst women, but this should not be confused with a general Jewish cultural predisposition that such knowledge should actively be encouraged. Thus for example Polish language and literature – a subject unthinkable for men – was included in the curriculum of the orthodox women's schools known as Beis Yakov in inter-war Poland (Rabinowicz, 1965, pp.90-91; cf. also Heller, 1977, p.227, p.325), and similar schools in modern Belgium also strikingly maintain this emphasis on a secular curriculum, for which there is no counterpart in the schools for boys (Gutwirth, 1970, pp.326-331). The men of the pious Chasidim communities still dress traditionally, in the head-gear and frock-coats of 17th-century Poland, but their women are encouraged to follow modern Gentile fashions in dress (provided such 'immodesties' as trousers, mini-skirts or decolletages are avoided), and indeed the ban on married women revealing their natural hair in public has today become a stimulus for such women to frequent the most elegant international salons specialising in wigs. Women from these communities are thus in a sense much more free, culturally speaking, to respond to the Gentile cultural environment than are men.

This is a point which needs to be carefully noted in considering the wider question of perceptions of Jewish socio-cultural change today. The prominence of women as agents of external influence on Judaism has probably always been quite pronounced, but this does not mean that women have thereby effected changes in their status within Judaism, or indeed that the system has necessarily changed at all. Rubin (1972, pp.261-2) has observed the process quite clearly amongst Chasidim in America: women are the agents of acculturation in the home, insisting for example that their children spend their evenings learning English rather than in religious study. Once the female-sponsored process has begun, the male does not necessarily attempt to curtail it. Quite the reverse: he absorbs and sanctifies it within his world-view, provided only that it can be legitimated in his halachic categories in the first place. Thus learning English is needed for earning a living (a principle endorsed by the halacha), hence the wife's interference on this point can be made acceptable. Women were likewise frequently used as a source of labour, not only in helping out in the husband's business but also in the wider free market. This is by no means evidence for an attitude of equality between the sexes – for men never sought to take up female roles, and women were often reluctant to admit that they were working at all. Women were simply exercising their potential freedom of manoeuvre which could be drawn upon to widen their cultural experience without affecting the system. After all, traditional male learning consisted of disinterested halachic knowledge; practical knowledge, even including the ability to run a business, was the sort of knowledge considered not inappropriate for women – precisely because it did not conflict with the halachic definition of the male preserve. Thus the suggestion (Gans, 1958) that in contemporary American Jewish middle-class suburbia men are effectively only night-time and weekend Jews, leaving housewives in effective control of the community during the daytime, does not imply the existence of a feminist revolution; women are merely providing the additional labour required during their husbands' absence - as sociological baby-sitters, if one may coin a phrase. It is, in short, not especially difficult to argue that the surface appearances of women's new prominence in Jewish community life is an illusion, in that it leaves the traditional system more or less intact; women's experience, despite its cultural diversification, is as peripheral to a male view of Judaism as ever it was.

Such a view would however remain ethnographically unsatisfactory. For the fact is that a new generation of Jews has arisen, particularly in the United States, that is already socialised into a secularised value-system and into a sense of alienation from the habits of traditional orthodoxy. Halacha as Jewish culture, rather than as divine service, means in effect a movement away from religious activities by adults in favour of a much greater emphasis on the education and socialisation of children. 'Jewishness' is the new concept, defined - ideologically and institutionally - in terms of what is felt to be the most appropriate for a child's future needs. Now the crucial implication (clearly explained by Gans, 1958) is a shift in community self-identification from one based on the traditional male world-view to one based on that of the female. It can be assumed that this is not simply because women play the major role in child-raising, as Gans supposes, but because there has come about a new sense of legitimacy for a non-halachic outlook on the world generally. It has always been the female population that has carried such an outlook and that moreover has probably possessed cultural resources better than those at the disposal of the male population to do so responsibly and effectively should it be given the opportunity to act it out.

Hence the cumulative effects of the crucial position of women as agents of acculturation in the home should not be underestimated. For example the progress of Jewish intellectual emancipation beginning in 18th-century Germany may well have been attributable in part to the salon life eagerly greeted and successfully hosted by cultivated Jewish ladies. More important and influential perhaps - at least as far as the 20th century is concerned - was the role of the well-educated middle-class Jewish mother (e.g. in pre-war Poland; cf. Heller, 1977, pp. 241-4) who was not satisfied merely to have her children learn the local vernacular in order later to be better able to earn a living, but wanted to instil into them a love for that language and its literature, even to the point of asserting its superiority over Jewish culture. In a domestic context of this kind husbands and wives took up new stereotyped positions. The secularised womenfolk became the intermediaries between the traditionalist fathers - now seen as outmoded, in dress as much as in their outlook on the world generally - and their modernist children. Doubtless because of their stronger secular education (and their considerably weaker religious education) women came to be more accomodating towards the religious and cultural changes amongst their children than were their fathers, and probably shouldered much of the blame also. The image of the 'yidishe mama', the peace-making Jewish mother, pivot of domestic unity (and psychoanalytic preoccupation) much loved in modern American popular literature, would have derived from this background. Certainly many of the inter-generational conflicts that have marked, at the family level, the general process of change towards modern liberal values seem to enact a perception of traditional Judaism as 'male', in opposition to the 'female' search for a newer cultural identity – an identity intended to be both distinctively 'Jewish' but also realistically 'modern' at the same time.

In the transformation of the modern Jewish community the position of women is thus decisive. From a sociological point of view it can almost be said that the status of halacha varies in inverse proportion to the status of women and the status of women's experience of Judaism. The ordination of women as rabbis, and the adaptation of synagogue ritual so as to provide for mixed seating, ritual honours for women, and female 'Bat-Mitzvah' ceremonies for girls at puberty (to correspond with the Bar-Mitzvah for boys) – have all come about not as 'gestures' but as empirical changes designed to recognise the critical new position of women in modern Jewish life [7]. Indeed the communities (mainly in America) that have introduced such changes have sensed the urgent need for some empirical adaptation: inasmuch as mothers, and not fathers, have (according to the halacha) the sole right of transmitting Jewish status to their children, careful preservation of women's commitment to Judaism is therefore of utmost importance. If women today no longer practise such traditional virtues as modesty (particularly in dress and sexual reticence), if they no longer regard the preparation of kosher food as a domestic domain possessing intrinsic value, then a restructuring of their status enabling them to move out of the private domain into the public domain represents a cultural adaptation that is valuable evidence for the understanding of Jewish survival in the modern world. The trump card, so to speak, has been played: women, traditionally held back in reserve, have been mobilised as a population resource in its moment of difficulty. And the statistics available confirm their willing response: Jewish women today marry Gentile men far more rarely than Jewish men marry Gentile women.

Jewish custom has often come to override Jewish law. Polygamy fell into disuse many centuries before the halacha came actually to forbid it. There is, therefore, every reason to suppose that it is only up to a certain point that halachic interpretations of Jewish social life can continue to prosper without any reference to changing empirical conditions. On the other hand, the modern American Jewish community, though far and away the largest in the world, can easily be dismissed as atypical of Jewish adaptations to contemporary circumstances: witness the well-documented failure of Israeli Jews, even on the kibbutz, to accomplish sexual equality – despite a Zionist ideology apparently committed to this principle (Tiger and Shepher, 1975; Hazleton, 1977; Bowes, 1978). Moreover there is no uniform set of contemporary circumstances applicable to what is a great diversity in Jewish life today. One fifth of the world's Jews are closeted in the Soviet Union, whilst elsewhere there have been substantial migrations during the 20th century, notably those of the Oriental and Arab Jewish communities to countries of the Western world. 'Reform' is far too generalised a term to cover the variety and subtlety of all these adaptations world-wide, particularly since strong pockets of orthodox Jewish society, of the Eastern European, German, Arab and Oriental traditions, are to be found in many advanced Western countries. The Chasidim women of Antwerp, London and Brooklyn, for example, or the North African women of Marseilles and Paris, have also made their adaptations, but of a different kind to those made by 'reform' women. These orthodox women may in a sense be more 'modern' today in their grasp of the outside world than were their mothers and grandmothers, but such cultural change is seen as ephemeral, cosmetic perhaps, and not at all as 'reformist'. Its importance is purely illusory when it is set against their orthodox belief in the change-lessness of halacha and the constancy of Jewish social structure and social relations. Indeed their very flexibility in the face of changing cultural circumstances, based ultimately on a virtual indifference to the linguistic and physical appearance of the outside world, may go some way to explain their retention of traditional Jewish values in the modern world. The strength of halachic ideology, particularly in its popular recensions, seems to offer 'orthodox' women both the cultural security and, at the same time, the cultural freedom not to feel it necessary to rise up against it in their voluntary participation in communal life.

So the question whether reform feminist ideology is actually needed to make explicit the empirical aspect of modern Jewish social change remains unresolved. There can be no doubt that communities that have moved away from the halacha, whilst declaring the emptiness of women's traditional life as home-makers, have effectively confronted their women with the new responsibility of becoming transmissors of Jewish identity. But is this - or should this be - the norm? Has Jewish life today reached that point where halacha must perforce renew itself? The evidence is not uniform; a consensus is lacking; and the internal debate continues.

Notes

My grateful thanks are due to Shirley Ardener and Pat Holden, who encouraged me to write this paper in the first place; to Margaret Rubel, for her comments on an earlier version; and to Vera Grodzinski and Lionel Kochan for some useful bibliographic suggestions. I hope I have not let them all down.

1. It is not in any case the technique of the Talmud, which records discussions and disagreements amongst the early rabbis on all subjects, systematically to combine isolated conclusions into a coherent framework. The status of women is no exception: fundamentals are discussed in the same way as details, and the many inconsistencies are not always noticed, let alone reconciled. Certainly it must be made clear that the mere occurrence of this or that opinion in the Talmud (or later responsa) is no guarantee of its status within the system of halacha as a whole.

2. In contrast with the popular belief that sex is a man's right and

160

a woman's duty, the halacha tends rather to view marital relations as the duty of the husband and the privilege of the wife. For a thorough exposition see Feldman, 1968, esp. pp. 63-4.

3. The four headings suggested here have been drawn from R. Loewe's brief but excellent survey of the subject, which can be recommended to the interested reader. Most of the examples in the paragraph above are from those given by Loewe, though some I have classified differently.

4. For a useful review see Meiselman 1978, passim; for example pp. 52-7, on the halachic inaccuracy of the feminist claim that women's ritual duties are so meagre as to constitute a genuine handicap to spiritual achievement.

5. A useful source for this literature is the collection edited by Koltun 1973.

6. I am grateful to Dr. N. Lowenthal, of the Lubavitch Chasidim Jews of North London, for a clear exposition of this point (personal communication). The Lubavitch Chasidim are very active today in their attempt to re-educate the wider assimilated Jewish public, and especially the female population.

7. The going has not been easy. Some innovations, such as the Bat-Mitzvah ceremony, have gained fairly widespread acceptance, even amongst non-reform communities. (Because some measure of religious knowledge is required of those who undergo the ceremony, this innovation at least pays lip-service to the importance of the idea of providing religious education for girls, a principle which is today by no means restricted to reform Judaism.) But the granting of equality has often remained no more than programmatic, as the contributions to Koltun 1973 significantly reveal. This may in part be due to a fear that the new participation of women in synagogue life, for example, will cause men to withdraw on the ground that such participation is no longer an honour for them; for a discussion of this point by a group of British women rabbis see Nave-Levinson et al. 1981. But clearly there is a great deal at stake here: inasmuch as men traditionally retained control over the public character of the individual nuclear family, membership of Jewish sub-groups, of the Chasidim for example, would usually be transferred from generation to generation through the male members of the community; a wife is normally expected to conform to her husband's sub-group norms and social identity. Now the fact that this is to a great extent synagogue-based means that resistance to sexual egalitarianism in the public rituals may be quite marked, even on points of comparative detail.

References

Abrahams, Israel. (1896) Jewish Life in the Middle Ages (second edition, ed. Cecil Roth), London, Edward Goldston, 1932

Bowes, Alison. 'Women in the Kibbutz Movement', The Sociological Review, Vol. XXVI, 1978, pp. 237-262

Falk, Ze'ev W. Jewish Matrimonial Law in the Middle Ages, London, Oxford University Press, 1966

Feldman, David M. Birth Control in Jewish Law: Marital Relations, Contraception, and Abortion as set forth in the classic texts of Jewish Law, New York, New York University Press; London, University of London Press, 1968

Gans, Herbert J. 'The Origin and Growth of a Jewish Community in the Suburbs: A Study of the Jews of Park Forest', in Marshall Sklare (ed.), The Jews: Social Patterns of an American Group, New York, The Free Press; London, Collier-Macmillan, 1958

Gutwirth, Jacques. Vie juive traditionnelle: Ethnologie d'une communaute hassidique, Paris, Editions de Minuit, 1970

Hazleton, Lesley. Israeli Women: The Reality Behind the Myths, New York, Simon and Schuster, 1977

Heller, Celia S. On The Edge of Destruction: Jews of Poland between the Two World Wars, New York, Columbia University Press, 1977

Kahana, K. The Theory of Marriage in Jewish Law, Leiden, E.J. Brill, 1966

Koltun, Liz (ed.), The Jewish Woman: An Anthology, Response, no. 18, 1973

Loewe, Raphael. The Position of Women in Judaism, London, S.P.C.K., 1966

Meiselman, Moshe. Jewish Women in Jewish Law, New York, Ktav Publishing House and Yeshiva University Press, 1978

Nave-Levinson, Pnina et al. 'Women and Judaism', European Judaism, Vol. XV, 1981, no. 2, pp.25-35.

Rabinowicz, Harry M. The Legacy of Polish Jewry: A History of Polish Jews in the Inter-War Years 1919-1939, New York and London, Thomas Yoseloff, 1965

Rubin, Israel. Satmar: An Island in the City, Chicago, Quadrangle, 1972

Tiger, Lionel and Joseph Shepher. Women in the Kibbutz, New York and London, Harcourt Brace Jovanovich, 1975

Trible, P. 'Nature of God in the Old Testament', in The Interpreter's Dictionary of the Bible (Supplementary Volume), Nashville, Abingdon, 1965a

_____ 'Woman in the Old Testament', in The Interpreter's Dictionary of the Bible (Supplementary Volume), Nashville, Abingdon, 1965b

10 WOMEN EXCLUDED?   MASKING AND MASQUERADING IN WEST AFRICA

Elizabeth Tonkin

Masks Transform

The title of this paper points to more than one puzzle. Masking and masquerading tend to exclude women; if they are important religious activities, what does this mean for the women concerned? They also tend to be secret, so how can we discuss them? And, although the material I discuss sounds very particularistic, I should stress that there are comparable examples not only in Africa, but in many parts of the world. If one is to treat African mask events as religious, one has also to consider the nature, and reportability, of religious experience – problematic subjects everywhere and always.

Masks are found in every quarter of the world, and where we have evidence of the more distant past, we often find masks there. In Africa, their use is widespread – certainly not universal, always subject to change, but still very frequent especially in the West, in Central Africa and across to its eastern sides. In Western Africa today masked figures vary in significance: appearing publicly in some communities from time to time as elements of entertainment, they are in other communities crucial elements of social life, the medium and idiom of many different kinds of social action.

I talk of Mask use, and it is often difficult for those only familiar with African masks as art objects, hung up in museums as part of primitive art collections, to realise that these objects were made for use, and were worn on a person as part of a striking costume. Masking everywhere is, and has always been a social activity and it is the action of masking, the assumption by a carrier of the mask and his appearance in performance that we need to understand if we are to explain the phenomenon of mask creation itself. The aesthetic qualities of a wooden mask may contribute to the effect of the performance (though one must be thoroughly sceptical of the accounts of these effects which are put forward by most commentators on masks as African Art). Some of the Western artists who were influenced through their appreciation of formal features also understood something of how a mask's power worked [1], but this cannot really be predicated from the object alone, as a part cannot explain the whole.

163

It is the **action** of masking which gives the mask - as object - its power. The carrier or wearer is actually transformed by assuming a mask and so it is not surprising to find that this transformation is believed to be something more than ordinary dressing up. The manifestation of mask, carrier and costume together is more than the carrier's ordinary self. For these reasons I talk about the action and not just the physical object. When I use the word Mask I mean the whole assemblage, unless the context clearly means the object alone. This usage, by the way, also occurs in some of the languages of African Mask users, and I think accounts for the Nigerian English meaning of 'masquerade', which can refer to the masked figure as well its performance.

Masks Generate Power

Since the Mask - in my total sense - is no longer an ordinary self, it may embody a spirit, often an ancestor, or like the gods of Greece and Rome both represent aspects of life and have power to intervene in human affairs. Using such terms it is easy to call Masks religious, but only by setting up equivalents - I would be talking about something which can be compared to others accepted as religious in Western eyes. Deeper understanding comes from getting behind familiar labels and so from looking at masking in its fundamentals, to see if one can identify what is going on. Kenelm Burridge has pointed out that 'religions ... are concerned with the systematic orderings of different kinds of power, particularly those seen as significantly beneficial or dangerous' (1973, p.5). Religions he says, are 'concerned with the truth about power', but also, 'any concern with the truth about power is a religious activity' (p.7). This is because power is of many kinds. Fertility, energy, coercion, force - these are all recognisably aspects of power which is differentially connected in different cosmologies and scientific theories. A belief in Heavenly Powers, for instance, locates an external source for these mysterious but stubbornly real kinetics of human life.

Religious actions are designed to or have the effect of producing power [2] for their participators. I have argued elsewhere that:

Every Mask is part of an event, which can only be intelligible when understood as a performance with complex interactions between Masks and non-maskers. Indigenous explanations show that these are seen either as the actions of power or as the actions needed for its production. Power, all reporters agree, resides in the Mask (and often also in the mask on its own). The Mask is the exponent of power, which is manifested in all its actions - not just those which may be deemed instrumental, exerting 'social control'; to express power is to make power. The mask carrier is said to assume power, the aim of a mask cult is to channel, elicit or transmit power, and so forth (Tonkin 1979, p.243).

Of course, a label like 'religion' refers to many things: insofar as it is institutionalised, for instance, religion shares features with other institutions, including multifunctionality. Moreover, as Burridge says, 'there is no human activity which cannot assume religious significance' (p.4). If one focuses on the transforming power of the Mask, which is due to its paradox - that it is simultaneously two and one, a face transformed by removal and replacement - it is possible to locate this religious quality in any performance, not just those which could be described as 'religious ritual' or the incarnating of ancestor and other spirits. As I have mentioned, some West African masks can simply entertain, or as in ancient Greece, be dramatic. The relationship between masks and acting is complex indeed (see e.g. Tonkin, 1979). They can be processional like the carnival Masks of Europe and the New World. I must stress that Mask occasions in West Africa are very varied, and the repetition of a name, like the 'Poro' and 'Sande' which I go on to discuss, does not mean the occasions are identical at all, while closely comparable activities may have different labels. Like any other important event Mask events are complex, and I am sorry that there is no space here for extended description and illustration (the magazine/journal African Arts is a good general source from which to get a sense of Mask events).

Bounding Secrecy

I concentrate here on a few aspects of women's masked associations, often called Sande or Bundu, which are found alongside men's associations (usually Poro) in Sierra Leone, Guinea, Liberia and Ivory Coast [3]. Such parallelism is rarely found further east, e.g. in Nigeria and Cameroon, and it provides us with important evidence about women. My main source is the work of D'Azevedo on the Gola people of Western Liberia.

They are usually called secret societies, but this is a misleading name for Westerners if one considers that usually every member of the community becomes socially adult by initiation into Poro or Sande. But they are secret, in the sense that many of their activities are not public, and are confined to one sex - indeed to the initiated members of that sex. They are also graded associations, so that progressively fewer members know more and more, and few reach the status of leader (sometimes called zo). You can be punished for telling Poro or Sande secrets to the opposite sex, or for seeing what you are not supposed to see, but male and female zos may well know some of each others' secrets. Female zos for instance have to be present at certain Poro events. D'Azevedo explains that among the only men permitted to see some of the Gola Sande secrets are the carvers of their wooden masks.

Secrecy, then, is virtuous in these communities. In a sense all social life consists of communicative acts, and so the shape of society will be very different according to the openness or closure of its lines of communication. In societies which practise Poro or Sande, type and extent of knowledge must vary by age and sex, so knowledge is a component of hierarchy. Such variations also obtain elsewhere; they are not always, as here, justified on ontological grounds.

Secrecy is a great problem for scholarly investigators. I do not know of any outsider who has published Poro or Sande secrets, and if an investigator is initiated into membership, he or she of course will be bound by the rules of secrecy too [4]. However, we should not take secrecy to be simply an observer's problem (and then consider it as crucial or irrelevant according to one's theoretical perspective). In even the simplest, tiniest communities, some member is excluded from some social knowledge and activities, in most communities some classes of member are excluded much more than others.

Prohibitions of secrecy therefore make boundaries explicit. They also encode a universal condition of life, which is that everyone experiences, but no-one can experience for anyone else. My experiences are unique to me - they indeed are me, and communicating them is not the same as experiencing them. It is sometimes said that non-religious people cannot possibly understand religious events because they do not share religious experience. While it is true that the agreements we reach, the recognitions that occur when we hear other people's reports of experience, all point to a common existence of perception and memory, there is <u>no</u> guarantee that anyone will experience the same as anyone else.

The great social analysts understood this very well. The breakthrough to grasping, analysing a specifically social dimension came I think from considering that the human person is like a coin, composed of two indivisible sides, the uniquely individual and the social. It is the social side which tells us which language to use, how to behave, in short makes me an amalgam of genes and upbringing, a distinct personality who is also socially recognisable in terms of class, accent and gender. This amalgam is a dynamic formation since some of its components come from involvement with others, so the social analyst could look at the larger events in which the individual is involved, to consider, for instance, the structures of church organisation or the formulation of doctrine or the nature of religious symbols, and by the systematic consideration of variability, to show how individuals must be constrained in some ways by their social condition, else there would not be recognisable patterns of choice, situation and response.

Given these contrastable configurations, it is then possible to infer that individuals at some level agree on what they must be meaning, and at least to accept that some types of experience are more or less likely for a given context. For certain schools of social thought it has been sufficient to say that the resulting collective representations are the only proper subjects of analysis or even to assume that since experience is inaccessible, it effectively does not exist, or is insignificant in social explanation. I do not accept this conclusion, but I don't think we have yet a methodology to overcome it completely.

What then can be said about women's experience of masking and its meanings for them? Logically, no more and no less than about anyone's experience, but in this case the sorts of knowledge on which to base inference are limited in comparison to those in non-secret conditions. The outside analyst cannot, for example, hear accounts from other women or even go through the same events, so as to understand some of their components. A possible inference derived from negative evidence would be that <u>indigenous</u> analysis, which demands the systematic articulation of experience, would be unlikely when such experiences are as it were introverted into intense but closed-off occasions. But we do not even know, for instance, whether initiands discuss their fearsome initiations together. They have sometimes reported some of the sequences to outsiders and since they were ideally and in the past often really taken out of the community for three or four years, to live together in humble communitas (cf Turner, 1969) they would have time to collectivise their experiences. Later in life, some of them will certainly learn that what might have been experienced alone was undergone by all, and as <u>zos</u> they may even create the initiation experience for others. Some women in a Sande society will know what it is to <u>be</u> a Mask.

What <u>is</u> an experience, even in oneself? We cannot say that it is simply <u>direct</u> or directly remembered. It can be reglossed and reunderstood over time, re-remembered in fact as if it were quite a different experience. It can change, and so continually alter in its meaning for, or effect on our lives. The most famous literary examination of this process is Proust's. In his researches into lost time, he endlessly revolved the question of how far experience is remade by redefining it. In one volume, Marcel, the narrator, on his first visit to the theatre, starts to discover:

> the touch of genius in Berma's acting a week after one has heard her, in the criticism of some review, or else on the spot, from the thundering acclamation of the stalls ... the more I applauded, the better, it seemed to me, did Berma act (1924, I, p.29).

And this was only the beginning, because Marcel's opinion changed as he continued to talk to others about the performance; even his evaluation of Berma continued to change - so was his initial experience recoverable?

Masks, Myths and Gender

Returning to the Gola men, women and children described by D'Azevedo, <u>masking</u> is for them part of a pervasive and repetitive experience which is enacted through participation in Poro and Sande and made into an all-encompassing explanation of life and time. D'Azevedo says that:

> the greatest public dramas of life are played out in the cycle of ceremonies connected with the recruitment and maintenance of membership in the all-powerful and universal male and female secret associations. The major theme of these dramas is the unresolved

rivalry between the sexes and the unrelenting struggle of the ancestors - together with their ancient tutelaries among the nature
spirits - to ensure the integrity and continuity of the community.
The actors are the uninitiated youth, all the adult men of Poro, all
the adult women of Sande, the sacred elders representing the ancestors, and the masked impersonators of the nature spirits who
are allied with the founders of the country (1973, pp.126-7).

Methodologically, D'Azevedo must have made these inferences in a
(necessarily) circular way from the evidences themselves by compar-
ing the results of every day observation, the sequence of performance and the Gola charter myth which explains how:

> in the beginning ... there was Sande. Women were the custodians
> of all ritual and the spiritual powers necessary for defending sac-
> red tradition in the interests of the ancestors. The initiation and
> training of females for their roles as wives and mothers was a
> central task in which the entire community participated. The gener-
> ations spring from the wombs of women, and it is the secret
> knowledge of women which ensures the fertility of families, of the
> land, and of all nature (p.127).

Into these 'ancient days of peace and perfect order' (p.129) came
Poro. For terrible wars came to the country, which women could not
withstand. They resisted the men's attempts to mobilize for defence,
because it interfered with Sande, instead of letting Sande's powers a-
lone protect the land. Men then searched the forests to find a special
monster, which they tended and subdued, so that it became the great
spirit of Poro, too fearful for women to look on. This allowed men
to subdue the women and take away their sons to teach them loyalty
and cooperation exclusively among males. They did however agree
that Poro and Sande should share control over the country. So Poro
rules for four years, Sande for three with a year or so in between
'so that the country can rest' (p.130).
Gola men and women each have their own association and Masks;
the cycles of Poro and Sande alternate forever in Gola understanding,
providing an image of time, a definition of relations between the
sexes, and a lived justification of gerontocratic authority (D'Azevedo, 1973, a, b, 1978).
When Sande rules the country, fines are levied on the men for
their misdeeds in the previous period of Poro rule. Men often have
to cope for themselves as women leave the domestic hearth for Sande
affairs. Gola women are unquestionably organised, and by the means
that Tiger has argued are normally confined to men in groups
(1969). In this respect then, my title would be incorrect, for Gola
women are not excluded any more - or any less - than men are.
This symmetry is, as I have said, rare: it is far more usual for
men alone to organise themselves in graded 'masking' associations,
and even when female Masks appear, they are in fact carried by
men. On many occasions, women are forbidden to see the Masks, or
sometimes even the masks on their own. (These prohibitions are re-

ported for Poro areas too). Just as day masquerades are more often public than night time ones, so are the Masks in their imagined home territory of forest or bush more dangerous than when they come into the public space of the community. In the forest the dangerous male power of the Mask attacks female power though sometimes the attack can be neutralised by the reversing action of initiating a woman who has inadvertently seen it into the men's association. In the town festival, however, the male Power of the Masks is often thought to communicate life, and barren women will seek to be touched by them.

From the earliest reports onwards, one learns that Masks are intended to coerce and control women, who are ignorant of the carrier's identity. The reporters, who like their informants were male, accepted this thesis, while sometimes doubting that the corresponding dogma of women's ignorance could be true in fact. As my examples show, the truth must at least be rather more complicated, and there are also theoretical objections to social control as a final cause (I argue this in Tonkin, 1979, and show that the cognitive creativity of Masking can be put to many uses).

In Africa, male initiations generally transform children into adults; while female initiations do the same, they are not made 'voters' or soldier citizens, but rather have their primal powers of fertility regulated for the needs of the social world. In men the attributes of adulthood have as it were to be manufactured. Where male initiations transform them into warriors, we could say that war is thereby institutionalised, and as a form of male aggression. All these themes are present in the Gola myth, which also has a characteristic presentation of 'women's secrets'. The importance of women's secrets is to do with the life-giving femineity of women, as Shirley Ardener has pointed out (1975), this perhaps is why men's only riposte is that women betray the men's (more commonplace) secrets.

Widely dispersed communities in West Africa have aetiological accounts of Masks which, as in the Gola myth, attribute them first to women, but claim that men stole them later. Griaule recounts different versions of a Dogon story which all agree in stating that women were at first dominant, and that men stole the Masks to get this source of power for themselves, and thus to control the women instead of vice-versa. Adam is so to speak created out of Eve's rib. Masks in such stories mediate, locate and differentiate Power, and distinguish the aspects that should belong to male and female. One might also say that the tales describe a conflict of priority, for while women are the sources of fertility men also have a claim to be generators.

It is important not to reduce into some hard and fast analysis what are really complex and subtle operations, stories and events capable of different interpretations, and understood too in relation to other aspects of life. The evidence does at least suggest that West African masking explores the differences between men and women, and frequently defines, creates or enacts 'maleness' as the most socially marked state. It follows from the nature of the Mask that sex and gender are conceptualised as different aspects of Power [5]. Masks then are a focus for pondering on sexual divisions and also for bounding or neutralising the powers of women which, simultaneously, they present.

Female Experience: Ideology vs. Exclusion?

In trying to infer female consciousness we must take into account the character of their life trajectories, their changing access over time to knowledge and action by reason of age, position and sex. In an article on Women Power and Art, in <u>African Arts</u>, Anita Glaze argues that by focusing on the visually exciting male masquerades in a Senufo village one will miss the subtler involvement of women. In this Ivory Coast community Poro and Sande are not experienced as parallel and self-contained institutions, but have interactive, dynamic qualities. A male and a female must act jointly to found a new Poro grove, whose 'true' but not I think executive head is a woman. As elsewhere she is an older woman, a postmenopausal woman as may on occasion be inaugurated into men's associations.

Glaze also claims that girls share in much but not all Poro training. The organisation which is in many ways parallel to Poro is not Sande in this case but Tyekpa, a woman's society which cares for the effigies of lineage ancestors – female ones in a largely matrilineal society. Sande has an order of mostly women diviners and 'is more an inner, closed arena where the individual grapples with daily problems and his relationship with the unknown' (Glaze, 1975, p.64). Glaze describes a social interlacing which is at first sight very different from the echoing alternation of the Gola world – but it might not seem so different to older Gola women. She draws attention to the validatory presence of Sande leaders. As she rightly says, if you look at one of her photographs in her text your eye is drawn to the male masks, and you actually miss these unobtrusive female bystanders, standing on the periphery in their everyday cloths.

It is quite possible that such examples are not unique, and that a male-focused observer may literally not see women, so reporting that there are none. But what sort of experience is it for the women concerned? Glaze points out that they do not act 'to diminish in any way the legitimate authority of the male in the socio-political order'. Similarly the ideology of complementarity does not mean equality for Gola women. Senufo women can apparently be <u>eminences grises,</u> but because of their diffused and in many ways circumscribed involvement, they would seem to experience public religious occasions with Masks in a detached, or limited, way. This unarticulated and unobtrusive female status is of course a familiar one.

Glaze is anxious to point out that there is a fundamental honouring of motherhood which is repeatedly enacted through Poro ceremonial. Her case is not unique; the word Poro is often said to mean earth, a <u>female</u> earth just like <u>Ogboni,</u> the name of a mainly male Mask cult which is important in some Yoruba areas of Nigeria. It is not uncommon for earth, motherhood and the male initiation society to be identified with a monster female Mask who swallows initiands and gives birth to them, clawing them with her mark for ever.

I can think of no single expression of Senufo language which better communicates the ideological core of woman power or more intimately touches the very heart of their religious thought than the phrase 'at our Mother's work'. This phrase forms the nucleus of a combination formal greeting/secret password used wherever members are engaged in the affairs of Poro. The words refer to the initiated Senufo's status as a child of divinity conceived of as a being distinctly on the distaff side and under whose control human activity finds wisdom, creativity, and order (Glaze, 1975, p.29).

The Senufo central deity is said to be bi-partite, called by two names – I presume male and female respectively – in its aspects of 'divine creator' and 'protective nurturant being'. Glaze does not distinguish between male and female understanding of Senufo religious thought, but this nexus of meanings must surely be understood by both sexes.

Masks therefore can give value to women's powers, but they can also justify women's subservience to men. They do so in the stories I have mentioned, and the justification is the authority of the Masks as autonomous sources of Power. But I do not believe [6] they are autonomous. I do not believe myself in supernatural beings, and I think though Masks do indeed release powers, they are not the sorts of Power that is claimed in Mask doctrines. Masks do not bring the dead to life, they do not reincarnate spirits of the wild. It is neither Masks nor God who legitimate authority, but men, and sometimes women as well. I don't think one can discuss women's share in or exclusion from a particular 'religious experience' without the most careful thought about the source and status of that experience.

If certain communities use masks to exclude women, or have myths which explain why women have been rightly deprived of the authority that resides in the ownership of masks, then Masking is an ideology which has the effect of justifying women's secondary place in the social world. But there is a nice contradiction here, for if women are so excluded they should consequently be ideologically freer. Their experience may not lead them to accept the male message of the Masks. It is possible – who knows – that women do not always cower in their houses when the Masks go by outside, even though the men would like to think so. It is certainly possible to turn the myths around and conclude that they do not justify men's supremacy but simply describe an unjustifiable but everyday history of male coercion, justified by a crude trickery in a logic which would only convince foolish and self-interested men. Yet again, however, women often comfort themselves with the idea that 'men are but children of a larger growth' and it would be just as dangerously lulling to conclude from a myth which explains how men are really cheats and liars that it is not worth bothering about their coercive power over oneself.

Insofar as women are excluded from the mysteries of the Masks, they are excluded from the exercise of certain rights in society which are implemented through Masks, since Masks in some communities act as judges, but this exclusion may extend to men, especially junior ones. Again, masking is both lived philosophy and profound spectacle, so to be excluded from it is to be deprived of cognitive and imaginative opportunity. It can also be an englobing form of experience, which enables the growth of wisdom but not of detached speculation [7]. Gola women must share the religious assumptions of men – in the broadest sense of the word religious: they can also celebrate their own worth in an arena and a medium which is res-pected by men; do they in consequence <u>lack</u> a bleaker view, one untrammeled by the warmth of male rituals <u>and</u> so more realistic? Michael Jackson has argued that the similar dual cult rituals of the Kuranko in Sierra Leone enable their members to 'bring into focus an abstract image of their social ideology and to tolerate a dramatic re-hearsal of the contradictions within it' (1977, p.201). If this is so, tolerance may replace rebellion, and the drama of the Mask help to perpetuate the contradictions of society.

Notes

1. For instance André Malraux quotes Picasso as saying 'If you give spirits a shape you break free from them. Spirits and the sub-conscious ... and emotion – they're all the same thing. I grasped why I was a painter' (i.e. from the discovery of negro 'fetishes'). This is part of a passage translated by P. O'Brian in his life of Picasso (1976:37) because he thinks it is one of the artist's reveal-ing statements.

2. Here again I use the capital letter to refer to the 'total' con-cept.

3. D'Azevedo's (1962) map of 'the Poro cluster' could be extended by further research (and there is more new work being reported) but these questions of identity, comparability and change will have to be very carefully considered. Jones (1979) reviews some of the earlier literature on Poro, which was first mentioned in 1616. Dap-per's famous account (1668) also mentions Sande, which tended to be ignored later; Cessou (1911 as Ceston) has another interesting account of its importance for the Gola. Research on these topics is now increasing, see e.g. the special issue of <u>Ethnologische Zeitsch-rift Zuerich</u>, I, 1980.

4. Cultural norms against talking about 'society business' are strong, so that researchers have generally been hypercautious in their investigations. Accounts therefore are derived from public asp-ects, deducing functions and meanings. Bellman (1975) joined a dif-ferent, minor society to get evidence on cultural secrecy.

5. Cf. Bloch and Guggenheim who argue that 'the birth that baptism effects and the social relationships thereby formed are under the control of men, because it is a birth into and by the religious – political community, a birth which involves the symbolic denial of the procreating power of birth by women.' Communities practising Poro/-Sande do not deny female procreative power, but their male initia-tions – as elsewhere – articulate 'the religions – political community' as male, not least by their greater elaboration (1981, p.280).

6. Like 'experience', 'believe' is a philosophically disputed term

(see e.g. Needham 1973). I mean by it here 'hold to be true, actual'; we are talking of faith.

7. Cf Biebuyck's account of the Lega bwami cult (1973) which can be seen as a set of closed processes reverberating off one another so that different kinds of learning are experienced simultaneously, transforming the initiate emotionally, but neither speculative, ratiocinative or heuristic. Such cults are profoundly educative, but not in directions supportive of political leaders or development experts.

References

Ardener, S. 'Sexual Insult and Female Militancy' in S. Ardener (ed.) Perceiving Women. London, Dent/Malaby; New York, Halsted, 1975

Biebuyck, D. Lega Culture: Art, Initiation, and Moral Philosophy Among a Central African People. Berkeley and Los Angeles, University of California Press, 1973

Bellman, B. L. Village of Curers and Assassins: On the Production of Fala Kpelle Cosmological Categories. The Hague and Paris, Mouton, 1975

Bloch, M., and Guggenheim, S. 'Compradrazgo, baptism and the symbolism of a second birth' Man 16.3 (1981), 376-86

Burridge, K. New Heaven, New Earth. Oxford, Blackwell, 1973

Ceston, le P. J. M. 'Le "Gree-Gree Bush" (Initiations de la Jeunesse chez les Negres – Golah, Liberia)'. Anthropos, 6 (1911), 729-54

Dapper, O. Naukerige Beschrijvinge der Afrikaensche Gewesten ... Meurs, 1668

D'Azevedo, W. L. 'Some historical problems in the delineation of a Central West Atlantic Region', Annals of the New York Academy of Sciences, 96, I (1962) 512-38

———— 'Mask Makers and Myth in Western Liberia', in A. Forge (ed.), Primitive Art and Society. Oxford, Oxford University Press, 1973

———— 'Sources of Gola Artistry' in D'Azevedo, W. L. (ed.), The Traditional Artist in African Societies. Bloomington and London, Indiana University Press, 1973

———— 'Gola, Poro and Sande: Primal Tasks in Social Custodianship'. Ethnologische Zeitschrift Zeurich, I (1980) 13-23

Glaze, A. J. 'Women Power and Art in a Senufo Village'. African Arts 8.3 (1975) 24-29, 64-68, 96

Griaule, M. Masques Dogons. Institut d'Ethnologie Travaux et Memoires 33, Paris, Universite, 1938

Jackson, M. The Kuranko: Dimensions of Social Reality in a West African Society. London, Christopher Hurst and Co., 1977

Jones, A. A History of the Galinhas Country, Sierra Leone c. 1650-1890. Ph.D. University of Birmingham, 1979

Needham, R. Belief, Language and Experience. Oxford, Blackwell, 1973

O'Brian, P. Pablo Ruiz Picasso. London, Collins, 1976

Proust, M. Within a Budding Grove. Vol. I Remembrance of Things
    Past (1910) tr. C. K. Scott Moncrieff 1924, London, Chatto
    and Windus imp., 1966
Tiger, L. Men in Groups. London, Nelson, 1969
Tonkin, E. 'Masks and Powers'. Man 14.2 (1979), 237-48
Turner, V. The Ritual Process. London, Routledge and Kegan Paul,
    1969

11 MEN, WOMEN AND MISFORTUNE IN BUNYOLE [1]

Susan Reynolds Whyte

The Nyole of Bukedi District, Eastern Uganda, are a Luyia-related group of peasant agriculturalists who explain suffering in terms of dislocations in social or ritual relations. This model of misfortune is a representation of Nyole society referring to social categories such as patrilineal clans and local agnatic descent groups, as well as to particular types of social relations between individuals. Analysis along these lines, however, reveals an interesting peculiarity of the Nyole model. There are two explanations for misfortune which are unlike all the others in that they do not make any direct reference to relationships within Nyole society. They explain suffering as the result of attack by unrelated 'little spirits' or foreign spirits met fortuitously on the road. Moreover, while all other etiologies of misfortune can be applied equally to the problems of men and women, these unrelated spirits are particularly associated with women.

The Nyole model of misfortune

Like most people, Nyole have various symptomatic treatments for such misfortunes as illness and reproductive disorders. These include local herbal preparations or Western medicines obtained at the dispensary. But when misfortune is severe or persistent, symptomatic attention must be supplemented by etiological treatment. Of such severe afflictions, Nyole say 'there is a reason', and they attempt to determine the cause in order to attack the problem at its roots and cure it. In the same way, death always has a 'reason'; it is never natural or accidental. Although death cannot be cured, it is still important to determine its cause in order to take steps to avoid further danger.

The reasons for misfortune are usually determined through divination, and by working with diviners one can soon grasp the outlines of the Nyole 'theory' of misfortune. Diviners and their clients manipulate a set of explanations which relate suffering to some set of relationships in the sufferer's world. They do so not simply for the intellectual pleasure of understanding but in order to discover which ritual remedy is appropriate for the problem.

The main Nyole model of misfortune posits a number of different causes for suffering, but behind them all lies a single general principle. That is the assumption that suffering is related to personalised agents which act as subjects in bringing misfortune to a given individual. Some are thought to be living people, cursers or sorcerers, who make use of mystical powers to harm others. Very often, the agent is said to be an unseen being, a ghost or spirit. Yet even in these cases, the agents are like people in important respects. They act out of motives which are comprehensible though perhaps not admirable. They usually are thought to have some kind of relationship with those they attack.

This general principle has been discussed by Horton (1967) as a common characteristic of African theoretical idioms. He suggests that in African traditional thought, the raw material for explanatory models is people and their social relations (1967, p.65). Where Westerners invoke abstract forces such as luck or genetics, or depersonalised entities such as viruses, Africans often speak of relations between people or between human beings and personalised spirits. In so far as misfortune consists of physiological processes such as illness, death or reproductive difficulties (by far the most commonly found to have a 'reason'), there is a kind of inversion of Levi-Strauss's analysis of totemism. Whereas totemism consists of the application of a natural model to society, we have here a social model applied to natural processes. Individual physiological experience is made the occasion for enacting a statement about social relationships.

The vision of society contained in this Nyole model of misfortune is continually dramatised and re-presented because it is tied to unavoidable and universal natural events. The Nyole word for 'to suffer' (ohuwonawona) means literally 'to see-see', or 'really to experience', and suffering is associated with a way of perceiving or experiencing Nyole society. Inasmuch as treatment is given on the basis of what is 'seen', that vision is enacted and made to seem real. The ideological reproduction of the Nyole system of social relationships is thus linked to the explanation and treatment of individual 'natural' disturbances.

The representation of social relationships

One explanation for such troubles as barrenness, impotence, the sickness or death of children, marriage difficulties and crop failure is the power of senior relatives to curse. It is believed that offended senior consanguines can invoke the ancestors to punish wrongs committed against them. The ancestors are by definition moral and it is thought that they will support the legitimate rights of their children to bridewealth shares, and to respect and obedience from their descendants. The ability to curse is not lineal. One can be cursed by a mother or father or by grandparents or parents' siblings. In Lunyole these are collectively referred to as 'parents', and in the ideology of cursing they are represented as people with whom

176

one has an asymmetrical relationship. Misfortunes attributed to cursing emphasise these relationships by pointing to some alleged neglect of the legitimate rights of 'parents' over their children.

By contrast, ancestral ghosts (emigu, j'abafu), when they act on their own initiative (not by invocation), bring suffering unilineally, to their descendants through males. Like living senior relatives, the dead also have rights over their children. They should be honoured in an elaborate second funeral ceremony and should receive periodic sacrifices. Since it is male descendants who are primarily responsible for these matters, neglected ghosts remind them of their obligations by sending misfortune upon them and their families. They may cause both adults and children to be ill; they may cover people with sores that will not heal; or they may affect livestock and crops. The interpretation and relief of ghost-caused misfortune re-presents the local minimal lineage, the group which traces descent from a named ghost. Like cursing, it calls attention to the moral obligations of kinship, but it stresses a kin principle of agnation rather than bi-lateral relationships to parents and grandparents.

Every Nyole clan, of which there are over 200, and which are exogamous and dispersed, is associated with one or several clan spirits (ekuni). These are also believed to be agents in certain mis-fortunes, such as illness, strange behaviour, reproductive disorders or crop and livestock problems. The agency of clan spirits in mis-fortune emphasises clan categories, for a person can be affected only by the spirit of his own clan. Although they cause suffering, clan spirits are no more evil than ancestral ghosts. They have rights to sacrifices and ritual attention from clan members and are thought to act as legitimately even as the ordering of society in clans is right and proper.

Thus cursing, ancestral ghosts and clan spirits all provide explanations of misfortune which invoke notions of kinship and the obligations and morality of kin ties. The ceremonies which deal with these agencies are open and clear assertions of kin relationships and kin categories. A curser lifting a curse invokes the ancestors saying 'Grandmothers, grandfathers, if I am the parent of this child who is suffering ...' Prayers to the dead beg for blessings on their descendants, and their wives and the children of their daughters. Supplications to clan spirits ask that all members of the clan may prosper.

Sorcery as an explanation of misfortune is clearly of another sort. Although its use is often suspected between kin, it is not clearly identified with the bonds of kinship as are the other misfortune etio-logies. In dealing with sorcery, there is never any explicit statement of relationship, even when its source is thought to be a kinsman. Moreover, ideology makes no association between particular types of relationship or kinds of people and sorcery. Sorcery medicine is available to anyone who cares to purchase it. It is a force to which all have equal access, unlike the power of cursing which resides with senior relatives. The person who suspects he has been affected by sorcery can and usually does respond in kind, manipulating medicines against the sorcerer. There is thus a kind of symmetrical reciprocity in sorcery, which contrasts with the complementarity and asymmetry of other etiologies. One cannot strike back at a ghost or spirit nor can one curse a senior relative in return, as one can return sorcery upon the sorcerer [2].

Although sorcery is not explicitly attributed to particular categories of people, it is still very much an expression of social relationship. A sorcerer is always someone you know. Sorcerers are thought to act out of hatred, malice, jealousy and the selfish pursuit of their own interests. They act for particular reasons, because of quarrels, insults, conflicts over resources or people. As fits the principle of symmetry, typical sorcerers are thought to be in positions of structural equivalence to their victims. They are competitors with conflicting interests – co-wives, brothers, neighbours, fellow students or colleagues. Sorcery expresses the negative side of a relationship, and because it is immoral it presents the very conflicts it expresses as harmful. Most of these conflicts are determined by social organisation as surely as the rules for access to resources. But the ideology of sorcery presents them instead as the evil result of individual malice.

Little Spirits

In addition to the clan spirits, a variety of other spirits are thought to strike people with misfortune. Of these spirits we can distinguish two groups which differ fundamentally from all others in the Nyole model. Cursing, sorcery, ghosts and clan spirits all postulate some kind of disturbed relationship as the root of misfortune. But 'little' spirits and foreign spirits are thought to strike people with whom they had no pre-existing relationship. They 'catch' victims and cause suffering until the sacrifice they require induces them to release their unwelcome hold. Then the victim 'says goodbye' to his spiritual captor and has no further connexion with it at all.

The 'little spirits' (obusambwa) are a category of named mystical beings: Mukama, Nahitutuwusi, Nalulama, Ndulundulu and Namatango. They attack individually or in various combinations with one another and they affect women and children exclusively. Their ritual remedies are carried out by a hired practioner, not by a kinsman, and take place either in the house or, in the cases of Nahitutuwusi and Nalulama, in the bush. For Mukama and Ndulundulu, temporary shrines are established in the home. Later a final ceremony breaks the temporary association and sends the spirit away for good. There are no congregations of devotees for these spirits, no enduring shrines nor regular priests nor mediums. In these respects, they stand in clear contrast to ghosts and clan spirits.

This lack of a lasting relationship is even more marked in the case of the foreign spirits (the term is mine, not a Nyole one). These include Muslim spirits (amajini from the Arabic jinni) and Ganda, Soga and Swahili spirits (emisambwa miganda, misoga, miswahili). It is said that such spirits are picked up accidentally on the road; a person just walking somewhere just happens to run into them and is attacked and made ill. Although other spirits have no doubt come into Bunyole from elsewhere, only this group is distinctively conceived as foreign. They bear foreign names and are said to possess their victims and cause them to speak foreign languages. People say that these spirits came on the roads which Europeans built. Treatment is again a matter for a hired practitioner. One sacrifices to them at a crossroad and sends them on their way. Inevitably the sacrifices they demand include items associated with foreigners (for instance, coffee beans for Ganda spirits) and shop merchandise such as teacups, sugar or cloth and cash.

Occasionally these foreign spirits are said to attack because they want their victim to become a diviner. If he or she chooses to do so, a permanent relationship is established with the spirits and they assist in divination. It is only in such cases that foreign spirits attack men. Otherwise and far more commonly, they attack women and are sent on their way as quickly as possible.

If we look at the logic of the Nyole model and its various etiologies as a whole, these unrelated spirits present an interesting analytical problem. They seem to negate the conceptions of social articulation presented in the other etiologies. While one could argue that the category of foreign spirits symbolises Bunyole's relationships with the world beyond, yet the link is represented as one which is accidental, which did not exist before the attack and which should not exist.

Notions about morality are related to conceptions of relationships. Sorcerers are alleged to act immorally while the ancestral ghosts, clan spirits and cursers act morally to enforce legitimate rights. Together these explanations of misfortune make a statement about the moral nature of Nyole society. No moral judgment is possible where no relationship exists and the little and foreign spirits are amoral.

One of the most important contributions of Evans-Pritchard's pioneering study of Zande witchcraft was, as Gluckman has several times stressed to show how witchcraft explains 'the particularity of misfortune' (Gluckman 1965, p.218). Old granaries sometimes collapse and occasionally injure people sitting under them. What the Zande are concerned to know is ' ... why should these particular people have been sitting under this particular granary at the particular moment when it collapsed?' (Evans-Pritchard 1937, p.69). This is the question to which the Nyole theory of misfortune also addresses itself and it answers it, as does Zande theory, in terms of particular agents who have specific reasons for attacking given individuals. I am cursed because my mother's brother did not receive a share of my bridewealth. I am affected by my clan spirit because, as a clan member, I have an obligation to sacrifice which I have not fulfilled. The particularity of suffering is explained by evoking membership in social categories or relations to individuals. The exception is the case of the little and foreign spirits. As an etiology, they alone cannot explain why a granary should fall on one person rather than another. Because these latter spirits are represented as being beyond the realm of social relations, they have no particular motives when they (so to speak) push granaries over on some people rather than others.

Points of view in ideological discourse

The analytical problem presented by the Nyole little and foreign spirits has been discussed extensively by Lewis (1970; 1971). He contrasts central morality cults, generally dominated by males, with cults of peripheral spirits not articulated to the central cult. His distinction applies most clearly to the difference between Nyole beliefs in clan spirits and ghosts on the one hand and the little spirits and foreign spirits on the other. Documenting the prevalence of such cults, he shows that it is generally women or marginally placed men who are possessed by peripheral spirits. Lewis suggests a congruence between the marginal political and economic positions of the spirits' victims and the peripherality of the cults to the central religious concerns of the society. Peripherality often has a geographical sense also in the spirits' alleged foreign provenance (1971, p. 32). Lewis's general approach is based on the assumption that different aspects of religious belief and practice must be explained in terms of the different placement of social categories such as men and women within the society. Centrality and peripherality are aspects of both social position and ideology.

In an article by Feuchtwang (1975) attempting to formulate a Marxist approach to the study of religion, several of these same concerns reappear in a different guise. Feuchtwang emphasises that although ideology as a whole may have internal logic and coherence, different social categories are differently presented to the ideology. Moreover (a point which Lewis neglects) ideology serves to formulate social identities for individuals. It is a system of representations which tell people what society is and who they are as social beings. Where social hierarchies exist, 'part of society controls the whole and represents the whole to itself' (1975, p. 70).

The relation of Feuchtwang's remarks to Lewis's work and to the Nyole material becomes clear in Feuchtwang's treatment of religion in late imperial China. He describes an ancestral structure and a god structure which formulate two different social principles having to do with lineality and residence (1975, p. 78). In contrast to ancestors and gods, there exists a third category of orphan ghosts or demons which he describes as being 'outside structure', 'beyond the social pale' (1975, p. 80). Logically, orphan ghosts and demons are the negation of ancestors and gods. They are outside the central structure represented by ancestors and gods just as Lewis's peripheral spirits are marginal to the central morality cult. And interestingly, the dominant group of landowners and administrators are very little concerned with the category of orphan ghosts and demons, while they are the focus of much attention from the peasantry. For Feuchtwang, religious ideology formulates a picture of social relationships, a set of social identities for everyone in the society. But it does so from the point of view of a dominant group which is upheld by principles represented as structurally central. What is central and what is peripheral obviously contains some kind of assumption about points of view.

The first step in understanding the Nyole misfortune model is to see it as a kind of discourse about Nyole society. Then we may note with Auge that 'there is no discourse without a subject and society is not a subject' (1975, p.xix). We are led to inquire what or who is the subject; from whose point of view is the model elaborated? The answer has already been suggested by Lewis in his association of women with the peripheral spirits. They are, of course, peripheral from the point of view of a centre which is defined and dominated by men. Society as a whole is represented from the perspective of one group within it - the adult males.

This is one of the points brought out in E. Ardener's analysis of the Bakweri mermaid cult (1972) and in a later comment upon that analysis (1975). The mermaid cult seems to associate Bakweri women with certain aspects of nature, an association which must be interpreted in terms of the '... "bounding" problem presented by women in a situation in which the "bounds" of society are themselves defined by men' (1975, p.23). The general view of Bakweri society elaborated from the dominant male position represents men as central and identifies them with the essence of society itself. Women are defined as 'other' than men and their otherness is emphasised in the male model by placing them peripherally in nature. Bakweri mermaids are 'beyond the social pale' in the same sense as Feuchtwang's orphan ghosts and Lewis's peripheral spirits. All are represented as marginal from the point of view of that structure and those groups which are the subject of the discourse and therefore presented as central.

The problem is still more complicated, however, and some of the interesting complexities have been brought out in S. Ardener's discussion of 'dominant and muted structures' (1975). If we attempt to understand ideology as a discourse elaborated from the perspective of one section of society, an important question has to do with the effects of this orientation upon other non-dominant groups within the society.

S. Ardener suggests that the dominant model is shared by the whole society in the sense that it is established as the general mode of interpreting all experience. Members of the non-dominant group must so express themselves in terms of the dominant model if they are to be 'heard'. However, since this muted group is placed in a different existential or social position, the model may not 'fit' them so perfectly as it does members of the dominant group (S. Ardener, 1975, p.xii). The interests and perspectives of the subordinate group might be better expressed in a counterpart set of representations. Yet the structure of dominance renders the formulation of alternative representations very difficult. The 'dominant model may impede the free expression of alternative models of their world which sub-dominant groups may possess, and perhaps even inhibit the very generation of such models' (1975, p.xii). Thus the sub-dominant group is rendered less articulate, 'muted' or even silent.

The Ardeners have argued that in spite of this phenomenon of mutedness, a 'counterpart' model may occasionally be expressed. Such was the case with the Bakweri mermaid cult, and also with certain women's movements in the Cameroons (S. Ardener, 1973). In these situations, the point of view in the ideological discourse or its related ritual practice must be assumed to shift to the hitherto muted or non-dominant group. It is as if the dominant model relaxes its hold under certain circumstances and at certain points, allowing a specifically female view to come through and be glimpsed by the analyst.

It seems reasonable that we should look for these counterpart models at those points where there seems to be some discrepancy or anomaly in the general model. In certain ways the Nyole little spirits and foreign spirits do not seem to fit neatly into the general Nyole model of misfortune. Having established that we should look at the Nyole model as a discourse with more than one point of view, we may now suggest that the little and foreign spirits express orientations which are specifically female.

Male and Female perspectives in the Nyole model

The argument that the Nyole model of misfortune can be treated in terms of male and female perspectives gains strength from the importance of gender in Nyole society as a whole. The distinction between men and women is the primary social distinction, the fundamental organising principle for the Nyole social system. It is crucial in the specification of descent (through men) and its associated recruitment to kinship groups and categories. It regulates access to land and livestock in that only men have rights of disposal and only men can inherit. It determines post-marital residence - a woman goes to live with a man on his father's land. It is important in the division of labour and even more so in the control exercised over the products of labour. Women have rights over food in the granaries while men tend to control cash and livestock. The important institution of bridewealth and its associated exchanges rest on an opposition between men and women and wealth such that women and wealth pass between men. Since wealth is a metaphor for women [3], it is in a sense opposed to and separated from women [4].

As a kin-based system, Nyole society incorporates the biological difference between the sexes in a very fundamental way. The ability to produce and suckle children, for example, gives women a unique structural value which is not in contradiction with their productive work and which is much more apparent and openly recognised than it is in our own society [5]. This emphasis on female reproductive ability was very clear in the sorts of things that were taken as misfortunes to be explained. Women's reproductive problems and the illness of children were the most common of all, and were misfortunes for the men involved just as much as they were for the women and children - even if in different ways.

Since Nyole society is thus organised primarily on the basis of a distinction between the sexes, men and women are placed differently within Nyole social structure. If we accept that the Nyole model of misfortune is a representation of their society, a discourse upon the nature of social relationships, then it seems quite reasonable that the sex distinction should also be important here. In Bunyole we do not find the difference between men and women explicitly discussed in the content of ideology. There are no myths which explain why men inherit land and women do not. Rather we find that the sex difference is relevant to an understanding of the point of view contained in ideological discourse.

It is in the ideas and practices surrounding ancestral ghosts that men are most clearly seen as the subjects of the ideological discourse which is the Nyole model of misfortune. This is not in the least surprising in view of the fact that the ghosts represent the principle of agnation.

Denich has called attention to the 'patrilineal paradox' engendered by the ideology that a group is reproduced through its men (1974, p. 260; and also M. Whyte, 1974). In Bunyole, this ideology is not carried to an extreme, for women are recognised symbolically and ritually as having a part to play in the furtherance of agnatic groups. But the ghost complex makes it very clear that their part is a secondary one. Women are represented as important because of how they relate to men and because they produce children and sister's children for men.

The elaborate second funeral ceremony may honour dead mothers as well as fathers, but it is never done for women alone (nor by women alone). It is primarily organised by sons for their father and paternal grandfather; mothers are given attention in the process. The ritual focuses upon the graves and ancestral shrines located on land held by the male descendants of the dead. These men, known as 'owners of the second funeral', provide the bulls slaughtered in honour of the dead fathers. The ghosts of mothers are honoured with goats – both less expensive and less prestigious. As priests, guardians of the shrines and leaders of local descent units, men dedicate the animals to the ancestors, pray for blessings upon the group and distribute the meat. Occasionally daughters present goats to the ghosts of their mothers and grandmothers, but even in these cases, dedication and distribution are under the supervision of older men.

The prayers which accompany the sacrifice reveal the dominant male perspective of the ghosts cult.

> We are begging here for wealth, we are begging that the children here may study and learn, here we also would like a motorcar to drive. Wherever we plant millet, wherever we plant sesame, wherever we plant sorghum, may it come quickly and soon. Here let us elope with women, we are begging here for facility in getting wives, here we beg for reproduction, may we strike two by two so that we may have a twin ceremony everyday. Let us be well, you give us life and let us be free from cold.

While these prayers have no fixed form, they always cover certain points such as 'getting wealth', 'getting children', and 'getting wives'. If an inexperienced person makes the initial dedication of an animal he or she has provided, others call out cues to help them through the prayer. Thus it can happen that women in this ceremony may adopt the male perspective and ask the ancestors for the ability to get wives.

The idiom of the second funeral ceremony is agnatic descent and it is in these terms that people are symbolically represented. At several points sacramental food (ebigwasi) of millet porridge, sesame and the internal organs of the sacrificial animals are distributed. This food is divided into three portions for three different groups of people. The first portion is said to be that 'of the clan' and is eaten by the men who are the 'owners' of the second funeral and their fellow clansmen. The second is said to be for 'clan daughters' and is eaten by women of the clan including married women who have returned home for the ceremony. The final portion is for 'clan wives', women (necessarily of other clans) who are married to men of the clan. Here it seems clear that the basic term in the discourse is male; they are the 'we' who are classifying women according to the women's relationship to themselves, whether as wives or daughters. If it were not so, then both men and women would eat the portion 'for the clan' for both may be members of the clan.

Ghosts are thought to inhabit the ancestral shrine located in a man's courtyard. The essential components of these shrines are stones passed from father to son. A dead man's ghost, after wandering in the bush for a period after his death, returns to the land and to the shrine stone which the dead man received from his father and which is now held by his sons. The ghosts of dead women, however, do not return to shrines in their father's compound. They remain in their married homes where their children should care for them. But instead of sheltering in the ancestral shrine with the ghosts of their husbands and fathers-in-law, women's ghosts congregate under the eaves of the house of the senior man's senior wife. Women's ghosts are thus virilocal as women are and their attachment to a place does not have the same permanent quality that men's does. The shrine stone, at least in theory, is permanent over time and represents the lasting attachment of those men to that land. Houses in Bunyole are much less permanent; they fall down or are deserted when people die.

Moreover, since the focus of the sacrifices is the ancestral shrine, and the main stage is the open courtyard where people congregate, female ghosts are marginally placed. The main dramas of prayer by the senior men and the offering of sacrificial blood at the shrine, the dancing and music in the courtyard all define a spatial centre to which the eaves of a woman's house are peripheral. As ghosts, women are certainly present, but they are there secondarily, marginally.

Inasmuch as the agnatic idiom of ghosts is a male discourse supporting men's rights to property, women are muted. Their use of the discourse is restricted because it is not elaborated from their point of view nor in their interests. It is their husbands or their brothers or their fathers who 'speak the language' with ease, who take decisions and make plans about the ceremonies. They cannot speak up as women to say, for example, which of two brothers should act as priest for a shrine. But their very exclusion from direct expression makes them appropriate vehicles for another form of communication. For the ghosts possess women and speak through them to pronounce their wishes or express dissatisfaction with the way men have conducted the ceremony. In this way, women may speak, but not as women, thus maintaining the representation of an agnatic descent group to which women are marginal and in which they do not have the same rights as men.

If we look at how ghosts operate in explanations of misfortune, it is clear that they emphasise relations within the local agnatic descent unit. Almost invariably ghosts are thought to attack males. However, here as in most other etiologies, we find an innocent victim pattern whereby a person can be attacked <u>through</u> dependants. Thus the illness of children or of a wife are attributed to a man's failure to fulfil obligations to his ancestral ghosts, especially failure to perform the second funeral ceremony. The children or women who are actually suffering are thus represented in terms of their relationships to a man. They are extensions of the man with whom the ghosts are annoyed and it is he who takes the necessary step to remedy the misfortune. It is instructive that no men are ever made to suffer because their wives have failed to fulfil an obligation to the ghosts.

In fact, this innocent victim pattern holds equally for cursing, sorcery and clan spirits as explanations of misfortune. Women can suffer because of some conflict or oversight of their menfolk, but men are never afflicted because of their relationships to women who have failed in their obligations or conflicted with a third party who wanted to hurt them. Women's sufferings may be interpreted from the point of view of men and their social relations. The reverse does not occur.

It will be recalled that clan spirits also explain misfortune by emphasising an agnatic category. Such afflictions dramatises an individual's clan membership just as ghosts emphasise local descent units. But while the latter have to do with the transmission of property, the former are primarily marriage categories.

Clan spirits are thought to attack men as well as women, though according to divination records, women are attacked more than twice as frequently. Here too, the different 'presentations' of men and women to the ideology is clear. When the illness or peculiar behaviour of a man is attributed to clan spirits, it is said that the spirit has caught him because it wants him to assume the role of priest or medium in the clan spirit cult. These spirits are associated with sacred groves and ideally there should be yearly celebrations in which the spirit possesses his medium and sacrifices are made at the grove. Only a few clans actually carry out these rituals regularly, but everyone is aware of them and many Nyole have attended such ceremonies. The have much in common with second funerals. Men address the spirits, entreating them to bless all members of the clan with good crops, many wives and children. As in the ghost cult, the subject in the discourse is male; the prayers asked for wives, not for husbands. And here too women may be possessed by the spirit, although they never become priests or mediums in the clan spirit cult.

More commonly, clan spirits visit misfortune upon female clan members and in these cases the ritual is quite different. Typically, a recently married woman's illness or psychological disturbance is attributed to her clan spirit. The remedy is not, as in the case of men, the activation of a clan cult. Rather the woman goes <u>ohung'-ong'a</u> - to bring a sacrifice of a spear and a chicken to the home of her father who offers them on her behalf to their clan spirit. The nature of a woman's obligation to her clan spirit is associated with her marriageability. One piece of evidence for this is the strikingly high incidence of clan spirit affliction of newly married women. Furthermore, it is said that all the daughters of the clan are the 'wives' of the clan spirit. When they go to marry men of other clans, the spirit must be compensated for the loss of its 'wife' and so it sends misfortune upon her in order to enforce its claim.

Again it seems that this aspect of the Nyole misfortune model defines women in terms of their relations to men. The remedial ritual represents women as articulated to their clans through their fathers. They go to the paternal home bringing chickens (which women cannot eat) and spears (which women do not use) and men speak on their behalf. Of course it is true that males are also articulated to their clans through their fathers, but there is no equivalent ritual asser-tion for men. Nor are men defined and represented in terms of their marriageability as women are, in spite of the fact that clans are mar-riage categories for men and women equally. This makes sense if we accept that that entire discourse is drawn from a male point of view. They marry women and have rights in women who go to be married. Although women also marry men, whatever perspectives they might have upon men in this regard are muted.

In some ways the explanation of misfortune in terms of foreign spirits parallels the clan spirit etiology. Like clan spirits, foreign spirits may attack men in a supposed effort to establish those men in new ritual roles. But most commonly, the foreign spirits attack women, often young women of marriageable age or older women whose marriages are in difficulty. Both foreign spirits and clan spirits are acceptable explanations of women's psychological distur-bances or illness. Men accept these attacks as real dangers that threaten their wives and daughters and no doubt from the male point of view it all makes good sense. For men, standing at the core of a patrilineal, virilocal society, women must in some ways resemble the foreign spirits which possess them. Like the spirits who travel on the roads, women move from one place to another. Like foreigners, wives and mothers come from somewhere else. Indeed the Nyole sys-tem has no difficulty accepting women from other tribes who marry into Bunyole. By contrast, foreign men cannot be so easily absor-bed.

Women move from one place to another, but for men the whole point about women's movement is that it must be controlled. If it is not, the bridewealth exchanges which are keyed to the movement of women become problemetic. If a woman does not 'stick in marriage', her fathers and brothers are hesitant to accept bridewealth because they will have to return it as soon as the woman leaves. Likewise the husband is reluctant to give bridewealth if his wife has already left several previous husbands. Of such women it is said that they wander (Bagendahugenda - they go and go) and perhaps that they are 'harlots' (malaya).

The notion of foreign spirits that wander can be seen to represent the danger of uncontrolled movement of women. Perhaps for men, the ceremonies which 'say goodbye' to foreign spirits affirm that women are saved from the road, from the dangers of casual encounters that do not lead to lasting affinal relationships. Foreign spirits symbolise the opposite of proper marriage. For wandering cheats men of the exchange relationships which are a basic principle of Nyole social organisation.

Women, too, desire to be settled in a firm marriage - for different reasons. They can stay with their children, establish usufruct rights in land, form lasting friendships, attain the respect which marriage and children bring. At the same time, however, casual relationships have certain rewards such as independence, less heavy responsibility, and the gifts which a woman may ask of her lover. These gifts are often shop wares and cash of the very kind that appear in the foreign spirit rituals. The colonial and post-colonial period have offered men the chance for education and cash and political participation. Few women have benefited in the same way. For most, the only realistic possibility for contact with 'foreigners' and the larger context beyond Bunyole is to establish sexual relations with men - either Nyole who have such contacts or 'foreign' men. Through these relationships they can also gain access to the manufactured wares sold in shops.

For women the foreign spirits must represent this possibility. Denying the Nyole social structure and the rights men have over women, they symbolise a direct and temporary relationship between a woman and other men, a relationship not involving her brothers, father or mother's brother. There is no doubt that this type of relationship can be attractive to women. It is well to remember, however, that foreign spirits are treated by being sent away. They are dangerous and what they represent is shown to be undesirable. In this sense the ideology ulitmately reaffirms Nyole social structure and its control over women.

We have seen that the foreign spirits are 'foreign' precisely with respect to what is represented as Nyole, the 'central morality cult' of ancestors and clan spirits. If we turn now to the 'little spirits', we find that in the same way they are 'little' compared to 'big' spirits which represent social principles such as clanship. The word obus-ambwa is the diminutive of emisambwa, the ordinary word for spirits. Little spirits which attack women and children are thus marked by their very name as secondary and less significant. The little spirits have to do with reproduction in the sense of conceiving and bearing children and bringing them safely through the first dangerous years. In the idiom of little spirits, this is seen as a special concern of women. Here children are represented as belonging to their mothers, not to the men who paid bridewealth and own the land.

The ceremonies which deal with the little spirits are relatively simple. A curer, who can be male or female, comes to the home and treats the afflicted woman or child, performing rituals in which the woman is the key figure. Her husband is usually present and assists if he is asked. If a baby is ill, the curer may bathe it in medicine and address the afflicting spirit with a prayer such as the following: 'Let this child be well. Tonight may it sleep upon its mother's breast, so that in the morning, the mother may say - oh, at last I have slept a little' (from a ceremony for the little spirit named Kiryawire). In the case of another little spirit, Mukama, the woman must show the curer the place in the banana plantation where she delivered her child and the spirit Mukama which was supposedly born with it. Part of the ceremony must take place at that very spot. Such points - a mother's sleeplessness when her child is ill, the place where she gave birth - are a special concern of women, and of relatively little interest to men.

A number of the items used in the ceremonies are also typically associated with women. Instead of spears we find winnowing trays and potsherds. The curer puts medicine in the damp hollow under the waterpot, a spot which women certainly know best since it is they who fetch the water daily, lifting and lowering the pot from and to its place. The curer may sprinkle the interior walls of the house with medicine as well as applying it to the bed where the woman sleeps.

It will be recalled that the association of women with the house was also made in the ghost cult, where the ghosts of women were thought to congregate under the eaves of the senior wife's house. In that case the house was peripheral to the ancestral shrine in the courtyard where the spirits of deceased male agnates were of central concern. But in the little spirit ceremonies, the house is a central focus of ritual activity. But in the little spirit ceremonies, the house is a central focus of ritual activity. The house may lie in a compound with other houses of co-wives and mothers-in-law whose formal social articulation is symbolised by the ancestral shrine. But that fact is ignored in the little spirit ceremonies.

In the ghost cult, senior males sacrifice on behalf of the ghosts' descendants and represent the group as a whole. There is no part for these elders to play in dealing with the little spirits, for the latter have nothing to do with descent relationships. In fact, the very nature of the little spirits excludes them from treatment by any senior kinsman. Nyole protocol and feeling about modesty between adjacent generations concerning sexual matters would never permit senior men the kind of intimacy with the house in which a specialist indulges. A woman's bed could never be approached by her father-in-law; a parent cannot even enter the house of a married son or daughter because it is there where the sexuality of his child is expressed.

This leads us back to the analytical problem presented by the little spirits and the foreign spirits in general. Their peculiar characteristic is that they do not explain misfortune in terms of particular social relations with given individuals or kinship groups.

The exlusion of senior male relatives from their treatment is one aspect of this peculiarity. Another is lack of an 'innocent victim' pattern in misfortunes explained by little and foreign spirits. The spirits do not attack men by causing wives and children to suffer. Instead the person who suffers is considered the real object of attack. Thus the suffering victim is not represented in terms of relationship to and dependency upon another person. Women are represented as individual women, not as wives and daughters.

The alternative vision expressed in the little and foreign spirit etiology is thus not another view of the same structure represented in the rest of the Nyole model. The counterpart picture asserts that women are not articulated in the standard structure at all. Here alone women seem to be the subject of the discourse, and they are represented as autonomous and unconnected, instead of being defined in terms of their relations to men.

Shared Models and Social Differences

Perhaps the most fascinating general problem raised by this excursion into the ethnography of Nyole misfortune has to do with the sharing of models by groups placed very differently within society. As a discourse upon the nature of social relations, much of the Nyole model has a male subject. Social structure is defined from men's point of view and it is therefore women who are represented as peripheral, foreign, secondary and so on. At a few points in the model, the subject of the discourse seems to switch and women express a counterpart view, not of social structure but of their own lack of connexion to it. Yet while the subject of the discourse may be one or other group, the model as a whole is shared. Men are as well aware that little and foreign spirits cause misfortune as women are of the agencies of clan spirits and ghosts. Both men and women are conscious of the model as an integrated whole, and as such, it can be elicited from either men or women in its entirety.

One of the mechanisms which militates for a sharing of the model is its practical use in providing explanations and remedies for misfortune. Suffering is universal, not only in that it can happen to anyone, male or female, but also in that the misfortune of one person touches others. A woman's barrenness is not her private problem, but the concern of her affines as well as her own family, her male as well as her female relatives. In fact, it is considered very bad to keep a misfortune and/or its cause secret from the relatives and neighbours who would sympathise with the sufferer. People coming home from a funeral are asked whether they found out what caused the death. This is a way of asking whether they were treated in friendly confidence by the mourners (and given much to eat and drink). In Bunyole as in the West the most common greeting asks 'How are you'. Yet Nyole expect a real response, not our automatic 'Fine, thanks'.

Thus at a general level the model is shared by men and women. What is not shared is the orientation towards it, the points of view built into it, and the particular meaning which the little and foreign spirits have specifically for women. It is that particular significance which may be interpreted as the female counterpart to the dominant male model.

It is important to understand that the implication of ideological dominance is precisely that the ideology is shared. The representation of social relations in the Nyole model of misfortune supports a number of male rights crucial to the organisation of Nyole society. Men's rights to bridewealth and land and children are unquestioned by women. They accept, indeed they support, this state of affairs by sharing the ideology of misfortune and explaining their own sufferings in these terms. Women's own counterpart vision is added on to the dominant male model as one more explanation of misfortune, an alternative within a set of alternative etiologies.

Thus we cannot speak of separate realities, exclusive male and female models. If we accept the argument that little and foreign spirits express a specifically female point of view, we are left with the fact that this counterpart vision is in some sense still determined by and subordinated within a discourse having a male subject. As S. Ardener has put it, 'counterpart models ... are not generated independently of those of the dominant structure, but are to some extent shaped by them' (1975, p. xiii).

The general model distinguishes Nyole (and big) from foreign (and little). The counterpart model does not directly challenge or oppose this distinction. The little and foreign spirits do not offer an independent vision of men articulated to women, nor of women linked to other women through men, nor even of female solidarity. Through them women express their own interests and concerns not by challenging the dominant model as such but by elaborating an element of that model. The element which they elaborate is simply the logical contrast to the representation of social relations in the rest of the general model. Although the little and foreign spirits can be seen as a repudiation of the male-centered view of social relations, they nevertheless remain a dependent part of the general model, rather than a complete alternative to it.

Repudiation or negation at the logical level must not be confused with real opposition. The little or foreign spirits are not associated with any actual feminist challenge to male domination in Bunyole. Lewis speaks of peripheral-spirit cults as loci of revolt (though not revolution) in which women are able to express discontent and frustration and at the same time gain a temporary improvement in their position (1970, p. 294-5). It is not clear to me that these functions are met by the Nyole rituals for little and foreign spirits. Rather, I would emphasise the way that these spirits reject male domination at a <u>logical</u> level and give <u>symbolic</u> expression to female interests and viewpoints. I would equally stress that they are a part of a broader model of misfortune and are shaped by that larger ideology which is shared by men and women although it in fact functions to support male rights in people and property.

Anthropologists have long spoken of representations as collective, implying that the members of a society have equal interests in the

190

ideology. Those such as Turner who have been aware of divisiveness have still seen the symbol system as a neutral shared focus for the harmonising of conflicting interests [6]. Recent work has taken us a step beyond this type of formulation. By seeing representations as a discourse with a subject, we can solve particular analytical problems such as the one discussed here. But the more general consequence is that we are brought to specify the definitional centre from which the representations are made, to link them to positions within the society. This seems to me a fruitful way of relating semantics to social structure, allowing us to say more interesting things about them both. Such an approach can be seen to lie within the 'post-structuralist' context discussed by Hastrup (1976).

Notes

Fieldwork was carried out in Bunyole from February 1969 to April 1971 with the support of a grant from the United States National Institute of Mental Health. This article was inspired by discussions with the members of my seminar on Sex Differences and Social Structure at the Institut for Etnologi in Copenhagen. I would like to thank them very much. In addition I am grateful to Kirsten Ramlov, Kirsten Hastrup and most especially Michael Whyte for their helpful comments on earlier versions of this paper.

1. This article first appeared in Man (N.S.) Vol.16 No.3 1981. The Editor wishes to thank the Royal Anthropological Institute of Great Britain and Ireland for the permission to reprint.

2. Harwood (1970) has shown this same principle of reciprocity very clearly in Safwa sorcery.

3. O'Laughlin (1974) has developed this notion in an article which relates certain aspects of ideology to the social organisation of sex differences.

4. I would not deny that bridewealth involves a distinction between older men who control wealth and the younger men who depend upon them to obtain a wife. I am merely asserting that the gender distinction is the basis for it.

5. Leleur (n.d.) argues that even cultural expressions which seem to denigrate women (ideas that women are dangerous, polluting and need to be controlled) are infact reflections of the structural importance of female biological capacities for kin-based social organisations.

6. 'Contradictions which may not be resolved on the level of politico-kinship relations among the Ndembu, may yet be resolved, or rather transcended, on the plane of ritual' (Turner 1968: 283).

References

Ardener, E. 'Belief and the Problem of Women' in J. S. La Fontaine, (ed.) The Interpretation of Ritual. London, Tavistock Publications, 1972

_____ 'The 'Problem' Revisited'. in S. Ardener, (ed.) Perceiving Women. London, Dent Malaby, 1975

Ardener, S. 1973. 'Sexual Insult and Female Militancy', in Man 8, 422-40.

_____ 1975. 'Introduction'. in S. Ardener (ed.) Perceiving Women. London, Dent Malaby, 1975

Auge, M. Theorie des pouvoirs et ideologie. Paris, Hermann, 1975

Denich, B. 'Sex and power in the Balkans', in M. Z. Rosaldo and L. Lamphere, (eds.) Woman, Culture and Society Stanford University Press, 1974

Evans-Pritchard, E. E. Witchcraft, Oracles and Magic among the Azande. London, Oxford University Press, 1937

Feuchtwang, S. 'Investigating religion'. in M. Bloch (ed.) Marxist Analyses and Social Anthropology. London, Malaby, 1975

Gluckman, M. Politics, Law and Ritual in Tribal Society. Oxford, Blackwell, 1965

Harwood, A. Witchcraft, Sorcery and Social categories among the Safwa. London, Oxford University Press, 1970

Hastrup, K. 1976. 'The Post-Structuralist Position of Social Anthropology'. Ybk social Anthrop. I

Horton, R. 1967. 'African traditional thought and Western science' I, Africa 37, 50-71.

Leleur, A.n.d. Vaginal magt og kvinde foragt. Unpublished ms, Copenhagen.

Lewis, I. M. 'A structural approach to witchcraft and spirit possession', M. Douglas (ed.) in Witchcraft Confessions and Accusations (A.S.A. Monogr. 9). London, Tavistock Publications, 1970

_____ Estatic Religion: An Anthropological Study of Spirit Possession and Shamanism. Harmondsworth, Penguin, 1971

O'Laughlin, B. 'Mediation of Contradiction: Why Mbum Women Do Not Eat Chicken', in M. Z. Rosaldo and L. Lamphere (eds.), Women, Culture and Society. Standford, Univ. Press, 1974

Turner, V. W. The Drums of Affliction: a Study of Religious Processes among the Ndembu of Zambia. Oxford, Clarendon, 1968

Whyte, M. A. 'The Ideology of Descent in Bunyole'. Thesis (Ann Arbor University Microfilms.) 1974

INDEX